Sweatworking

The Mastery Guide to Revolutionizing Your Life &
Professional Relationships Through Wellness

SEAN BURCH

WELLNESS
INSTITUTE
PRESS

First published by Wellness Institute Press 2025

Sean Burch asserts the moral right to be identified as the author of this work.

Rights & Use Disclaimer. Copyright © 2025 by Sean Burch. All rights reserved.

No part of this publication may be reproduced, stored in a retrieval system, or transmitted in any form or by any means, electronic, mechanical, photocopying, recording, or otherwise, without the prior written permission of the author, except for brief quotations used in reviews, educational instruction, or non-commercial reference, provided proper attribution is given.

The content, frameworks, and original terminology presented in Sweatworking: The Mastery Guide to Revolutionizing Your Life & Professional Relationships Through Wellness are the intellectual property of the author and are protected under applicable copyright and trademark laws.

The tools, exercises, and frameworks in Sweatworking: The Mastery Guide to Revolutionizing Your Life & Professional Relationships Through Wellness were designed with both individual transformation and organizational impact in mind. This material may be used internally within your company or institution to support leadership development, culture change, team engagement, and wellness integration, so long as such use remains non-commercial, non-derivative, and does not imply authorship or endorsement by the author without express written consent. Please attribute the source clearly when referencing or sharing materials from this guide.

If you plan to deliver Sweatworking content publicly, repackage it for commercial purposes, or certify others using these methods, please contact the author to request official licensing or collaborative partnership.

For licensing, partnership, training, extended curriculum, facilitator support, or content adaptation inquiries, contact at: www.SeanBurch.com

Jacket Design: Sean Burch
Author Photograph: Paul Lara

First edition
ISBN Paperback: 979-8-9932135-0-7
ISBN ebook: 979-8-9932135-1-4
Library of Congress Control Number: 2025920362
Wellness Institute Press, Tucson, ARIZONA

To those who desire to live by the mantra: Your health is your wealth

Contents

Preface iv
Your Moral Code vi
You Can Feel Young Again xi
1 Open Your Door, Unlock The Way 1
2 Wake Up, Your Network's Dead 12
3 The Evolution of Networking 27
4 Company Convergence of Your Relevant 34
5 The Corporate Incentives (Bullet Points) 46
6 Wellness for Winners (and Those Who Want to Be) 56
7 Sweat, Smile, Repeat: How Exercise Rewires Your Brain 62
8 The Samurai's Guide to Not Losing Your Mind at Work 71
9 Fear: The Silent Architect of Your Life 83
10 Your Corporate Pitch Cheat Sheet 89
11 The Great Unveiling: 1st Session 94
12 Mountains to Climb and Pitfalls 103
13 All-Day Movement: Sitting is the New Smoking (But
   Less Cool) 109
14 Sessions Activity Roulette: Beat Boredom 118
15 Juggling Chainsaws (aka Life) 132
16 Brain in Motion = Couch in Defeat 140
17 The Art of Doing Everything in Half the Time 148
18 Dripping with Ambition: The Science Behind Your Sweat 152
19 Curb Your Enthusiasm: Let's Walk and Talk Before
   We Burst 164
20 Zen and the Art of Not Losing Your Cool at Work 169
21 Conference Case Analysis With Solutions 181

22	SB 1 Minute Mindfulness	185
23	Your Venue Voodoo: The Essentials	187
24	Sweatworking Boundaries Guide: How Not to Get Fired	199
25	Case Study - How SoulCycle Became the Boardroom on a Bike	208
26	Genuine Relationships: Where Ghosting Goes to Die	215
27	Plotting World Domination: Your Promotion Magic Formula	225
28	Sweat, Tears, & Logos: Branding While Breaking a Sweat	230
29	The Future of Productivity: Your Wellness Is The New ROI	241
30	One Breath To Your Freedom	248
31	The Hero Is You. The Time Is Now	252

Author's Note on Appendices — 258
Appendix A: Sweatworking Sessions - Adrenaline Outdoors — 260
Appendix B: Sweatworking Sessions - Strength and Camaraderie — 273
Appendix C: Sweatworking Sessions - Hyper-Connected — 289
Appendix D: Sweatworking Sessions - Sane in the Membrane — 301
Appendix E: Sweatworking Sessions - Low-Impact Gentle Giants — 314
Appendix F: Sweatworking Master Class Outline #1 — 324
Appendix G: Sweatworking Master Class Outline #2 — 329
Appendix H: Expected Sensory Experiences — 333
Appendix I: Funding Options for Sweatworking Sessions — 336
Appendix J: Hiring Options — 338
Appendix K: Detailed Marketing of Your Sweatworking Session — 340
Appendix L: Strategic Planning Sessions — 343
Appendix M: Starting Your Own Sweatworking Business — 345
Appendix N: Sweatworking Session Employee Sample Evaluation — 348
Appendix O: Timeline for Your Sweatworking Business — 350
Appendix P: Quick Stress-Relief Techniques — 352
Appendix Q: Stress-Release Techniques — 354
Appendix R: Nutritional Tips for Sustained Energy — 357
Appendix S: Proper Ergonomics — 359
Appendix T: Clothing — 364

Acknowledgments 367
About the Author 370
Also by Sean Burch 372

Preface

In this book, you will be provided the tools and insights needed to become a champion of living, both personally and professionally. Consider it your trusted mentor, coach, and reference, a resource you can rely on time and again.

- **Boost your career**
- **Strengthen your home life**
- **Overcome fear and depression**
- **Break free from complacency**
- **Prevent future diseases**
- **Feel and look younger**

You will notice some redundancy in the chapters. This was done for two reasons:

1. **Each chapter is designed to be self-contained**, allowing readers to appreciate it independently if needed, without requiring them to read every chapter to fully understand the narrative from start to finish.

2. **Repetition can be a good thing and aids in instilling positive habits**, so treat this as an enhanced learning exercise and you'll improve that much more and quicker than the average habit.

A Note on Data

You'll find some data and statistics woven into this book, but I've intentionally omitted formal citations. Why? Because trust matters. If a claim gives you pause, I encourage you to verify it—I'd do the same. Every figure here has been vetted, so you can focus on the concepts rather than flipping to footnotes. After all, whether in business or life, trust isn't given; it's earned. Consider this your invitation to take what resonates and question what doesn't. The truth holds up.

Your Moral Code

At the foundation of every meaningful transformation, whether in life, wellness, or professional relationships, lies a moral code: a set of guiding principles that shape your actions, decisions, and interactions. Before embarking on the journey outlined in this book, it's essential to define and embrace your moral code that will serve as your compass for personal and professional growth.

The Essence of Your Moral Code

A moral code is more than a list of rules; it is a living commitment to integrity, compassion, and authenticity. It is the quiet force that guides you when no one is watching, the standard you uphold in both triumph and adversity. As you strive for mastery in wellness and relationships, your moral code becomes the lens through which you view challenges, opportunities, and the people around you.

Core Principles: RICH CARS™

This book challenges you to refine your personal values. In navigating life, consider the principles of **RICH CARS**, a framework for a meaningful existence.

'RICH' represents the richness of your inner character: **Respect, Integrity, Compassion,** and **Honesty.** These cultivate a substructure of inner wealth and authentic connections.

'CARS' signifies the active demonstration of these values: **C**onsistency, **A**ccountability, **R**eliability, and **S**elf-awareness. Just as a car transports you, these principles drive your actions, ensuring your moral code translates into a powerful, positive impact in the world.

R.I.C.H.

Respect: Treat every individual with dignity, regardless of their background or beliefs. Recognize the inherent worth in yourself and others, and approach every relationship with openness and humility.

Integrity: Live in alignment with your deepest values. Let your actions reflect your beliefs, even when it is difficult or inconvenient. Integrity is the bridge between intention and impact, ensuring that who you are inside matches how you show up in the world.

Compassion: Extend empathy and kindness, even when faced with differences or conflict. Compassion fuels understanding and creates the space for healing and collaboration.

Honesty: Speak the truth with courage and clarity. Transparency in communication builds trust and fosters genuine connections, both personally and professionally.

C.A.R.S.

Consistency: Uphold your values across all situations and relationships. Consistency breeds credibility and sets a powerful example for those around you.

Accountability: Own your choices and their outcomes. When you make mistakes, acknowledge them, learn, and make amends. Accountability is the bedrock of trust and growth.

Reliability: Be dependable. Honor your commitments and be someone others can count on, in both words and actions.

Self-Awareness: Celebrate your achievements, but recognize the contributions of others and the role of circumstance in every success. Remain teachable and open to new perspectives.

Living Your Code in Wellness and Relationships

True wellness is not just physical health; it is the harmony of mind, body, and spirit, achieved through conscious choices aligned with your moral code. In professional relationships, your code becomes the basis for trust, collaboration, and mutual respect. Whether you are leading a team, supporting a colleague, or nurturing a friendship, your moral code is the invisible thread that weaves strength and authenticity into every interaction.

Your moral code is not just a private matter; it is your personal brand, the legacy you build with every decision and every relationship.

Making Your Code Your Own

While RICH CARS offers a blueprint, your moral code must be personal and authentic. Reflect on the values that resonate deeply with you. Write them down. Commit to them. Revisit them often.

Imagine waking up each morning knowing exactly who you are and what you stand for, no matter what the world throws your way. In today's fast-moving, often unpredictable society, your moral code is more than just a set of ideals; it's your anchor, your shield, and your guide. It shapes how you respond to challenges, how you treat others, and how you see yourself when you look in the mirror.

We live in a time when the lines between right and wrong can seem blurred by pressure, competition, and the constant noise of social platforms. It's easy to get swept up in trends, to compromise your values for quick wins, or to lose sight of what truly matters.

Your moral code is your most valuable asset. It's what sets you apart and gives you the strength to make decisions you can be proud of, even when no one is watching.

Why does this matter for your wellness and professional relationships? Because every meaningful connection, whether at work or in your personal life, depends on trust, respect, and authenticity. People are drawn to those who are consistent, honest, and compassionate. You inspire confidence, foster collaboration, and create a ripple effect of positivity in every space you enter.

In a world that's always changing, your moral code is your constant. Make it count. Embrace your code. Live it boldly. Let it be the foundation for your journey to mastery in wellness and relationships.

I know this may sound dramatic, but I say it with purpose—fully understanding the weight and importance of your moral code is essential. As your mentor, I care deeply that you recognize how this foundation can shape every decision and direction that follows.

You Can Feel Young Again

Ah yes, a morning when you wake and your bones don't creak and your joints are not a weather report for the next incoming storm. Miraculous, almost suspicious, you rise from bed and find yourself whole and unscathed, not yet gnawed by a disease or ailment, unfortunately making the rounds of some friends and colleagues. Your body, once an aging jalopy, now purrs along the road instead of sputtering in the ditch.

You hit the company gym to meet up with a group from work, where your body moves and your mind sharpens. You see people as they are, stripped of pretense and perfume. You're making new friends, new allies, sometimes new adversaries, and you do it face to face, the way our species has done for thousands of years. As your muscles grow, so does the circle of those you trust, those you might call upon when the river rises. To be healthy and fit is to be ungovernable, to be strong is to be free, and making new contacts through sweat and effort reclaims a bit of the fierceness and energy that today's civilization tries so hard to stamp out. You know you're meant to be a creature of sinew and spirit. That is how you endure, and more, how you live.

And then it's time for your workday. Your handshake is firmer, your conversations seem less polluted by the stench of corporate jargon, the camaraderie seemingly more legitimate, of shared effort, not shared misery. You listen to your associates' stories, their gripes, their small victories, and you find yourself, God help you, enjoying it. The world is an everyday expedition into the unknown, as it was when you were a child and the universe was new and the possibilities infinite.

You are, in short, happy. Not the plastic, grinning happiness hawked in commercials and Instagram posts, but the unvarnished joy that comes from being alive, from being present in your own skin, from knowing that you are here. You are grateful for the job, for the company, even for the commute. Yes, even that, because it means you are moving, breathing, participating in the grand spectacle of existence.

And when the day is done, you go home, not to collapse in defeat, but to revel in the company of family, in the small rituals and comforts that make life bearable. You survive by thriving, by refusing to be cowed by the slow encroachment of decay. Tomorrow? Who knows. But today, by God, you are healthy, happy, fit, and strong, and that is enough. That's a rare and radical act in a world intent on making us soft, sedentary, and sedated. You are a creature of flesh and spirit, fortunate to be alive in this world, ready to make history.

1

Open Your Door, Unlock The Way

John, a student in my Everest Workout™ class, stood out for his quiet demeanor. Unlike the business professionals and weekend warriors who lingered to socialize after sessions, he would swiftly gather his gear and exit before conversations had even begun. This consistent habit made him an enigmatic presence, one who participated fully in class yet avoided the communal aspect that others embraced.

I understand that completely. I am shy around people I don't know and hesitant with making new friends, and maybe you are, too. At times, you may feel trapped in your solitary world because you're afraid of judgment or misconnection. It's as if you're stumbling through the dark, colliding with your insecurities—the loneliness, the hunger for belonging, the fear of rejection. That's why I appreciated having John in my classes. He was diligent and hardworking while exercising, yet if he chose not to socialize afterward, who was I to question it? His quiet presence was enough.

It was around the sixth or seventh session when he finally approached a small group of us who communed regularly after each workout, hesitantly asking a question about one of the exercises we'd done. Shy and reserved, he seemed cautious. Perhaps he worried our characteristic energy and outgoing nature, the spirited demeanor I aim for in my students in every session or workshop, would overwhelm him. His words hung with us, a small but meaningful breach of his usual silence.

Locking eyes with him, I offered a smile and responded to his query. Almost immediately, another voice chimed in, full of admiration for John's incredible box jumps on the towering risers. The way he moved, practically flying like Michael Jordan, brought an instant wave of shared amusement. That moment of collective laughter and smiles forged a connection. Within five minutes, John felt like one of our own. He'd become a part of our tribe.

John's initial reticence gradually gave way to open sharing with the group, both during and after our sessions. Within two months, a natural outgrowth of our camaraderie, sparked by post-class conversations about workouts and professional lives, led to a remarkable opportunity for John. A mate in class facilitated an introduction to his company's CEO, resulting in a successful product sales pitch and a subsequent collaboration on a government contract. For John, the collective energy of people working together, sweating, shouting, and striving as one had become an undeniable catalyst for change. It was evident that this experience had profoundly changed him as a person.

Though John may not have consciously realized it, his decision to join my classes tapped into three deep-seated desires:

- To cultivate well-being and a positive self-image
- To forge connections with others who shared his passions
- To build his professional contacts

He achieved all three.

A Passage Beckons

As you navigate a city's cadence of corporate suits, slacks, and business routines, imagine yourself breaking free from the conventional. What if corporate networking wasn't about stale handshakes over coffee but connections built through sweat and shared goals? A substitute from "Let's do lunch" to "Let's conquer this workout." The future of networking lies in experiences that inspire, challenge, and go beyond the boardroom.

In this new world, the conference room would become an exercise room, and the boardroom a battlefield of wits and endurance. This wouldn't be about turning your network events into a scene from *Mad Max*, but harnessing the raw power of shared physical challenges to forge bonds that could withstand the storms of business and the trials of life.

At Present

As a society, we're currently careening headlong into a business future where the only companions we'll have are the cold glow of screens and the sterile hum of machinery and cloud servers. We spend our time looking at life through a phone but not actually participating in it. Each day we're trading in our souls for an existence devoid of warmth and community, forsaking genuine human connection for the hollow comforts of isolation.

People today seem to want to sell out—their business, their personal life, anything and everything for attention and the almighty dollar, so that they can do what, buy more things, be noticed, or spend more time in a virtual world? What happened to one's ethics and morality? Those who resist the temptation to betray their principles are becoming increasingly rare. This will be our undoing unless we make some drastic changes in the way we live our lives.

In the fast-paced world of business, you should be on a quest to connect, collaborate, and build relationships that truly matter. 'Sweatworking,' which seamlessly integrates wellness with networking, will not only help you forge meaningful bonds with like-minded professionals, it will also lead to a more balanced and fulfilling life.

Sweatworking is your wellness solution for longevity and social connection, both personally and professionally. Unlike traditional networking, this approach focuses on cultivating positive habits that help you reconnect with your natural rhythms in a world that has become increasingly disrupted and impersonal. It is the key to your salvation in this godforsaken rat race we call modern business.

Tyranny of Time

Time is a cruel mistress. She doesn't discriminate between the CFO in her corner office and the janitor cleaning the wastebaskets after hours. We're all slaves to her whims, dancing to the tune of ticking clocks and buzzing watch alarms. But here's the rub—while you can't control time, you can damn well choose how you spend it.

In this age of endless meetings and mind-numbing Zoom presentations, we've forgotten what it means to truly connect with our fellow humans. We hide behind screens, tapping away at keyboards, deluding ourselves into thinking we're being productive. But from my experiences, there's more wisdom to be found in a single bead of sweat rolling down your brow that you truly earned than in all the emails you'll send in a day.

Forget everything you've learned about time management from those self-help gurus and so-called productivity experts. Their color-coded calendars, AI applications, and prioritization matrices are just another form of chains, binding you to a desk and a computer screen. We're all working with too many apps. True time management isn't just about squeezing more tasks into fewer hours. It's about making the most of the time you have and creating experiences that enrich your life and your work simultaneously.

Wilderness of Corporate America

The corporate world is its own kind of wilderness. Predators lurking around every corner, ready to pounce on the weak and unsuspecting. But unlike the natural world, where survival of the fittest actually means something, the corporate world rewards people who play the game better or kiss the right asses or just keep their heads down, instead of being good at their jobs.

I want you to reclaim that primal edge. I want you to prove your worth not through a virtual presentation, but through sheer personal determination. When you're out there on a trail, scrambling up an incline with your potential business partner, you're not just burning calories, you're forging a bond that goes deeper than a meaningless LinkedIn connection.

Illusion of Efficiency

Now, you may be thinking. "I don't have time for such paltry activities. I have quarterly reports to file and stakeholders to appease." To that, I say: horseshit. You've been sold a bill of goods. This obsession by a majority of corporations with their supposed efficiency and productivity is nothing but a smokescreen, a way to keep you chained to your desk while the world burns outside your office window.

Many of us choose to live in a world of illusion because the pain of reality is just that bad.

True efficiency isn't about how many emails you can send in an hour, how many posts you can 'like,' or how many meetings you can cram into a day. It's about the quality of the connections you make and the depth of the ideas you generate. And there's no better incubator for revolutionary thoughts than the shared commitment to a session of physical movement.

There's a reason the world's top CEO's are health-conscious. According to one recent study, 97% (485 out of 500) of Fortune 500 CEO's exercise at least 5 times per week. While the exact percentage can vary depending on the study and definition of success, it's clear that a significant majority of highly successful people incorporate regular exercise into their lives. It's one of the most important things they do in their day.

Zen of Sweat

There's a Zen-like harmony in moving in unison with your peers, your bodies and spirits merging into a seamless continuum, each stride and breath a shared rhythm of collective energy. It's a profound connection, about individual effort and about becoming part of something greater, a living, flowing testament to unity.

As you inhale and exhale, your mind empties of the trivial concerns that usually occupy it. Gone are the worries about market fluctuations and profit margins. In their place comes a clarity of thought that can become transcendental.

In these moments of physical exertion, the artificial hierarchies of the corporate world melt away. What beauty it is to be on an equal playing field. The COO and you are colleagues in your struggle against gravity and fatigue. It's in this stripped-down state that true innovation can flourish. After all, it's hard to maintain pretenses when you're both covered in sweat, questioning your life choices.

Environmental Imperative

Let's not forget the bigger picture here. While you're out there networking and sweating, you might remember there's a whole world beyond your office walls. A world that's slowly being choked to death by the very industries we all serve.

Sweatworking isn't just about your personal or professional gain. It's about reconnecting with the environment as well. It's about remembering you're part of something larger than your company's stockholders. Maybe, as you're exercising, you'll have an epiphany about how your company can reduce its carbon footprint or develop more sustainable practices.

Work-Life

You've been fed the idea of work-life balance as if your life can be neatly compartmentalized into little boxes. Life isn't a pie chart (although I do provide one for your corporate pitch in Chapter 5 to appease the executives!). It's a messy, interconnected web of experiences and relationships.

By combining networking with wellness, you're not just making better use of your time, you're integrating different aspects of your life in a way that's more natural, fulfilling, and whole. You're no longer a piston in the corporate machine, you're a human being with a body that needs movement and a spirit that craves connection.

Competitive Edge

In this competitive world of business, everyone's looking for an edge. There's no better way to stand out from the crowd than by being the person who suggests a functional exercise workout or trail run instead of a coffee meeting. You'll be remembered as the maverick, the one who dares to break free from convention.

And while your competitors are growing soft and complacent in their ergonomic chairs, you'll be honing your body into a lean, mean, deal-making machine. There's something to be said for the confidence that comes from knowing you can outrun or out-climb your business rivals.

Social Skills

Real conversation—the kind that leads to breakthrough ideas and lasting relationships—doesn't happen in nonproductive office environments. It happens in moments of shared experience. It occurs in the pauses between breaths as your team tackles a wellness routine or pushes through the last mile of a jog. The usual barriers to communication fall away. There's no hiding behind corporate jargon or carefully crafted personas. You're stripped down to your essence, and in that vulnerability lies the potential for genuine conversation.

Legitimacy Factor

In our digital age, we're suffering from an authenticity deficit. It's talked about constantly on how to be an 'influencer.' We've become so busy curating our online personas that we've forgotten how to be real. I aim to fix that by getting you back to basics.

In today's world of fake news and corporate doublespeak, the word 'authenticity' (more on that word in another chapter) is more valuable than ever. Especially when terms like that are thrown around by people in business so frequently that they mean nothing. There's nothing more authentic than seeing someone drenched in sweat, red-faced, and appreciating the air we breathe more. This raw, unfiltered version of you, your colleagues, and clients can lead to more honest and productive relationships. When you've seen someone at their most vulnerable, pushing through physical discomfort, you develop a level of trust that's hard to achieve in a meeting room.

Innovation Incubator

Some of the greatest ideas in history came not from brainstorming sessions or focus groups, but from moments of bodily movement, of physical exertion.

1. Isaac Newton's theory of gravity was inspired by observing an apple fall while walking in his garden.
2. Albert Einstein's theory of relativity he reportedly conceived while riding a bicycle.
3. Nikola Tesla's idea for alternating current struck him while walking in a park in Budapest, later stating he walked 8 to 10 miles daily to stimulate innovation.
4. Marie Curie's insights into radioactivity often came to her during long bicycle rides with her husband Pierre.
5. Jane Goodall's revolutionary observations of chimpanzee tool use were made while trekking through the forests of Gombe.
6. James Watt's improvements to the steam engine were conceived during a Sunday afternoon walk.
7. Many of Friedrich Nietzsche's philosophical insights came to him during long walks in nature.
8. Barbara McClintock's Nobel Prize in Physiology or Medicine came from the discovery of genetic transposition, which was conceived while working in corn fields.
9. Charles Darwin's theory of evolution was refined during his daily walks on the 'thinking path' at his home in Kent.
10. Steve Jobs conducted walking meetings, believing movement fostered candid dialogue, and his biographer noted these mobile discussions often yielded Apple's most pivotal decisions.

11. Ludwig van Beethoven composed symphonies in his head during long, solitary walks through the Vienna woods, relying on motion to untangle musical ideas.
12. Charles Dickens walked relentlessly, often covering 12 to 20 miles nightly through London, remarking that his novels' vivid characters and settings emerged from these nocturnal rambles.

There's something about the combination of increased blood flow to the brain and the meditative state that can come from rhythmic physical activity that creates the perfect conditions for creative thinking and calming your mind.

By taking your networking sessions out of the office and onto the trail or into the gym or conference room, you're creating an environment where innovation can flourish. The next big breakthrough for your company might come not from a R&D lab, but from a moment of clarity during a bike ride.

Antidote to Digital Overload

You're drowning in a sea of digital communication: emails, instant messages, video calls. They're coming at you from all directions, a never-ending barrage of information that leaves you feeling overwhelmed and disconnected.

Sweatworking is stepping away from the screens and engaging with people in the real world. It's using your body for something other than typing and swiping.

Legacy Factor

At the end of the day, what legacy do you want to leave? Do you want to be remembered as the person who got a large paycheck, attended the most meetings, posted the most photos, and built a comfortable, virtual world in which to hide your true thoughts? Or do you want to be remembered as the pathfinder and innovator who dared to do things differently? Who brought a sense of adventure and credibility to the world by infusing your industry with bold innovation and genuine passion?

Sweatworking isn't just about advancing your career or closing deals. It's about creating a new paradigm for how you work and interact.

Join The Inner Circle

Corporate warrior, the choice is yours. You can continue to waste away in your climate-controlled office, slowly sacrificing your health and your humanity on the altar of perceived productivity, or you can be a fraction of the next business revolution.

First, realize that only one person is keeping you from being your absolute best, and you look at it in the mirror every day.

In the following chapters, you'll embark on a journey to explore how Sweatworking can revolutionize the way you connect, collaborate, and conquer in the business world. Embrace the vulnerability and raw humanity of it all. It's time to answer the call. Here's your plan on how.

Your Mantra: Things that occur in life happen *for* me, not *to* me

2

Wake Up, Your Network's Dead

You know that feeling, right? That little internal groan when a business associate launches into the weather or some other pleasantry that feels miles away from anything concrete? And then there's the enthusiastic handshake, a finger point in your direction, and "Looking forward to it!" that evaporates into thin air the moment you try to actually connect. It's like, were we even in the same conversation?

Honestly, sometimes those superficial interactions we've all experienced can feel more draining than a marathon. It seems everyone's playing a role, and you're left wondering if anyone is truly present. And don't even get me started on conferences! You wade through a sea of buzzwords and forced smiles, and by the end of it, you're practically gagging on the sheer volume of… well, you know.

It makes you crave something genuine, doesn't it? A real conversation, a connection that goes beyond the surface. It's frustrating when those opportunities seem to be dangled in front of you, only to vanish like a mirage. You're left thinking, "Was any of this real?"

I've spent years, far more than I'd like to admit (okay, over twenty-five), schmoozing and head-nodding and eating and drinking with executives and company heads, telling stories of my expeditions.

- Fresh off a marathon win in -30 degree weather at the North Pole, I was challenged to an arm wrestle by a drunk, partially naked Russian.

- The experience of falling into a crevasse, alone, attempting a first ascent of a mountain in Greenland.

- How I stood down a bear out in the wild on Kodiak Island while cameras were rolling during a National Geographic show.

- How I managed to get 'Donkey Man' inspired enough to continue the expedition when, if he left, would have put the entire two years of planning and execution of the expedition in dire jeopardy.

- How I successfully led diverse, non-English-speaking teams and porters across Nepal, Tibet, and Mongolia by adapting my leadership to unite groups and achieve expedition goals.

- How I set ambitious goals, meticulously planned each step, and achieved them at the highest levels, leading teams of all sizes to success.

Many of those people wanted to hear the backstories and chronicles of events for sheer enjoyment, for insight, for the secret sauce on leadership, or for implementing a goal for themselves, no matter how audacious and challenging. Whatever it was, I was more than happy to oblige. Witnessing individuals triumph over obstacles and realize their aspirations brings me joy.

I also wanted the next job, the next speaking gig, the next leadership workshop. And yes, this type of networking did pay off, but with an extremely low ratio. It was like trying to obtain sponsors when I first started attempting adventure world records. You talk to one hundred companies in hopes of getting a five to ten percent return.

I remember when I returned from Nepal after becoming the first Virginian to climb Everest, and an investment banker asked me out to lunch at the Ritz-Carlton in Tyson's Corner, VA. When I showed up, I was staring into the eyes of some of the biggest high-impact leaders and hedge-fund managers in the Washington DC area, including the owner of the Washington Capitals and Washington Bullets (Wizards).

I told some stories and ate some incredible shrimp cocktail and bloody rare steak. Everyone got some great laughs, a few jaws dropped, and they appreciated the insane tales from my experiences climbing alone on Everest without supplementary oxygen, and the process and journey I took to get there. They marveled at my black fingers and toes. But in the end, that investment banker, the one who invited me to lunch, was trying to play favor with these men to get in their clique. I was his sideshow. I was the entertainment. This was merely the first tremor in a series of such engagements yet to come.

I must confess, the greatest yield on my time, the most lucrative consulting gigs, did come not from lunches, or conferences, or dinners with high-powered suits or boardroom strategists, but from those unassuming participants to whom I taught wellness classes, and the business professionals who sought me out with a singular goal: to be reshaped, reborn, and rejuvenated from the inside out.

Then it struck me, this is what networking should be for everyone: sweat-drenched, soul-stirring, and built on the unshakable camaraderie of kindred spirits where life burns brighter than any transactional exchange. The genuine community and heartfelt bonds you cultivate form the bedrock of a life worth living. It's the shared moments of toil and triumph that can truly set your soul alive.

The current, invaluable 'networking' you've been taught to worship like some false god of career advancement is, for the most part, made up of sterile connections. Traditional networking events, such as cocktail parties, conferences, and formal dinners, have long been the staple of professional relationship-building. They can be fun and pay off on rare occasions, I'll admit that. Who doesn't like an open bar?

The problem is that you think and hope you're building relationships, but instead, you're just wasting your time, sipping watered-down cocktails and exchanging meaningless platitudes with strangers who couldn't give two shits about you. It's mostly a charade. Sure, you may wrangle a few contacts, but those are few and far between. The forced nature of many traditional networking events can lead to superficial interactions, making it difficult to form genuine connections.

Think about all the business connections you've made over time. How many of those feel like truly deep relationships? And honestly, how many of those people do you think would genuinely show up at your funeral? It's a thought-provoking way to consider the quality versus the quantity of your professional circle.

Real, deep-meaning connections aren't forged in disinfected conference rooms or over rubber chicken dinners and dried-out farmed salmon. They're born in the wild, in the perspiration of honest work and shared struggle. You want authenticity? Go hike a mountain, sweat next to your EVP, or howl at the moon with a pack from your work team around a fire pit. That's where you'll find your tribal instincts. That's when you'll discover the us-against-the-world-business formula is more of a proven potion.

The Sweatworking framework is that formula.

If you want a real purpose, then get out there and fight for something that matters. Defend and pursue your dreams, rage against the dying of the light, and maybe you'll find confidantes who are worth a damn and of your time, and who are viciously loyal to one another. The rest is just noise, a distraction from the raw, blood-pumping soul of your life.

Have you attended a conference like this?

Annual "Schmooze & Snooze" Networking Conference

Where Ambition Goes to Die

Day 1: The Grind Begins

8:00 AM - 9:00 AM: **Registration & Badge Pickup**

- Start your day by standing in line with strangers who avoid eye contact while fumbling with their phones. Bonus points if someone spells your name wrong on your badge.

9:15 AM - 10:30 AM: **Opening Keynote: "Unlocking Your Potential in a Digital World"**

- Translation: A tech CEO will drone on about blockchain or AI for 45 minutes while three-fourths of the audience checks their email, and you wonder if you can sneak out for more coffee.

10:45 AM - 12:00 PM: **Breakout Sessions (Choose One)**

- Room A: "Leveraging Synergy for Cross-Functional Collaboration"
- Room B: "Optimizing Your Workflow for Maximum ROI"
- Room C: "Buzzwords That Impress No One but Sound Cool Anyway"
- Spoiler alert: All sessions are basically the same Google Slides deck with different clip art or fake AI images and avatars.

12:15 PM - 1:30 PM: **Networking Lunch**

- Sit at a round table with eight strangers and try not to spill salad dressing on yourself while awkwardly asking, "So, what do you do?" Someone will inevitably dominate the conversation by talking about his or her startup that no one asked about.

2:00 PM - 3:15 PM: **Panel Discussion: "The Future of Innovation in Business"**

- Four panelists will disagree politely while a moderator reads questions off index cards like some kind of game-show host. You'll leave with zero actionable takeaways but plenty of time wasted.

3:30 PM - 5:00 PM: **Speed Networking Session**

- Imagine speed dating but somehow even more uncomfortable. You'll meet 20 people in rapid succession, forget all their names instantly, and leave with a stack of virtual business cards you'll delete by next week.

7:00 PM - 9:00 PM: **Evening Reception & Cocktail Hour**

- Free drinks! But don't get too excited. This is where everyone clusters into groups they already know or that they're already a part of, while you hover awkwardly near the cheese platter, pretending to text someone important.

Day 2: The Snooze Continues

8:30 AM - 9:45 AM: Morning Keynote: "Disrupting Industry Norms Through Thought Leadership"

- Translation: Another executive will use buzzwords like 'disruption' and 'thought leadership' without ever explaining what they really mean in the business world. You'll leave more confused than inspired.

10:00 AM - 11:15 AM: Workshop Session

- Pick from thrilling topics like 'Maximizing KPI Alignment' or 'The Art of Strategic Pivoting.'
- Spoiler: Both involve group exercises with a drone-like, monotone-sounding moderator that makes you not want to participate, but you'll pretend you do.

11:30 AM - 12:45 PM: Networking Lunch (Again)

- Same salad choices and meat cuts, same awkward conversations, same guy still talking about his startup from yesterday.

**1:00 PM - 2:15 PM: Closing Keynote: "Achieving Excellence in an

Ever-Changing World"

- By this point, half the audience has left early to catch their flights. You are too tired to care about achieving anything except getting out of the room alive.

2:30 PM: **Adjournment: Farewell Mixer**

- One last chance to stand around holding a cup of bad coffee or sugary soft drink while pretending you're having fun. You grab your tote bag full of branded pens and make a beeline for the exit.

Why Traditional Networking is Outdated

This whole digital revolution has turned the business world on its head. It used to be that you had to schmooze your way into the right circles just to get a whiff of an opportunity. Now? Information's flying around faster than a peregrine falcon with its tail feathers on fire. By the time you've polished your elevator pitch, some kid in a garage eating Doritos and Cheetos has already disrupted your entire industry.

And let's talk about those hierarchies you've been destined to climb. In this new world of remote work and gig economies, the organizational chart looks less like a pyramid and more like a plate of spaghetti that's been tossed off the Grand Canyon. Golfing with your network of buddies, the wine and cheese happy hours, and checking LinkedIn and Facebook for your old high school or college friends are fun, but are they a useful way to make long-standing connections?

Deeper Relationships

Now, I'm not saying these types of relationships don't matter. Hell, even a mountain whore like I am knows the value of a good companion when you're lost in the backcountry. But the nature of those relationships is changing. It's not just about who you know anymore. It's about what you know, what you can do, and most importantly, why you do it.

And let's talk about diversity for a moment. In today's global marketplace, conformity can be a death sentence. The companies that are thriving are the ones that are bringing together people from all walks of life, all backgrounds, and all perspectives.

Younger Generations

But it's not just technology making your Rolodex obsolete. It's a fundamental shift in how we view work and success. The up-and-coming generations don't give two shits about our country club membership, long hours, and traditional job roles. They care about building a life of deep, considered purpose, about social impact, about leaving this world a little less screwed up than they found it.

While business executives have been busy trading business cards and perfecting their power handshake, the world's been burning. Literally, in some cases. And the younger generations are waking up to the fact that maybe there's more to life than climbing the corporate ladder. They're looking for leaders who can navigate the choppy waters of climate change, social upheaval, technological revolution, and overall well-being.

Too Slow in a Fast-Paced World

But perhaps the biggest nail in the coffin of traditional networking is the simple fact that it's slow. Painfully, glacially slow. In our world where markets can shift in the blink of an eye, where a tweet or Instagram post can tank a stock price faster than you can say 'insider trading,' the idea of slowly building relationships over years of small talk and favor trading is endearingly out of touch.

How many years do you have left on this earth to sit and email twice a month the contact who's been telling you, "We're going to do something together", and then snuffs out the air and your job? It's like trying to capture a fart with chopsticks. This type of traditional networking has nearly bankrupted me, monetarily and psychologically, as I'm sure it has for you and many other working professionals, colleagues, entrepreneurs, consultants, and the self-employed.

Adaptable

I realized the future belongs to the quick, the malleable, the innovative. It belongs to those who can spot talent and opportunity wherever it may lie, not just within their pre-existing social circles. It belongs to those who can build teams and partnerships based on shared values and complementary skills.

So what's replacing this antiquated system of backslapping and martini lunches? Well, for one, social media. For all its faults, it has democratized access to information and opportunities in ways that would have been unimaginable just a decade ago. A brilliant engineer in Bangalore can now collaborate with a visionary entrepreneur in Northern Virginia without ever having to set foot in the same room.

Technology is a double-edged sword though. More on that later.

Mind Shift

But it's more than just technology. It's a fundamental shift in mindset. The most successful organizations today are those that foster cultures of openness, of continuous learning. They're the ones who are willing to look beyond traditional credentials and connections to find the best talent, wherever it may be.

And let's not forget about the power of shared purpose. You're facing unprecedented challenges, from climate change to income inequality to the erosion of democracy. People are increasingly drawn to organizations and leaders who stand for something more than just profit. You should want to be part of something meaningful. Something that makes a difference.

The old model of top-down, command-and-control leadership needs to give way to more collaborative, inclusive approaches. Leaders who can inspire and empower their teams, who can navigate complexity and uncertainty, and who can build coalitions across traditional boundaries. Wouldn't you want that for a leader?

And believe it or not, this isn't just some pie-in-the-sky idealism. It's the cold, hard reality. Companies that cling to old ways of doing things, that rely on outdated networks and chains of command, are finding themselves outmaneuvered and out-competed at every turn. They're the business equivalent of a giant tortoise trying to outrun a Ford F-150. It ain't gonna end well.

I can hear you protesting. "Burch, you're whining. This type of conventional networking forms connections." And you're not wrong. You are 100% correctamundo. Humans are social creatures, no doubt about it.

But the nature of those connections is changing. It shouldn't be about superficial association built on mutual back-scratching anymore. The focus should be on genuine connections based on shared values and shared goals for the future. The type of relationship where you could happily hang out with that person in a tent for a month while on an expedition.

Think about it this way: in the old model, networking was like building a wall. Brick by brick, connection by connection, you'd construct this barrier between yourself and the masses. The higher the wall, the more exclusive your circle, the better off you were. But today? What you need isn't a wall, it's a bridge. A bridge that can connect you to ideas, to talent, to opportunities that you never even knew existed.

And do it in person. Honest-to-god communication.

And here's the beautiful part. Building those bridges doesn't require you to be a smooth-talking, glad-handing extrovert. It requires curiosity, openness, passion, and a willingness to engage with ideas and people outside your comfort zone.

I'd argue that your most valuable networking occurring in the future won't be in boardrooms or at conferences. It will occur in Sweatworking, collaborative workspaces, and in grassroots community organizations.

I'm not saying it's easy. Change never is. If you've built your entire career on the old model of networking, or segued into online meetings and virtual conversations, this shift can feel like trying to trek the Himalayas without a map. But let me tell you something, the view from the other side is worth it. There's a whole world of possibility out there, just waiting for you to be brave enough to explore it.

Executives & Managers & Employees

For C-Suite folks, this means rethinking how you build and lead your teams. It means looking beyond the usual suspects when you're hiring or promoting. It means fostering organic collaborations that value wellness, diverse perspectives, and encourage innovation.

For middle managers, it means to stop playing politics and start focusing on results through your employees' overall well-being. Your ability to navigate office dynamics isn't going to save you when your whole industry gets disrupted overnight. What will save you is your ability to adapt, to learn, to bring together your team to solve complex problems.

For the rank-and-file employees? This is your moment. The playing field is being leveled in ways that were unimaginable just a few years ago. Your ideas, your skills, your passion—these are your currency in the new economy. Don't waste your time trying to schmooze your way up a ladder that's already starting to topple. Focus on developing your skills, getting healthier and fit, expanding your knowledge, and connecting with others who share your values and your vision. Your place is in the building where the C-level executives sit, if you want it bad enough.

Pursuit of Truth

Mother Nature doesn't ask if you're introverted or extroverted before she makes you sweat. Exercise doesn't care either, your heart pounds the same as mine. The noonday sun burns indiscriminately, and the wind cools all skin equally. In raw moments of effort, we're stripped down to the same essentials: breath, blood, and will.

Traditional networking events are just another way to segregate you, to keep the outsiders out and the insiders in. Sweatworking presents a more inclusive alternative, allowing professionals of all genders to participate on equal footing and bear the truths.

This is why Sweatworking can be a key to your success. It builds those bridges. It embraces the challenges and the uncertainty. That's where the sincere opportunities lie. That's where your future will be built, one connection at a time.

***

Because everything in the end will be taken away forever. The very rich and most successful will die too. Never base your life on those two false gods. In the grand scheme of things, your job title doesn't matter. Your corner office doesn't matter. Your stock options don't matter. What matters is how you feel inside, how clean your soul and thinking are, the impact you have, the lives you touch, and the difference you make. And you don't need a fancy title or a big network to do that. You just need passion, purpose, and the courage to chart your own course.

There's nothing quite like standing on the edge of the unknown, heart pounding, breath quickening, staring into the wild, uncharted horizon. It's like summiting a mountain no one's ever climbed before, watching the first light of dawn spill over peaks untouched by footprints. Yeah, it's terrifying. But oh, is it magnificent. And when you take that leap? You're not just stepping forward, you're planting a flag where no one else has dared to go. Armstrong on the moon? That'll be you.

Years from now, you'll look back on this moment as the time when everything changed. When you stopped playing by the old rules and started writing your own. When you got together with someone or a group of people, and started connecting. Success is not defined by some outdated playbook but by your terms. Success is measured not in dollars or titles, but in impact, in fulfillment, in the knowledge that you've made a difference, to yourself, your mental health, and the world around you.

Your Mantra: Ideas are cheap; execution is everything

3

The Evolution of Networking

Eighteen days into a month-long expedition, I found myself in the remote Humla region of Nepal, a stone's throw from the Chinese border. My mission was to climb a series of virgin peaks, each just shy of 6,000 meters, or for those of us who follow the imperial system of measurement, 19,685 ft. Leading a team of Nepalese and Sherpas, we ventured into territory where no Westerner had ever set foot. The rugged landscape of towering mountains and thundering rivers unfolded before us since leaving Simikot, the capital of the Humla District. We had been enveloped by the unspoiled Himalayas for over two weeks, with no other human presence since our second day out. This isolation heightened the sense of adventure as we pushed deeper into this far corner of Nepal, driven by the promise of untouched peaks and potential first ascents.

As we crested a ridge, a wisp of smoke curled lazily over a distant bend. For an hour, we trekked through the rugged terrain, that marker guiding our path until we stumbled upon a nomadic yak herders' makeshift camp. Their yaks grazed contentedly on the grasses, shrubs, lichen, and moss that clung to rocks and soil. With yaks consuming roughly 1% of their body weight daily in vegetation, it was clear that the herders would soon need to break camp and lead their livestock to fresh pastures in another verdant valley, a timeless ritual that has played out for centuries in these remote mountains.

Our arrival at the nomadic camp quickly transformed into an intimate cultural exchange. We found ourselves seated with the band's venerable elder and his wife, savoring rich, creamy yak butter tea and sampling tsampa, a traditional roasted barley flour. In this clan, age bestowed leadership and the right to speak for the group. Remarkably, within just thirty minutes, I was hugging the elder's wife as we all hummed melodic tunes together. The purpose of this impromptu musical gathering initially eluded me, but my Sherpa interpreter later revealed its profound significance: we were collectively singing for the safety of our expedition team, for our expedition team's secure return to Humla, and for the yak herders' continued prosperity. It was a touching moment of shared humanity, transcending language and cultural barriers.

The blessing would prove timely, as less than two days later, I found myself teetering on the brink of life and death, spending a harrowing night that tested my resolve and fortitude on the side of a mountain.

The dance is as old as commerce itself: connection, which leads to networking, which leads to friendships, which leads to opportunity, which leads to success. It's mostly performed now in suits and slacks on the stages of boardrooms and cocktail parties. Let me regale you with a take on this peculiar human ritual, one that's as bizarre as it's necessary in the world of business.

Primeval Networking

In the beginning, there was trade. Our ancestors, barely upright and still picking fleas off each other, realized that swapping a shiny rock for a chunk of meat was a damn sight better than clubbing each other over the head. This was the birth of networking—crude, simple, and honest.

As we crawled out of our caves and started building civilizations, networking evolved. The Egyptians, those pyramid-obsessed showoffs, turned it into an art form. Pharaohs hosted grand feasts, inviting nobles and merchants to shoot the breeze under the desert stars. Meanwhile, across the sea, the Greeks were perfecting the 'conference', i.e., getting sloshed and talking business.

Medieval Mingling

Fast forward a few millennia, and we find ourselves in the bustling markets of medieval Europe. Here, networking took on a new flavor. Guilds, those exclusive clubs of craftsmen and merchants, became the hot spots for business connections. Sweaty blacksmiths and portly bakers, huddled in taverns, swapping tales and sealing deals over mugs of ale. A ritual many still practice to this very day.

But it wasn't all fun and games. The church got in on the action too. Monasteries became centers of knowledge and trade, with monks doubling as the world's first LinkedIn profiles. "Brother Nathaniel, expert in illuminated manuscripts and fine wines, seeking connections in the parchment industry."

The Industrial Revolution

As the world started belching smoke and clattering with machinery, networking shifted gears. The Industrial Revolution brought us the joy of mass production and the misery of mass exploitation. But it also gave birth to a new breed of networker: the capitalist.

These top-hat tycoons turned networking into a blood sport. Gentlemen's clubs sprouted like mushrooms after rain, offering sanctuary for the elite to plot and scheme. It was in these smoke-filled rooms, over brandy and cigars, that empires were built and fortunes were made.

In late 18th-century Britain, the seeds of professional networking were sown as businesspeople began creating capital and credit networks. This increase in trust and collaboration among business leaders laid the foundation for future networking practices. As the Industrial Revolution gained momentum in the 18th and 19th centuries, the need for businesses to collaborate and trust a wider range of people grew significantly.

20th Century Schmooze-Fest

The 20th century saw networking evolve as fast as a lightning storm striking a tin roof of a mountain hut on the Matterhorn. As the world got smaller, thanks to planes, phones, and eventually the internet, networking went global.

The early 1900s saw the formalization of networking practices. In 1912, the first Chamber of Commerce was formed in Washington, D.C., marking the beginning of organized business networking in the United States.

By the mid-20th century, from the 1950s to 1980s, exclusive clubs and organizations, such as the Elks, the Links, the Lions, the Masons, and the Woman's Century Club, to name just a few, became popular venues for business meetings and networking events.

Address Book

In the post-war boom, the Rolodex became the holy grail of networking. These spinning wheels of contacts were the analog version of today's smartphone, minus the how-to tutorials and endless notifications. The fuller your contact list, the bigger your influence. The Rolodex became a symbol of a person's network value, with a fuller Rolodex indicating stronger connections.

Conference Obsession

Next came the era of conferences—those grand circuses of business cards, bad coffee, and overindulgent happy hours. Suddenly, networking had a schedule.

- 9 AM: Keynote speech.
- 10 AM: Coffee break and desperate attempts to corner the CEO.
- 11 AM: Panel discussion on 'The Future of Synergy in the Paradigm Shift of Innovative Disruption.'

Late 20th Century

The accelerating advances in technology and improvements of communication of all kinds in the late 20th century revolutionized networking, and so began a fast tumble down an avalanche-prone slope.

- In the 1980s the first Interop trade show was born, showcasing the growing importance of technology in business networking.

- By the late 80's, businesses saw the emergence of America Online (AOL), CompuServe, and Prodigy as the big three online service providers.

- In 1989, Tim Berners-Lee developed the prototype for the World Wide Web, which would later transform online networking.

Digital Flare of Intelligence

As the millennium turned, so did the page on traditional networking. Enter the internet, stage left. Suddenly, with video conferencing tools, you could network in your pajamas and reach across continents without leaving your couch. LinkedIn burst onto the scene, turning networking into a game of digital contact over consumption and connections, with a constant barrage of people pitching you unwanted requests.

COVID

The pandemic accelerated the digital transformation of networking into informal tea parties, where being socially tone-deaf and rude became more accepted norms in virtual events and online conferences, completely transforming how people network.

Present Predicament

And here we are, in the present day, drowning in a sea of connections but parched for real relationships. We've got more LinkedIn connections than we know what to do with, X followers up the wazoo, and enough Facebook friends to populate a small country.

But do you really know anyone? I can hear the chirp, chirp, can't you? Full crickets.

Modern networking has become a paradox. We're more linked than ever before, yet increasingly isolated. We may swap digital business cards as if we're building a valuable collection, but we're frustrated because the real value of these connections is about as substantial as a politician's promise.

THE EVOLUTION OF NETWORKING

Traditional networking is all about polish. Shiny shoes, pressed suits, and plastic smiles. It's as fake as a three-dollar bill and about as useful. We've lost the raw, honest connection that our cave-dwelling ancestors had when they swapped that shiny rock for a hunk of meat.

***

As you stand at the crossroads of networking evolution, it's clear that the current ways are harming you and us as a society. The future of professional connections lies not in shiny LinkedIn profiles or carefully curated tweets, but in the authentic, sweat-soaked interactions of real human beings.

A Sweatworking program isn't a fad or a gimmick. It's a return to your roots—your truth. Put your assumptions to one side and relearn how to look at your experiences. It's about building a network, not of contacts, but of healthy friends and true business associates.

Ask yourself:

- Wouldn't I rather be building real connections while building my core to help with my longevity?

- Wouldn't I rather discuss business strategy between push-ups and squats to build my cognitive functions and expand my brain?

- Wouldn't I rather seal a deal with an enthusiastic high-five instead of a handshake or a hangover?

- Wouldn't I rather get the same amount of personal and professional work done as before in less than half the time?

Your Mantra: Poteris modo velis (You can if you will)

4

Company Convergence of Your Relevant

As you wander through the vast expanse of adulthood, you may find yourself yearning for the unrestrained bliss and wonder of your childhood. It's as if you're searching for a hidden spring, a secret place where the essence of youth still flows, waiting to revive you. When you gaze into the mirror, you catch a glimpse of that young self you once knew so well. Though you may project an image of maturity, the child within you remains, reminding you that you're not just a grown-up, but also the dreamer and explorer you've always been.

You long to rediscover the world with fresh eyes, to find magic in the mundane and beauty in the overlooked. It's a journey of rediscovery, one not of losing your adult self, but of embracing the fullness of who you are, with both the wisdom of age and the curiosity of youth. And as you embark on this path, you'll find the world is full of hidden wonders you've disregarded for years, waiting to be uncovered.

For me, it's during those long, winding journeys up into the high mountains, the sweat on my body after a workout, or simply taking a walk at night to gaze at the stars in the dark sky, that I find myself rediscovering the essence of life, the beauty in exposure, of being and feeling truly alive. There are moments I feel the weight of adulthood lifting, and I'm reborn into a state of wonder, much like my uninhibited curiosity as a child.

Toxic Leadership

For four long years, my heart lay barren and cracked. Separation and divorce had left me lost in failure as a person. Till death do you part. The commitment was broken. I was so down and out for having failed, I didn't know how I'd get my life back. Life. Living. That feeling of wanting to live, to go on, was evaporating.

I decided I needed to retreat from the world of expeditions. I couldn't fathom going away on a mountain expedition in my present state of mind. I tried to escape my failing marriage by taking a path less traveled, accepting a role as the Director of Wellness at Mission Hills Resorts in Dongguan, China. Little did I know my boss was, to put it mildly, a shadow of darkness. A reminder that sometimes the most toxic landscapes are not those of nature, but of the human heart. We've all encountered such figures, haven't we? The kind of person who leaves you questioning the very fabric of humanity.

Each evening in my hotel room, I would sit with a colleague, a golf pro who shared my employer, and together we'd find solace in the quiet of the night, often numbing our frustrations with alcohol. We were both ensnared in our own personal struggles, a poignant reflection of the consequences when leadership neglects to foster a nurturing environment. The silence between us spoke volumes about the emptiness and disillusionment that can arise when those in charge fail to prioritize the well-being of their team members.

In the end, I emerged grateful for the lesson learned. She taught me leadership by illustrating its opposite—a harsh yet invaluable lesson in how not to lead.

Forewarning

Be cautious of managers, bosses, or executives in your company who make decisions and lead teams exhibiting any of the following behaviors. If you observe these traits, it may be wise to consider leaving as soon as practically possible, and 'run for the hills' when circumstances allow.

- **Ineffective Communication**: Does your boss struggle to clearly convey expectations or listen to feedback, leading to misunderstandings and confusion among team members?

- **Lack of Vision**: Does your manager fail to provide a clear direction or strategy for the team, resulting in a lack of focus and purpose?

- **Poor Decision Making**: Are your boss's decisions often arbitrary or uninformed, thus undermining trust and morale within the team?

- **Inability to Empower Team Members**: Does he or she not delegate effectively or provide opportunities for your growth and development, leading to stagnation and dissatisfaction?

- **Unprofessional Behavior**: Does your supervisor exhibit unprofessional behaviors, such as being consistently late, dismissive, or unresponsive to important issues?

- **Inequitable Treatment**: Are you and your team members treated unfairly (especially those who are foreign or of a different sex, etc.), showing favoritism or bias, which can create a hostile work environment?

- **Lack of Accountability**: Does your boss take responsibility for his or her actions or the team's outcomes, or is the blame often shifted to you or others?

- **Inadequate Feedback**: Does your manager fail to provide constructive feedback, making it difficult for you and your team members to improve or understand your performance?

When my employer exhibited all the above traits (hand to heart), I realized it was time to stop running from my problems and face them head-on. Instead of continuing to escape or isolate myself from poor leadership and personal issues, I decided to tackle the one thing I could control—my internal struggles. So, I said goodbye to China, including a wonderful Chinese girlfriend who, along with my golf pro friend, had brought the only enjoyment into my life while I was there.

Returning home with what felt like the last threads of myself still intact, I plunged into the darkness of my past experiences. It wasn't simple, but I was determined to uncover the lessons hidden within all that turmoil and come out stronger on the other side. Because I knew, I knew, what scared me the most was giving up, because doing that is so easy to do.

I immersed myself in the teachings of Buddhism, philosophy, my self-leadership principles, and wellness, embarking on a profound journey of introspection. It was also the simplicity and self-reliance of having a daily ritual of exercise that became my solace, grounding me in the present moment and reviving my spirit. These consistent practices served as a marker of hope, guiding me toward the gift of existence. In them, I discovered peace. A poignant reminder that even in the most desolate times, there is always a path forward for you, always an opportunity to rediscover and renew yourself.

Your Crossroads

You might find yourself at a unique crossroads, a place where your desire to stay active and healthy meets your drive for career and personal success, and a deep need for connection with others. It's in this blend of self-reflection, ambition, and friendship that you'll uncover a timeless truth: Your body, your career, and your personal and professional relationships are all intertwined. Like flowing rivers through fertile valleys, these elements are essential for your well-being and fulfillment. Embracing this connection can lead to a more balanced and enriching life.

We are a world gone mad with progress. A world where men and women alike shuffle from climate-controlled boxes they call homes to climate-controlled boxes they call offices, their muscles atrophying, their spirits dulling, their connections withering. It's a reality I've railed against through teaching and speaking for over twenty-five years. A world that threatens to strip us of our very humanity.

Before you dismiss this as the ramblings of a Gen Xer gone soft in the head from too much time at altitude and longing for the nostalgia for yesteryear, hear me out. There's a method to my madness.

Health: The Foundation of Everything

Let's talk about fitness, but not the superficial kind you see in glossy magazines or on perky TV reality series. I'm talking about real, functional physical capability that can change your life. Whether you've read my book on functional wellness and self-help, *Hyperfitness* (Penguin Random House), taken my classes, seen me on the news, or a National Geographic program, you already know my approach. But if you haven't, don't worry, the core principles are universal.

My philosophy is about developing the kind of overall wellness that allows you to tackle life's challenges head-on. Imagine being able to embark on a multi-day hike with just a backpack, all while maintaining a positive attitude and thinking, "I can do this all day, every day."

In our modern world of convenience, we've lost touch with a fundamental truth: our bodies are designed for movement, exertion, and yes, even sweat. This isn't just about looking good, it's about feeling good, being mentally powerful, living longer, and experiencing life to its fullest.

When I wrote the first book on a holistic functional wellness program to help people conquer their goals, I knew it wasn't going to be a quick fix or a fad. And why should it? It's about building a foundation of strength, endurance, and mental resilience that serves you in every aspect of life. It's about reconnecting with our evolutionary heritage as active, capable human beings.

A Goal to Shoot For

You should exercise so you're able to leave on an adventure tomorrow and be in shape to perform mentally and physically. I'm not suggesting a world-record expedition, like the ones I sometimes challenge myself with, but rather any adventure that encourages you to lengthen your inner borders. Who doesn't want that? Feeling good, healthy, and enjoying each moment better than you ever have before is a gift to give to yourself.

This isn't about vanity or fitting into smaller pants. It's about reclaiming your birthright as a physical being. When you exercise, you're not just burning calories or building muscle, you're reconnecting with a part of yourself buried under layers of civilization and convenience that's been gradually coming to the surface since your childhood. You're reminding your body and your mind of what's capable.

Bonus: This physical awakening doesn't just benefit you individually. It ripples out, affecting every aspect of your life, including your personal and professional endeavors.

More Than Climbing Your Corporate Ladder

During my speaking engagements and workshops on professional development, you'll never hear me talking about kissing ass and playing office politics. I talk about genuine growth, about becoming better at what you do and who you are, and how to go about doing it. I provide you with learning objectives with viable takeaways.

You don't want to play the game, you want to be the game.

In my years of experience, I've learned that true professional development isn't about accumulating degrees or certifications. It's about constantly challenging yourself, pushing your boundaries, and learning from those around you. It's about developing the grit and determination to see a project through, even when the odds are stacked against you. It's about teaching others what you've learned, and to never stop learning more about the world and yourself.

What makes for good professional and personal development—resilience, adaptability, and the ability to push through discomfort—are the same qualities developed through Sweatworking. When you're out of breath while hiking up a steep trail or doing 50 jumping jacks, you're not just working your cardiovascular system, you're building mental toughness, learning to persevere when a part of your being is telling you to stop.

Beyond Small-Talk

In our hyper-connected digital age, true connection has become a rare commodity. We've traded depth for scope, and meaningful conversations for likes and retweets. People are too focused on qualifying the buyer.

You need real, tangible connections with others to thrive. Not the superficial interactions that pass for socializing in many workplaces, but genuine bonds forged through shared experiences and mutual respect. In Sweatworking, the approach to interactions is with openness, not interrogation.

It's about changing up boardroom whiteboards for exercise equipment, Zoom presentations for hiking trails, boring and non-inspirational 'motivational' speeches for real, honest-to-goodness genuine stimulation and endorphin highs through wellness aspirations. It's about building professional relationships, not through pretentious small talk while holding expensive lattes, but through shared challenges and triumphs.

And you can go beyond small talk, which is subtractive, to big ideas and big talk, which is proactive. When you hear, "How are you?" from a fellow participant before/during/after a Sweatworking session, they will want you to say something deeper and more meaningful than, "Pretty good," or "Hanging in there." Communication through a Sweatworking session goes much deeper than mere platitudes.

Power of Shared Struggle

When you're both winded at the top of a hill, or encouraging each other through one more set of air squats, the usual barriers of title and status melt away. You're no longer VP of Marketing and Junior Associate; you're just two humans, pushing your limits collectively. This is true populist capitalism, where ideology comes second to loyalty.

This shared struggle creates a level of trust and camaraderie that's hard to replicate in traditional networking settings. When you've seen someone exposed, red-faced, sweaty, and on the verge of giving up, you develop a different form of respect for them. And when they've seen you in the same state, it creates a mutual understanding, a bond that goes beyond professional niceties.

It's time to strip away the superficial veneer of your so-called 'civilization' and confront the visceral essence of human connection. Sweatworking is a primal return to your true nature, a way to forge bonds that transcend the artificial constructs of your corporate world. You'll meet each other face to face, devoid of the masks and pretenses that plague your everyday interactions, free from the stench of being 'sold to'.

Breaking Down Hierarchies

One of the most powerful aspects and genius of Sweatworking programs is their ability to break down traditional hierarchies. In the office, structures of power and authority can stifle genuine interaction. You might have brilliant ideas, but feel too intimidated to share them with your boss.

But put you and your boss on a basketball court or a hiking trail, and suddenly the playing field is leveled. Physical challenges don't care about your job title or your corner office. They test everyone equally, creating opportunities for leadership and collaboration that might never arise in a traditional work setting.

Fostering Innovation and Creativity

In my years of writing and teaching, I've found that my best ideas often come not when I'm sitting at a desk, but when I'm out in my small, non-HVAC dojo sweating through a workout, or on a trail out in nature, my body engaged and my mind having the free will to wander. Physical activity unlocks creativity, which allows ideas to flow more freely.

The same principle applies in the business world. A few innovative companies (some of which I will discuss in this book) have already recognized this, creating spaces for physical activity and encouraging employees to step away from their desks and get moving.

When you join people from different departments, different companies, different industries, and engage in physical activity in unison, you'll create a fertile ground for innovation. Ideas are exchanged, perspectives are shared, and creative solutions emerge, all while getting the blood pumping and the endorphins flowing.

Exercise Tip: Keep a small notepad with you. Small enough that it's not intrusive and hampering your exercise, but with enough pages and space to write down some quick, creative ideas that will arise when you're exercising.

Building Resilience and Adaptability

If there's one thing the past few years have taught you, it's that life and the business world can change in the blink of an eye. This is where your lessons learned through Sweatworking become crucial and create a support network that can weather any storm. The resilience developed through physical challenges, the adaptability honed by trying new activities, the problem-solving skills sharpened by overcoming obstacles—all of these translate directly to your business world. You develop a level of trust and mutual respect that can withstand professional challenges and setbacks.

Companies Promoting Health and Well-Being

Let's not forget the most obvious benefit of Sweatworking: it's good for you. In our sedentary work culture, where sitting for long stretches is as healthy as eating fast food, anything that gets you moving is a step in the right direction.

But Sweatworking doesn't just benefit your health. It creates a culture of wellness that can permeate entire organizations. When leaders and influential figures in a company prioritize physical activity and make it a part of their networking strategy, it sends a powerful message to their employees. It says that health and well-being are valued, and that taking care of yourself is not just permitted but encouraged.

This focus on health and well-being isn't just good for you and your employees, it's good for business. Healthier employees are more productive, more creative, and more engaged. They take fewer sick days and bring more energy to their work. By promoting Sweatworking programs, companies are essentially investing in the health and productivity of their workforce, and success for their bottom line.

We've all experienced the feeling that we don't fit in with other people, or we feel distant from the world, even when we've become a part of a company. You're there, but you're not being seen.

Leaders: Do you care about your fellow employees? Stupid question if you're the type of person who wakes up every day thinking about how you can make your associates better, more productive, healthier, more motivated, and with a feeling of belonging. Because that aligns with their needs.

Your Mantra: Complacency kills

5

The Corporate Incentives (Bullet Points)

To combat obesity, boost productivity, and realign workplace values, corporations need to revolutionize their approach to wellness by treating it as a strategic imperative, not just an HR initiative. This means replacing pizza meetings with nutrient-dense meals, incentivizing movement, and redesigning workspaces to encourage activity. Leaders should model balanced behaviors, tie wellness metrics to performance reviews, and openly discuss mental health to destigmatize self-care.

With employee fatigue costing companies $322 billion annually, and 88% valuing well-being as much as salary, the corporate wellness playbook needs a significant overhaul that tackles obesity, productivity, and values directly.

Follow The Money Waste

- **Burnout's price tag**: $322B/year in lost productivity.
- **Gen Z crisis**: 59% have mental health struggles vs. 35% of boomers.
- **Investments surging**: 75% of firms boosted weight management budgets (+109% since 2023).
- **Tech takeover**: 97.8% of companies now use AI for personalized

wellness.

Yet, most company-wide wellness initiatives continue to fail because they ignore the root causes, such as sedentary work cultures, stress-normalized leadership, virtual embeds, and misaligned incentives.
Here's a summary of obesity trends statistics from the USA's top agencies, such as the NIH, from 1990 to the present.

Adult Obesity Trends (Ages 25+)

- 1990: 11.6% of U.S. adults were obese.
- 2022-2024: 31.3% of adults are obese, though some sources report higher figures due to differing methodologies.

This is nothing to say of the child and adolescent obesity trends that are rising exponentially each year. Obesity prevalence has doubled since 1990 in most age groups.

Projections for 2050:

- Adults: Obesity rates may reach 55.3% in men and 58.8% in women.
- Combined overweight/obesity could affect 81.1% of men and 82.1% of women.

Here are a few immediate suggestions:

- Treat employee vitality like a supply chain.
- Optimize wellness with real-time wearables data.
- Tie manager bonuses to team well-being Key Performance Indicators (KPI).
- Replace 'mental health days' with systemic redesigns that make healthy choices inescapable.

Companies that don't act risk losing top talent to rivals offering better wellness initiatives. The global wellness market will hit $72.7 billion by 2030, and the war for productivity will be won or lost at the intersection of company wellness and business strategy.

Mindless spending, whether on causes, political agendas, or crises, rarely delivers real solutions. Businesses are pouring billions into an epidemic that could be solved far more effectively by embracing Sweatworking, at a fraction of the cost.

1. Health as Your Competitive Edge

- You burn calories while building relationships.
- Exercise releases endorphins that boosts mood and well-being.
- A focus on your health demonstrates discipline—a trait all successful people share.

2. Genuine Connections Forged Through Shared Endeavors

- Facing challenges together creates bonds stronger than small talk.
- Your true personalities are revealed (you'll spot who's a team player vs. a quitter).
- Morning runners and evening bodyweight exercisers naturally connect as like-minded professionals.

3. Direct Your Focus, Direct Your Results

- Professionals report making valuable contacts through fitness.
- Deals happen organically with less pressure than traditional networking.
- Post-workout coffee can lead to "Hey, I know someone you should meet."

4. Idea Incubator in Motion

- Walking boosts creativity by 60% (Stanford study).
- Novel environments (hiking trails, obstacle courses) spark innovative thinking.
- Movement breaks down mental barriers to collaboration.
- Physical activity increases divergent thinking by 60% compared to sedentary brainstorming.
- Companies like Apple historically used walking meetings to spark innovation. Sweatworking escalates this process with higher-intensity movement sessions.

5. Social Skills Calisthenics for Adults

- Learn to read body language in real-time.
- Practice encouragement (the business world's most underrated skill).
- Develop grit, which translates directly to professional resilience.

6. The Ultimate Advantage: Zero Regrets

- No need for calculating, "Was that 2 drinks or 5?" the next morning.
- Wake up energized instead of reviewing embarrassing texts.
- Your liver and reputation remain equally intact.

7. Behavioral Interviewing in Real-Time

- Recruiters observe candidates' resilience, teamwork, and problem-solving during challenging workouts, metrics impossible to gauge in traditional interviews.
- Example: Cycle classes reveal how individuals handle stress (e.g., hill climbs = project deadlines).

8. Cross-Departmental Collaboration

- Workplace sessions break individual work categories by mixing teams (e.g., engineers + marketers in boxing classes), fostering organic idea exchange.
- 78% of employees report improved interdepartmental communication post-Sweatworking events.

9. Cost-Effective Client Retention

- Replace expensive dinners ($300+/meal) with $30 fitness classes, to yield 3x longer client engagement post-activity.
- Boutique gym partnerships (e.g., SoulCycle corporate memberships) have been shown to reduce entertainment budgets by 40%.

10. Demographic-Specific Networking

- Women-led ventures: Yoga/running groups cater to female professionals, avoiding alcohol-centric events.
- Gen Z recruitment: 68% prioritize employers offering fitness-integrated networking over happy hours.

11. Remote Team Bonding

- Virtual Sweatworking (e.g., synchronized Peloton rides with Slack debriefs) bridges hybrid work gaps.
- Wearable tech (Fitbit challenges) creates global leaderboards to motivate teams.

12. Unconscious Bias Reduction

- Hierarchies flatten in workout attire; 62% of employees report feeling more comfortable voicing ideas post-Sweatworking vs. boardrooms.

These incentives address unmet needs in talent acquisition, client relations, and operational efficiency, positioning Sweatworking as a strategic tool beyond wellness perks.

Tip: The best Sweatworking happens when you focus on the experience first. The business benefits follow naturally.

Underexplored Sweatworking Incentives

Beyond the obvious previous perks stated—wellness, networking, and productivity—Sweatworking harbors deeper, underutilized advantages that the corporate world hasn't yet leveraged.

Unfiltered Character Assessment
Watch how a colleague handles a hill sprint or a dropped weight. Their grit (or lack thereof) reveals more than any performance review.

Shared Challenges as Loyalty
Bonding, forged in sweat-soaked challenges, outlasts transactional happy-hour alliances. The bootcamp participant who didn't grab the last available water bottle? That's your next trusted partner.

Creative Sabotage of Stagnation
Ideas flow when blood does. A study on heat acclimation shows sweat primes the brain for endurance, both physical and mental. The sauna-suit effect: Clarity emerges when the body's pushed into uncomfortable territory.

Skin-in-the-Game Networking
There is no hiding behind tailored suits. Sweatworking strips pretense; your drenched T-shirt is an honesty meter. Proof that vulnerability sells.

Time Rebellion
An hour stolen from the weekly meeting purgatory becomes an act of defiance. The clock ticks more slowly when you're winded from running, actually moving forward together as a cohesive tribe, making deadlines feel trivial by comparison.

Sweatworking Positives by Wellness Dimensions

Sweatworking's Yin Yang X 4

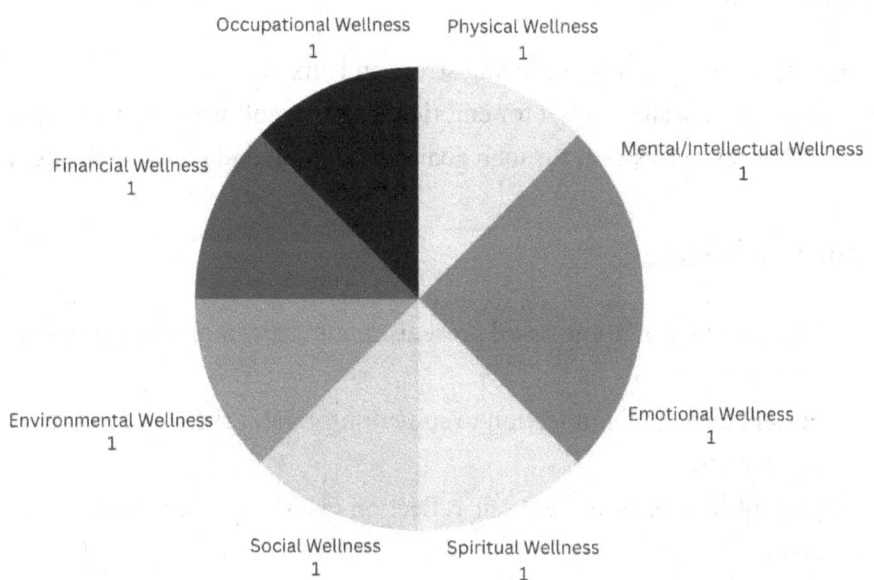

Physical Wellness

- Enhances cardiovascular health and endurance through regular physical activity.
- Promotes detoxification by flushing toxins from the body via sweat.
- Improves skin health by increasing blood flow and nutrient delivery to skin cells.

Mental/Intellectual Wellness

- Boosts cognitive function by increasing blood flow to the brain.
- Stimulates neurochemicals like serotonin and dopamine, improving focus and mental clarity.
- Reduces mental fatigue, fostering creativity and problem-solving.

Emotional Wellness

- Releases endorphins, reducing stress and anxiety.
- Provides a healthy outlet for emotional release and stress management.
- Enhances self-esteem through goal achievement and physical progress.

Spiritual Wellness

- Encourages mindfulness and present-moment awareness during workouts.
- Fosters a sense of connection to something greater through meditative movement.
- Promotes inner peace and self-reflection in a shared wellness environment.

Social Wellness

- Strengthens team cohesion through shared fitness goals.
- Facilitates networking in a relaxed, non-work setting.
- Builds trust and camaraderie among colleagues through collaborative workouts.

Environmental Wellness

- Encourages sustainable commuting (e.g., walking/biking to group workouts).
- Promotes eco-friendly fitness spaces (e.g., outdoor workouts, energy-efficient gyms).
- Reduces workplace stress by integrating movement into daily routines.

Financial Wellness

- Reduces healthcare costs by promoting preventive health measures.
- Lowers gym membership expenses if workplace facilities are provided.
- Enhances productivity, potentially leading to career advancement and financial gains.

Occupational Wellness

- Boosts workplace morale and engagement through team-based fitness.
- Reduces burnout by integrating physical activity into work culture.
- Attracts top talent by showcasing a company's commitment to employee wellness.

Your Mantra: Do the work, take chances, accept challenges, trust your gut

6

Wellness for Winners (and Those Who Want to Be)

You face unique challenges as you grow up, whether it's navigating family dynamics, dealing with bullying, having body image issues, or feeling insecure. For me, as I'm sure it was for you, growing up was a deeply emotional journey. As a sensitive kid, I often put on a brave face, but beneath the surface, I struggled with feelings of insecurity and a deep longing for connection and love. I felt profoundly lonely and misunderstood, like you and everyone else did.

While many childhood experiences may have been challenging, movement and activity likely provided a welcome respite, offering some of your genuinely positive moments. Remember those carefree days running around outside just for the joy of it? Growing up in Northern Virginia, I found being active wasn't just about ambitions, it was more about having fun, enjoying the outdoors, and feeling free.

As I entered my teenage years, exercise took on a new role. I found solace in sports. Through determination and perseverance, I excelled and found a sense of purpose. It was about doing my best when playing varsity sports like basketball and track & field. I'll admit, there was also a desire to feel more athletic and confident in my own skin. But what I discovered through exercise went far beyond physical benefits.

Exercise became a sanctuary, a daily escape from the ups and downs of adolescence. It taught me discipline, a quality that has been invaluable in navigating life's twists and turns. It also brought me mental clarity and resilience, helping me stay grounded even when things felt chaotic.

When I was in college and those first few years of adulthood, I found my anchor in exercise and martial arts. Whenever life felt like it was spinning out of control, hitting the mat or pushing my limits in training was the one thing that always steadied me.

Now, as an adult, I've come to appreciate exercise more than ever before. Exercising, sports training, and instructing groups have become my lifeline, helping me cope with daily life and giving me the strength to keep moving forward. In your often hectic and unpredictable world, having this simple, consistent practice can be incredibly comforting because it's something you can control. It reminds you of your inner strength and the beauty of taking care of yourself. Because you can still feel the fears and the insecurity of your youth when you're an adult.

Feeding Our Inner Monsters

In your quest for self-improvement, more specifically, weight-loss, it's easy to be drawn to the promise of quick fixes like weight-loss enhancing drugs that are becoming increasingly available. These medications offer the tempting prospect of reshaping your body to fit personal or societal ideals. While they may lead to weight loss, it's important to consider the potential side effects and long-term implications of gaining the weight right back once you've reached your desired weight and gone off the drug.

And it does nothing to strengthen or condition your body physically and mentally.

Sweatworking is not an exercise program for weight-loss. True transformation goes beyond physical appearance. Our journey towards self-acceptance and well-being is deeply personal and complex. It's not just about shedding pounds or obtaining a new trimmer wardrobe, it's nurturing your inner self and addressing the root causes of your insecurities and challenges.

You might achieve your desired weight, but if you haven't addressed your inner struggles, you will find yourself thinner yet still unfulfilled. Real, lasting change often requires looking inward, confronting your fears, and working towards self-acceptance and personal growth rather than taking a drug.

This isn't to discourage you from seeking medical help for weight management if it's needed. Rather, it's a reminder that your worth isn't determined by the number on a scale. True wellness encompasses both physical and mental health, and the most profound changes will come from the journey to obtain your highest self. This is where Sweatworking will shine for you.

Another Gadget or Exploitation?

You might be thinking that Sweatworking is just another corporate gimmick of our modern world, where even something as basic as sweating is being commercialized and leveraged for professional advantage. I encourage you to think beyond the boundaries of conventional norms.

This layering of two tasks is not some clever trick. It legitimately hits two of your targets with one arrow: maintaining that temple of flesh and bone while interacting with potential clients or partners. It's efficiency at its finest. It's a nod to society's obsession with productivity.

Sweatworking allows you to acknowledge your body, mortality, and connection to the earth beneath your feet. And if, in that moment of shared vulnerability and exertion, you make a business connection, well, so much the better. At the very least, you've tasted a morsel of what it means to be truly alive.

Skill Ninja Training

Instead of being cooped up in some air-recirculated hellhole, choking on someone else's exhaling bad breath, or even worst, your own bullshit, get out there in the wild, laugh your tail off, learn more about yourself, and actually live with presence. There's a certain poetry to discussing ideas while your lungs are expanding and your muscles are active. It's in those moments of physical exertion, when you're pushing yourself and feeling truly alive, that the real innovation happens.

Sweat, curse, laugh, and you'll find that the solutions to your problems, the innovations you've been chasing, have been out here all along. In the triumph of movement, you will rediscover a part of yourself you thought was long lost to the grind of a corporate entity.

It's a sad state of affairs when we need to invent reasons to move our bodies and talk face-to-face for the simple pleasure of physical exertion and genuine human interaction. But think of this as embracing 'old-school' priorities. It's good, it's justified, it's necessary.

The confidence boost? You're the most intricate wonder this planet has ever known: a living, breathing, feeling human being.

The personal fulfillment? You're Earth's masterpiece: a heart, a mind, and endless possibility in human form.

The Horizon Whisperer

Stuffy boardrooms and fluorescent-lit, white-walled rooms don't expand ideas. It's time to feel the ambition in your muscles and your mind. Sweatworking is what our ancestors did naturally, moving their bodies while conducting the business of survival. But in our mechanized world, it can become a revolutionary act. When you engage in wellness with folks, you open yourself up to a whole new world of ideas and possibilities.

The real challenge and opportunity lie in figuring out which of these fresh insights resonates with your aspirations. So, whether you're brainstorming with like-minded individuals or exploring uncharted territory with diverse thinkers, remember that every interaction can spark something amazing. Embrace the variety and see where it takes you.

Don't just follow the herd. You be the one to suggest these wild adventures. You be the one to push further, to take the path less traveled. That's how you stand out in this conformist world.

The cross-pollination of ideas and experiences through Sweatworking can lead you to:

- Exposure to different perspectives and approaches
- Opportunities for collaboration across sectors
- Insights into industry trends and innovations

This can't be sugarcoated. You must first get off your ass, out of that office, and into the gym or outside.

The act of exercising is 'beyond the human.' True balance is found in the tension between civilization and the natural world, between your ambitions and the beauty of working your body physically. You'll find that the 'growth' you're after isn't just about your career after all.

Mantra: Don't lay waste to your powers

7

Sweat, Smile, Repeat: How Exercise Rewires Your Brain

Love. Hurts so good, doesn't it? It's the ultimate rollercoaster of emotions. Love can be the best feeling on earth because it fills you with warmth, joy, and a sense of connection that makes life feel magical. It makes your heart race, provides meaning to the simplest moments, and reminds you that you're not alone in this big, chaotic world. To have a child is to know love in its most enduring form.

Love can also be the worst. When it's not returned or when someone you care about hurts you, it can leave you feeling hollow, shattered, and questioning everything. It's both beautiful and brutal. It can lift you to unimaginable heights and yet is powerful enough to bring you crashing down.

I was fortunate to have shared time and deep love with another human being. She was radiant and beautiful, intelligent and sophisticated, with a voice that could captivate anyone. She made me proud to stand beside her because she saw the beauty in my rough edges. She had a way of bringing out my confidence, not just in who I was, but in the kind of person I wanted to be.

Her presence brought a kind of peace. Even the simplest moments, like sharing a meal or sitting quietly together, felt special because we were by each other's side. There was an effortless connection, where conversations flowed naturally from silly jokes to deep, meaningful talks about life.

Being in love isn't about perfection, it's about partnership. It's knowing that no matter what life throws at you, you'll face it together. Being young adults, we fell into the immature trap of wishing the other could love us exactly as we needed. When we parted ways, my heart ached so deeply that I felt like the world would have been kind to just stop turning. A part of me had gently lifted away, leaving behind a sense of longing for time to reverse itself.

You know that feeling. It's a place you've been to at some point in your life. Maybe you're there right now. Depression wraps itself around you so tightly that all you can do to survive is retreat to your own space. The weight of it makes you feel like there's no escape, and it's hard to imagine ever breaking free. Everything around you seems to filter through this dark camera lens, and all you see is a negative.

When simple tasks feel overwhelming, navigating social gatherings like meetings or networking events can be particularly draining, leaving you feeling on the brink of collapse among forced smiles and superficial interactions. In these moments, the allure of unhealthy food and drinks offers a deceptive quick fix, providing temporary relief while ultimately exacerbating your discomfort and exhaustion in the long run.

I've been right there with you, just plodding through the passage of days while my inner world was screaming for help. My only thought was on how I could break this cycle.

I began to trust the process that had helped me so many times before, and forced myself to continue to teach classes and workshops. Eventually, it began to feel like I was discovering a hidden part of who I was, one movement, one bullet point, one session at a time. The physical activity and coaching cracked through my defenses, not all at once, but in small, consistent ways. And as my inner defenses softened, so did my perspective. I started noticing subtle, small wins and unexpected opportunities life offered when I was present enough to receive them.

This is how exercise healed my mind and restored my energy, and how it can for you, too.

Stress Reduction and Mood Enhancement

A good workout leaves you feeling lighter and more relaxed. That's the magic of endorphins—nature's built-in stress busters. When you bring that same energy into a conversation, even tense moments can turn into a more comfortable and productive exchange. People open up, trust grows, and suddenly, you're not just talking, you're connecting.

This approach allows you to transcend the superficial barriers that can encase you in professional settings, revealing a more genuine and compassionate side of yourself. That's how you build relationships that last, rooted in mutual respect and a little shared laughter and sweat.

Improved Cognitive Function

Studies show that regular physical activity can sharpen your memory, improve attention, and boost your problem-solving skills. These mental perks can make a real difference in professional settings and will help you stay sharp during meetings, contribute more effectively to your brainstorming sessions, and navigate negotiations with greater focus and clarity.

Exercise can also spark creativity and fuel innovative thinking. In workplaces where fresh ideas and novel solutions are highly valued, this cognitive boost can be a game-changer for you. Whether tackling a tough project or searching for unique insights, staying active will give you the mental edge needed to approach challenges with confidence and creativity.

Enhanced Self-Esteem and Confidence

When you start seeing what your body can accomplish, that confidence will naturally spill over into how you carry yourself at work. You'll notice you stand taller, make stronger eye contact, and just generally feel more put-together in professional situations.

And when you feel better about yourself, that newfound confidence will change how you show up at work. Suddenly, speaking up in meetings will feel way less intimidating, pitching your big ideas will come more naturally, and you might even find yourself volunteering for leadership opportunities you would've shied away from before. When you bring this kind of authentic, empowered energy to the table, work interactions will become way more dynamic and productive.

Building Genuine Connections

Traditional networking events often feel a bit stiff or overly formal, making it hard for you to truly connect with others. Sweatworking creates a more relaxed and natural environment where you can bond with people over shared physical activities. It's easier to strike up conversations when you're both focused on the same activity, rather than navigating the awkwardness of small talk in a crowded room.

What makes Sweatworking especially effective is how it allows you to connect with people on a personal level first, i.e., the wellness component, which often leads to stronger professional relationships later in the networking component.

Power of Vulnerability in Professional Settings

Sweatworking introduces an element of susceptibility to professional interactions by adding doses of actuality. When people exercise together, they're often in a more exposed state, both physically and emotionally, than they would be in a traditional business setting. That unpolished vibe tends to break down emotional walls.

And that little bit of vulnerability? It will help you. When people let their guard down, you'll see conversations stop feeling like rehearsed pitches and start feeling like genuine connections. Over time, you may become more comfortable sharing your thoughts, ideas, and even challenges, fostering a sense of trust and authenticity with the other members of the group.

Breaking Down Hierarchical Barriers

In a gym or fitness class, titles and positions often become less relevant. Everyone, regardless of their professional status, is there to exercise and improve themselves. That natural equalizer can soften the rigid structures of the workplace, making it easier to connect with colleagues as people, not just positions.

For junior employees or those new to an industry or company, this can be particularly beneficial. In a fitness setting, the playing field levels out, and conversations flow more naturally. Instead of worrying about rank, you're bonding over shared struggles—like that set of burpee jumps. It's a great way to build relationships with senior colleagues without the pressure of formal office dynamics.

Overcoming the Transactional Feeling of Networking

Interestingly, research has shown that many people, especially those who feel like they don't have much power at work, can see professional networking as morally sketchy or even soul-crushing. This psychological barrier can prevent individuals from engaging in networking activities, potentially hindering their career progress.

Sweatworking offers a unique solution to this problem. By framing networking as a mutual activity focused on health and well-being, it can help alleviate these negative associations. The shared experience of exercise can make networking feel less transactional, potentially reducing feelings of discomfort.

Endorphins

Ever notice how a good workout or time spent exercising leaves you feeling oddly happy? That's the magic of endorphins, your brain's natural mood boosters kicking in during exercise. These little chemicals don't just ease stress. They can make you feel a wave of euphoria, turning even the toughest sweat session into a mental reset.

The endorphin rush you feel creates positive vibes around professional interactions, making them feel less like a chore and more like something you actually look forward to. Over time, that mindset shift can transform your approach to professional relationships, turning them into opportunities for genuine excitement rather than obligatory small talk.

Long-Term Psychological Benefits

The psychological benefits of Sweatworking extend beyond the immediate effects of exercise. When you make these active meetups a habit, you're not just boosting endorphins in the moment, you're rewiring your brain for long-term resilience. Over time, that regular movement becomes your secret weapon against stress, helping you tackle work challenges with a sharper, calmer mindset, especially as the years stack up. It's leveling up your mental armor without even realizing it.

Conquering fitness goals alongside career milestones teaches you how to embrace the grind. Missed a personal fitness goal? No worries, you learn, adjust, and come back stronger, just like you would after a work setback. That persistence muscle you build in continued Sweatworking sessions? It translates directly to the boardroom. Suddenly, "I can't" becomes "I will, and just watch me."

Posture

We worry about our gadgets and gizmos, our cars and our careers, but what about the simple things? Like standing tall? Good posture is about refusing to let the weight of the world and time, literally and figuratively, bend your back. As you age, your spine begins to compress, your shoulders slump, and your head hangs low. But I say, resist this gravitational pull.

As you exercise your way through a cycle class or weight-training session, you can strengthen the very muscles that keep you upright. Your spine, usually curved like a question mark from hours of hunching over spreadsheets and staring at a screen, can be worked into alignment.

Sweatworking keeps your body in motion, resisting the relentless pull of office chairs. Your whole body can become misshapen by your desk-bound existence, so to straighten up as you jog alongside potential clients and associates or pedal furiously on stationary bikes while discussing quarterly projections will seem like a blessing. Stand up straight and shout to the world: "I'm still here. Bring it!"

I'm not advocating for some rigid, militaristic stance. It's about embracing your age with dignity and not letting the years weigh you down. So, take a deep breath, square your shoulders, and walk into a Sweatworking session with your head held high.

Aging

Ageism is not a fallacy. It's a universal and measurable form of discrimination that impacts individuals across all age groups, particularly older adults. It can manifest in various ways, such as workplace exclusion, healthcare biases, and societal stereotypes that undermine individuals based on their age. Globally, studies show that one in two people hold ageist attitudes toward older individuals, which contributes to social isolation, poorer mental health, and diminished quality of life. These biases deprive society of the valuable contributions of people across all ages.

Sweatworking's approach to aging seeks to cultivate community, purpose, and a confident mindset. This journey is not about you defying time, but about embracing it with grace and elasticity. It's about you recognizing that every stage of life offers its own unique beauty. As you age, you can find strength in your connections, your stories, and your shared humanity.

It becomes clear that your attitude toward aging can either nourish or wither you. The data shouts out how your beliefs can shape your health. Sweatworking can be a reminder that you're not a solitary traveler through your life, but rather a thread in a rich tapestry of human experience and social connection.

***

In this world of ours, you're witnessing a revolution in how we connect on a social, personal, and professional level. Sweatworking is the rebellious offspring of this new era. It's a holistic approach that doesn't just nurture your career but also your soul.

You can transform what was once seen as a necessary but often uncomfortable aspect of career development into an enjoyable and beneficial part of your routine. Your mind will get sharper, your mood will lift, and you'll walk taller with a renewed sense of self-worth. This shift has the potential to create healthier, happier, and more connected professional communities and companies, ultimately leading to more fulfilling and successful careers for you and your employees.

The continued evolution and adoption of Sweatworking may well redefine your understanding of work-life balance, career relationships, and the very nature of networking itself. In a world where mental health and physical well-being are increasingly recognized as crucial components of professional success, Sweatworking offers you a promising path forward. It's not just about efficiency or productivity, it's living a life that's full, vibrant, and true to who you are.

Your Mantra: Recognize what you can't control and what you can

8

The Samurai's Guide to Not Losing Your Mind at Work

I've long admired the Japanese. Not for their skyscrapers or bullet trains, but for the quiet strength of their culture. Respect, discipline, work ethic, politeness—these are virtues that transcend borders and time. Their dedication to craft and punctuality is my kind of poetry. In a world drowning in noise and nonsense, the Japanese show us what it means to live with purpose, to honor work as art and time as sacred.

I embarked on an expedition to Japan to learn more about the country and its people, and to attempt a winter speed ascent of Mt. Fuji (Fujisan), the nation's highest peak and a deeply revered symbol throughout its history. Mt. Fuji transcends its physical presence, serving as a philosophical, cultural, and spiritual cornerstone for the Japanese. As a sacred site, its significance is woven into the fabric of Shinto and Buddhist traditions, inspiring countless pilgrims and artists over the centuries.

Upon arriving at Haneda Airport in Tokyo in the evening, I spent my first night in Shinjuku. The following morning, I boarded a train to Kawaguchiko, where I arranged accommodation at a local hostel for several days. My expedition was in collaboration with The Fujisan Club, Japan's leading non-profit organization dedicated to preserving Mt. Fuji's natural beauty and combating environmental challenges.

During the summer months, Mt. Fuji attracts up to 400,000 hikers eager to reach its summit. In stark contrast, winter transforms the mountain into an unforgiving territory accessible only to seasoned climbers due to its treacherous conditions. Officially closed to the public during this season, winter ascents on Mt. Fuji aren't merely climbs, they are tests of endurance and survival. The risks include extreme cold with wind chills reaching -40°C, icy slopes, and unpredictable jet stream winds that often exceed 150 kph in the higher elevations. In 2024 alone, there were only 288 recorded off-season attempts, a testament to the mountain's formidable challenges and inherent dangers.

During winter, Mt. Fuji rivals the brutal conditions found on Himalayan giants like Everest. On the day I established the record for the fastest winter ascent, I had proof of just how fierce it was. A product sponsor provided me with a handheld weather anemometer, which showed wind speeds on Fuji's summit that were even higher than those recorded on Everest's summit that same day. Climbing in snowshoes from Umagaeshi Shrine, I battled frostbite, swollen hands, relentless high winds, and temperatures dipping below -20°F.

Before setting off, I had to submit a climbing form to the Yamanashi Police Department. They tried their best to dissuade me with warnings about the dangers of winter ascents, but being what many may call a fool, I said, "Arigatou," and pressed on. After completing the climb and confirming my world record time with Fujiyoshida City Hall's government coordinator, I celebrated in a way that reflected Japan's incredible hospitality. The owner of the hostel I'd been staying at invited me to dinner at his family home. A gesture that felt deeply personal despite our brief interactions during my stay.

This experience introduced me to 'Omotenashi,' Japan's unique approach to hospitality rooted in respect, harmony, and thoughtfulness. The family's kindness and their reverence for elders and community ties left a lasting impression on me. It wasn't just their actions, it was the cultural ethos behind them that captivated me. Their warmth and generosity made me feel like part of their family. Since then, I've been in love with Japan and its people, who embody decency and connection in ways that are both humbling and inspiring.

Japan's Approach to Employee Health

It's interesting how Japanese companies have integrated employee well-being into their operational fabric. Initiatives such as mandatory calisthenics, subsidized gym memberships, and meditation workshops are now common. Sure, boosting productivity is part of it, but there's a real human element too. They're acknowledging the demands of their work culture and offering these shared moments to look after both physical and mental well-being, fostering a sense of community and care within their often intense workplaces.

Honda began implementing exercise programs for assembly line staff that mirrored their job tasks before commencing work in the 1980s. This proactive strategy yielded considerable benefits, including a decrease in workplace incidents, employee absences, and medical expenses, alongside enhanced productivity. The positive outcomes of Honda's efforts motivated other Japanese firms to adopt similar practices, incorporating physical activity into daily schedules and cultivating a workplace culture centered on health and team spirit.

Japanese companies employ diverse strategies to promote wellness among their employees:

- **Rajio Taiso Morning Exercises**: This is a traditional exercise routine broadcast on radio, television, and streaming, that provides instructions for simple exercises during work hours. This routine in Japan has been practiced for nearly a century.
- **Health Checkup**: Annual health screenings are mandatory by law, enabling early detection of illnesses.
- **Government Initiatives**: Health and Productivity Management Programs are initiatives endorsed by Japan's Ministry of Economy, Trade and Industry (METI), which aim to improve employee well-being while aligning corporate wellness with broader economic goals.
- **Mandatory Group Exercises**: Companies like Osaka Gas require employees to participate in daily exercise sessions.
- **Subsidized Gym Memberships**: Many firms offer financial support for employees to join sports clubs or gyms.
- **On-Site Fitness Facilities**: Yoga, Pilates classes, and other physical activities are often available at workplaces.
- **Mental Health Support**: Counseling services and stress management workshops are widely offered.

Impact on Corporate Performance

Gross Profit Growth

Companies investing in employee wellness often see long-term financial benefits through reduced absenteeism and healthcare costs. For example, Honda's productivity gains contributed directly to its profitability.

Networking Opportunities

Group exercises foster collaboration among employees, enhancing teamwork and communication skills that are vital for business success.

Brand Image Enhancement

Organizations recognized for their wellness initiatives attract positive attention from stakeholders and the public. Companies with robust health management programs often report better stock performance compared to peers without such initiatives.

Otsuka Holdings Co., Ltd. emphasizes creating a supportive environment for employees' physical and mental health, offering health seminars, a cafeteria plan that rewards healthy behaviors, and measures to reduce long working hours.

The Subaru Corporation has a clear 'Subaru Health Declaration,' emphasizing the importance of employees' and their families' well-being as a foundation for the company's vision. Subaru focuses on physical health, mental health, and organizational health initiatives, including measures against smoking and promoting work-life balance.

The Organization for Economic Cooperation and Development (OECD) analyses suggest that workplace wellness investments yield a return of $4 for every $1 spent, emphasizing their economic viability.

Benefits of Workplace Wellness Programs in Japan

For Employees

1. **Improved Health**: Regular exercise has reduced risks associated with sedentary lifestyles, such as cardiovascular diseases and diabetes.
2. **Mental Well-Being**: Programs targeting mental health have alleviated stress and improved overall job satisfaction.
3. **Improved Employee Morale**: Wellness programs have fostered a sense of community within organizations. Employees feel valued when their employers invest in their well-being, which has boosted morale and loyalty.

For Employers

1. **Reduced Healthcare Costs**: Preventive measures such as fitness programs and health screenings have helped lower healthcare expenses by reducing the prevalence of chronic diseases.
2. **Enhanced Productivity**: Regular exercise has improved physical stamina and mental focus, leading to higher productivity levels. Japan Airlines implemented a comprehensive wellness program ('JAL Wellness 2025') with the explicit goals of improving employee health and boosting productivity.
3. **Lower Accident Rates**: Exercise routines tailored to job-specific movements have reduced workplace injuries such as seen in the case of Honda Motor's assembly line workers.
4. **Talent Retention**: Wellness initiatives have enhanced job satisfaction, making companies more attractive to potential employees while retaining existing talent.
5. **Reduced Absenteeism**: Fewer sick days have led to uninterrupted workflow and lower healthcare costs.
6. **Improved Corporate Image**: Wellness programs have helped attract and retain talent while enhancing brand reputation.

Healthy Habits, Happy Employees

The #1 Car Company in Japan - Toyota Motor Corporation

Toyota, Japan's leading automaker, purposefully integrates fitness into its operations, recognizing its power to boost employee performance, well-being, and networking. Rooted in their 'Respect for People' philosophy and commitment to continuous improvement, their programs cultivate a workplace culture that values physical and mental health, all while fostering stronger relationships among team members.

Key Illustrations

Group Fitness Programs: Toyota's TMMKFitness in Georgetown, KY, offers 35+ group exercise classes weekly, catering to diverse schedules and fitness levels. These classes aim to create a welcoming environment that feels like family, promoting both physical health and camaraderie among employees.

Health Education and Lifestyle Challenges: Toyota conducts periodic health education sessions for associates, such as the 'KENKO Challenge 8,' which focuses on cultivating eight healthy lifestyle habits. These initiatives include personalized feedback from annual health checkups, body composition analysis, and exercise recommendations to motivate behavior change.

Weight Reduction Programs: Programs using tools like body composition analyzers help employees visualize their progress in reducing body fat and improving fitness. These efforts have led to measurable improvements in health metrics and increased motivation among participants.

Wellness as a Networking Tool

Collaborative Fitness Culture: Toyota's group fitness programs encourage employees from different departments to interact in an informal setting, fostering teamwork and collaboration outside the workplace.

Empathy-Driven Leadership: Managers at Toyota are trained to address both physical and mental well-being, creating a supportive environment where employees feel valued. This empathetic leadership approach strengthens trust and enhances workplace relationships.

Global Engagement Practices: Toyota's global initiatives, such as digital tools for talent management and mentorship programs, further integrate fitness into broader employee engagement strategies. These programs ensure a balance between technological innovation and human connection.

Impact on Employee Well-Being

Physical Health Benefits: Regular fitness activities reduce risks associated with lifestyle diseases like metabolic syndrome while improving overall energy levels and productivity during Toyota's work hours.

Mental Health Support: Toyota provides resources like onsite counselors and flexible workloads to address stress or burnout. This holistic approach ensures employees remain mentally resilient while achieving their professional goals.

Employee Retention: By prioritizing wellness, Toyota maintains a turnover rate significantly lower than industry averages, underscoring the effectiveness of its employee-centric strategies.

Toyota's integration of fitness into its corporate culture exemplifies its commitment to holistic employee development. By combining physical wellness with opportunities for networking and personal growth, the company not only enhances individual performance but also strengthens its organizational fabric for sustained success.

Success in Action: Additional Case Studies

Honda Motor Co., Ltd.

For many years, Honda has been an integrator in incorporating fitness into its corporate culture, particularly for assembly line workers. The company introduced mandatory exercise programs designed to simulate job movements before employees began their shifts. These exercises aimed to improve physical readiness, reduce injuries, and enhance productivity.

Key Benefits

Reduced Workplace Accidents: By preparing employees physically for repetitive movements, Honda significantly lowered injury rates.
Improved Productivity: Workers became more efficient due to better physical conditioning and fewer disruptions caused by health-related absences.
Networking Opportunities: Group exercises fostered camaraderie among employees, creating a collaborative work environment that improved team dynamics.

Impact on Performance

Honda's approach resulted in fewer sick days and lower healthcare costs, directly contributing to operational efficiency. The program also enhanced employee morale, leading to higher engagement and loyalty. These outcomes have strengthened Honda's reputation as a forward-thinking employer.

Japan Airlines (JAL): Wellness Programs for Service Quality and Employee Satisfaction

Japan Airlines implemented comprehensive wellness initiatives to address the physical and mental health of its workforce. These programs include subsidized gym memberships, mental health seminars, and group exercise sessions. The airline's wellness program has significantly lowered absenteeism rates while enhancing customer service quality due to healthier employees.

Key Benefits

Enhanced Customer Service: Healthier employees exhibited higher energy levels and focus, improving the quality of customer interactions.
Lower Absenteeism: Regular fitness activities reduced sick days, ensuring consistent staffing levels.
Global Networking: By promoting wellness as part of its corporate identity, JAL has strengthened its brand image internationally, attracting partnerships and skilled talent.

Impact on Performance

JAL observed measurable improvements in employee satisfaction and service efficiency. The airline's emphasis on wellness has also contributed to its ranking as a 5-Star airline by Skytrax for many consecutive years and as a well-respected company in the global aviation industry.

Osaka Gas (now Daigas Group): Daily Exercise Routines for Productivity and Team Building

Osaka Gas mandates daily group exercises during work breaks as part of its corporate wellness strategy. These routines are simple yet effective in reducing stress and maintaining physical health.

Key Benefits

Boosted Productivity: Short exercise breaks improved focus and energy levels among employees.
Strengthened Team Spirit: Group activities fostered a sense of community within the workforce, enhancing collaboration across departments.
Corporate Networking: The company's commitment to wellness attracted attention from other firms in the energy sector, facilitating partnerships and knowledge exchange.

Impact on Performance

Osaka Gas reported higher employee engagement and reduced turnover rates due to its wellness initiatives. The program also contributed to the company's public image as an employer that values its workforce's well-being.

Your Mantra: Our shared culture is our greatest strength

9

Fear: The Silent Architect of Your Life

Fear. It's in your shadow that trails you from cradle to grave. It seeps into boardrooms, whispers in the ears of executives, and plants seeds of doubt in you and the hearts of those around you. Fear is a force so pervasive in your life that it shapes not only your personal choices but also the fabric of corporate culture.

But what happens when fear causes inactivity? When the corporate world, paralyzed by its own anxieties—fear of change, fear of failure—chooses to ignore solutions that could transform not only their businesses but their people? Yet fear keeps many companies from embracing this idea, preferring to cling to antiquated practices rather than risk stepping into uncharted territory that could inevitably improve their associates' lives for their lifetimes.

Weight of Fear

Fear manifests itself in you in countless ways: tightness in the chest during a presentation, sleepless nights before a major decision, or the gnawing anxiety that comes with uncertainty. Fear can often be expressed as overwork and perfectionism. A desperate attempt to control what cannot be controlled. You bury yourself in spreadsheets and projections, believing that if you work hard enough, push your team hard enough, and plan meticulously enough, you can avert possible failure. But this illusion of control comes at a cost: burnout, disengagement, and a disenchanted workforce that feels more like robots than human beings.

Fear doesn't just affect those at the top. It trickles down through every level of an organization. Employees sense their leaders' unease and mirror it in their own behaviors—hesitating to take risks, avoiding collaboration, and retreating into their comfort zones. The result? Innovation withers in a stagnant culture, while the heavy air of dormancy breeds unease and drains collective energy, leaving vital human connection to languish as an afterthought.

The cold hand of fear steers you away from risks, from connection, from your life itself.

Daily Manipulator

Fear's mastery lies in its subtlety. It doesn't roar, it murmurs. That promotion you didn't pursue? Fear of failure. The conversation you avoided? Fear of insecurity. The treadmill gathering dust in your basement? Fear of discomfort. Every 'no' to a new opportunity, every 'yes' to the safety of routine, every hour spent scrolling instead of speaking. These are fear's victories over you, small and silent.

Your corporate leaders, too, can bow to its rule. They'll cling to outdated hierarchies, reject comprehensive wellness initiatives, and prioritize profit over people. This is not out of malice, but fear. Fear of disorder. Fear of change. Fear of liability. Fear of the unknown. Fear of capital expenditures. The irony is suffocating. In their quest to mitigate risk, they breed stagnation. They retreat into cubicles and Slack channels, their bodies stiffening, their voices fading. The workplace becomes a home of unmet potential.

And what of your body? Fear keeps you sedentary. You sit for hours, hunched over keyboards or a phone, trading vitality for the illusion of productivity. Your muscles atrophy, your heart grows sluggish, and your mind fogs with the dullness of disuse. You rationalize: "Tomorrow, I'll exercise. Tomorrow, I'll call a friend." But tomorrow never comes. Fear, after all, is patient. It knows your laziness is its greatest ally.

Bleak Horizon

Picture a world where, because of fear, a concept such as Sweatworking remains a fringe principle, where your face-to-face interactions are a relic, and where traditional networking has transitioned to virtual—stiff, transactional, soul-crushing.

Physical Collapse

Your obesity skyrockets as your body, starved of motion, swells into grotesque parodies of its potential. Type 2 diabetes becomes a rite of passage, and cardiovascular disease is your universal inheritance. Gym windows prop up out-of-business signs while hospitals overflow with patients whose ailments were preventable. The polluted air grows thick with the labored breathing of human beings who forgot how and are too lazy to move.

Your children, raised on screens, inactivity, and sugar, lack the stamina to climb trees or run through fields. Their bones grow brittle, their postures crooked. Schools, desperate to adapt, replace playgrounds with virtual reality headsets. The young learn early: the body is a burden, a thing to be endured, not celebrated.

Social Wasteland

Your face-to-face communication fades into myth. Your relationships exist as curated personas on screens, devoid of distinction, stripped of vulnerability due to fear. Trust erodes. Misunderstandings proliferate. Familiar? Without the subtle cues of body language—a raised eyebrow, a hesitant smile—your empathy withers. Colleagues become strangers while your neighbors are ghosts.

In this fractured world, networking events persist as systematic acts of rehearsed elevator pitches that become echoes you can't believe or that no one wants to hear anymore. Authentic connections? Too risky. Better to hide behind LinkedIn comments and scripted small talk. Loneliness, once a private ache, becomes a pandemic.

Mental Rot

Your anxiety tightens its grip. Decision-making, already warped by fear, collapses under the weight of your chronic stress. Our leaders, paralyzed by the specter of failure and mistrust, default to soundbites and inaction. Mental health disorders soar as your friends, family, and colleagues become more isolated and sedentary, and lose the resilience that comes from physical exertion and genuine connection. Depression becomes our default state, a gray fog swallowing cities and suburbs alike.

Bleak? Absolutely. Where we're headed should deeply disgust you and wrench at your heart every day. I know it does mine.

Appeal

This future isn't inevitable, but averting it demands your active defiance. It requires you to tear down the temples of fear and build something real, alive, and unwaveringly powerful.

So here's my challenge to you: Let go of your fear. Embrace Sweatworking not as a gimmick but as a fundamental shift in how you approach employee wellness and company culture. You don't want to call it Sweatworking. Okay, call it something else: sweat-networking; exerwork; business wellness; wellness community. I don't care, just take action, start moving, and network with honesty and earnest intent.

You are a leader. Whether it be of yourself, your team, or your company. Start small, such as a weekly group workout or an on-site gym. Watch as your team's attitude transforms before your eyes when they realize you care about their wellness. You'll see healthier employees who are more engaged with their work; stronger relationships that lead to better collaboration; and perhaps most importantly, a culture where fear no longer holds sway.

Sweatworking must become part of you and your company's battleground. In the burn of muscles and the gasps for air, fear loses its power. Weakness can become strength while your bodies become instruments for connection.

Your face-to-face interactions must be reclaimed and more consistent. Replace transactional exchanges with shared experiences. Exercise together. Climb mountains together. Have monthly healthy meals together. Build something tangible. Trust is forged in these moments, not in the sterile exchange of virtual platforms and clickbait photos. Considering that studies suggest most people spend more time with their work colleagues than their families, companies need to treat their own associates as family as well.

SWEATWORKING

***

You possess a wellspring of untapped potential at every age, and the only way to unleash it and sculpt the life you envision is through conclusive action. Imagine life as the vast wilderness, with winding trails beckoning you to explore its hidden wonders and picturesque horizons. Hesitation and fear will keep you tethered to the familiar, preventing you from discovering the vibrant possibilities that lie just beyond your comfort zone. Embrace the chance to learn, evolve, and become the most authentic and capable version of yourself. Fear is the energy behind doing your best work.

The Earth doesn't care whether you live or die; it's just spinning on its axis within the vast stretch of the Milky Way galaxy among 400 billion stars, and it will continue to do so for billions of years. Deeply cherish how you live while you're here and profoundly appreciate the good fortune of your own existence. Choose connection over isolation, movement over stagnation, courage over fear. Build companies and lives that reflect the best of what humanity has to offer.

The choice is stark: succumb to fear's whisper and march into the void, or rise, sweat-soaked and unyielding, toward a stronger, freer existence. The wind doesn't care which way it blows, but you should.

Your Mantra: If you're passionate about your work, you have nothing to fear from life

10

Your Corporate Pitch Cheat Sheet

You're ready to pitch your Sweatworking venture to your company's corporate big cheese. Channel the spirit of rebellion against corporate mediocrity. Think of your pitch as more than just a presentation. It's a bold statement against the dullness of modern business. Grab your audience's attention and highlight the problem your idea addresses.

Step 1

Don't dare call it just an 'exercise session with networking'. Claim it for what it is: "To ignite people's lives within your organization and spark a revolution of productivity, communication, and community."

Make sure every word you say is like a drop of water in a desert—essential for the livelihood and success of the company.

During your pitch, let your voice be a bold escape from the monotony of corporate routines. This is your moment to spark something real, reminding those in the room of the significance of life and corporate energy, and inspiring them to break out and live bravely. Approach the advantages below with focus and passion, and embrace your creativity and individuality. This is your company's wake-up call.

Step 2

Focus your pitch by selecting the most impactful 'evident and untapped corporate incentives' from Chapter 4 that directly resonate with upper management's key motivations.

Step 3

Optional: Utilize the 'Impact on Corporate Performance' section and the 'Benefits of Workplace Wellness Programs in Japan' from Chapter 8 for more key organizational motivations that can be used in your address.

Step 4

As you leave the meeting, equip executives with a concise two-page, bullet-point overview of your discussion.

The first page outlines employer benefits, featuring components from Steps 2 and 3 that most resonate with your company's priorities.

The second page details employee benefits, utilizing the information provided below.

Physical Advantages

- **Cardiovascular Health**: Engaging in physical activities during networking sessions can lower blood pressure and reduce the risk of cardiovascular disease. This is particularly beneficial for professionals who spend long hours at desks.

- **Weight Management**: Sweatworking can help with weight loss and maintaining a healthy body composition. The physical activity involved burns calories and increases metabolic efficiency. This will then lower medical insurance costs as well.

- **Joint Pain Relief**: For those suffering from joint pain or conditions like arthritis, the gentle exercises often involved in Sweatworking can provide relief and improve joint health.

- **Improved Posture**: Physical exercise is beneficial for posture because it can strengthen core and upper back muscles, enabling the body to maintain proper alignment and reduce the risk of slouching and related injuries. Regular exercise, including stretching and strengthening routines, can also improve flexibility and balance, helping to correct posture imbalances and alleviate pain in the back, neck, and shoulders.

- **Improved Sleep**: Regular physical activity, even in the context of networking, can lead to better sleep quality. This is crucial for maintaining overall health and productivity in the workplace.

Mental Health Advantages

- **Stress Reduction**: Physical activity releases endorphins, the body's natural mood elevators. This can help alleviate stress and promote a sense of calm and relaxation, which is particularly valuable in high-pressure business environments.

- **Enhanced Cognitive Function**: Exercise improves brain health and cognitive function. Sweatworking can lead to increased mental clarity, sharper focus, and improved problem-solving skills. These are all essential for professional success.

- **Boosted Self-Esteem**: Achieving fitness goals and improving physical health can significantly boost self-esteem and confidence. This newfound confidence can translate into more effective networking and professional interactions.

- **Anxiety and Depression Management**: Regular physical activity has been shown to reduce symptoms of anxiety and depression. Sweatworking provides a supportive environment for managing these mental health challenges while building professional relationships.

Social and Professional Benefits

- **Authentic Connections**: Engaging in physical activities together creates a more relaxed and genuine environment for networking. This can lead to stronger, more authentic professional relationships.

- **Shared Experiences**: Participating in fitness activities provides common ground and shared experiences, which can serve as excellent conversation starters and bonding opportunities.

- **Work-Life Balance**: Sweatworking efficiently combines physical activity with professional networking, helping busy professionals maintain a better work-life balance.

Your Mantra: You don't know unless you try

11

The Great Unveiling: 1st Session

Ideas are as common as old plastic bags floating in the wind on the side of a highway, and just about as useful. You'll find that every suit-wearing manager, whether from Wall Street or Silicon Valley, has a head full of them, yet a significant number of these prove as empty as their assurances of your next raise.

Let's be clear: Your ideas are the catalysts for change, but without action, they're nothing more than you holding a sparkler. I learned this firsthand when I had the audacious goal of trekking across Nepal from east to west, faster than anyone ever in history. The mere thought and a few phone calls didn't magically transport me to the Himalayas; it was just a seed planted in my mind, waiting to be nurtured.

Two years of intense preparation followed. This included:

- Raising funds
- Finding a reliable logistics company
- Interviewing Sherpas and Nepalese for my teams
- Making travel arrangements
- Equipment
- Trying to obtain sponsors

- Making contacts within Nepal I could trust
- Working with government officials
- Training physically and mentally
- ...and on and on

Undeniably, the primary impediment to the Himalayan expedition would lie in the intricate logistics and the complexities of my team leadership. Navigating the remote terrain as well as interactions with local communities, where coming into contact with a Westerner was often a novel occurrence, generated unique logistical and intercultural challenges. Compounding this was the team's lack of prior experience with backcountry leadership, or substantial leadership of any kind, especially from a Westerner who lacked linguistic fluency. The expedition's route, stretching over 1,700 kilometers, from verdant valleys to soaring, unforgiving passes over 6,100 meters (20,000ft), presented a distinct array of challenges for both me and each member of my team.

In the end, the realization of this dream wasn't just about the physical feat. It was about embracing the unexpected, adapting to the harsh realities of the Himalayas, and pushing beyond one's perceived limits. This experience underscores that while ideas inspire, it's the relentless pursuit and action that truly bring about change and achievement.

One unexpected challenge during my journey through eastern and central Nepal was the relentless presence of leeches. The monsoon had lingered longer than usual and was the most severe in Nepal's history up to that time, according to members of Nepal's Rotary International, with whom I spoke the day before I left Kathmandu. For nearly three weeks, starting at the India/Nepal border, I traversed rain-soaked mountains and valleys, ranging from 5,000 to 10,000 feet in altitude.

As I navigated the waterlogged terrain, whether walking or running, these persistent bloodsuckers became unwelcome companions. They would stealthily attach themselves to my body, often unnoticed until later at night. The constant battle against these tiny adversaries added an unexpected layer of challenge to my already demanding expedition.

Every evening, I would burn them off from around my lower waist, under my armpits, on my feet and ankles, and around my groin area. Yea, that's right, the bloodthirsty creatures loved the family jewels. To combat the leech menace, I learned from my team to carry salt, tobacco, and a disposable lighter. All of which proved more effective than using knives to remove them.

Life will continually throw curveballs your way. You must learn to either dodge them or master the swing to hit them out of the ballpark. Sweatworking will teach you how to knock that ball over the iconic Green Monster at Fenway.

We all have dreams and goals, but it's your act of turning them into reality that truly ignites the passion and beauty of life. It's in the journey from idea to action that you find the bona fide magic.

Assuming the corporate brass approves the strategy detailed in Chapter 10, here's how you and your team can effectively incorporate your first Sweatworking session into your daily routines.

Planning Your First Session

Consider the varied states of physical degeneration among your fellow participants. We're not all cut from the same cloth, thankfully, so always keep that in mind. This is what makes this so wonderful and exciting. If everyone were identical, the only thing we'd have to gossip about is who ate the last donut.

Forget about any high-intensity sessions or marathon-type runs that'll leave half your group wheezing like they have emphysema. You want something that won't kill the poor bastards who may not have seen the light of day since they got chained to their cubicles. Tailor the exercises to your audience.

Start small: Begin with a lower-intensity workout that allows for conversation. Yoga, biking, a good old-fashioned power walk through nature's cathedral, or even a game of bocce. The goal here is to get your colleagues moving for a sustained period of time. You're not training for the apocalypse. Plus, it gives you a chance to observe your colleagues' fitness levels up close and personal.

Throw aside your suits and ties and choose comfortable, breathable clothing and athletic footwear. But no flip-flops or beach attire. Everyone is not on vacation.

Aim for the softer light of early morning or late afternoon for the time in which to hold the class. The strong midday sun can potentially create more challenging circumstances.

Most importantly, participate yourself. Don't just stand there barking orders like some fitness dictator. Get down in the dirt with your fellow humans. Show them you're all in when it comes to the perspiration and task.

The goal isn't to create Olympic athletes. It's to wake people up, to startle them out of their comfortable, air-conditioned coma. So, plan something that'll shake them up and build connections.

Overview:

- Considering participants' fitness levels

- Selecting an activity conducive to conversation
- Balancing exercise intensity with networking opportunities
- Addressing dress code implications
- Choosing the time of day and work schedule

Inviting Participants

Forget those stuffy email invitations that most likely will go directly to the Spam folder. Scrawl your message on a piece of actual, thick paper, and tape it to their office doors. If that's too subtle, try smoke signals from the parking lot. How about this one? Walk directly up to a colleague, look that person in the eye, and invite them. Well, okay, you might resort to the accursed 'electronic mail,' but only if you must. Be sure to follow up with each one that doesn't get back to you.

Be mindful of your environment. Ensure the Sweatworking session doesn't disrupt others or compromise professionalism.

Choose your first participants wisely. Seek out the restless souls with a glimmer of life in their eyes, not the automatons who've sold their spirits to the highest bidder. Look for those who fidget in meetings or gaze longingly out windows.

When you corner your targets, speak of the promise of endorphins, the thrill of defying gravity, new and improved friendships, and the sweet victory of outliving those chained to their desks. Paint a picture of sweat-drenched liberation and the bonds forged in the crucible of physical exertion. The more positive energy you radiate, the more it attracts and resonates with those around you.

Above all, promise them this: For a brief, shining moment, you'll feel more alive than you have in years, your heart pounding with something other than caffeine and deadlines. And in that moment, you'll glimpse the person you were meant to be before society stamped out your spirit and stuck you behind a desk and computer.

Overview:

- Determining group size
- Crafting effective invitations
- Managing RSVPs and expectations

Formalizing an Agenda

If you're shooting for a session beyond just walking or a leisure yoga session, start with a warm-up. Maybe a few jumping jacks, jogging in place, or burpees as a reminder that you're all human beings with a beating heart.

For the main event, pick something that'll challenge them physically and mentally—a bodyweight or resistance bands circuit, or an active hike/walk ought to do it, though not a stroll. You want everyone to walk with purpose, not stop to smell the flowers.

During the activity, pair people up randomly. Force them to rely on each other, to communicate without their precious smartphones. Nothing builds trust like depending on someone else to keep you from falling off the edge of a steep hill or getting lost in the woods. Use natural breaks in the action for quick introductions and exchanges of ideas.

Finish with a cool-down that brings everyone back to earth, like some basic stretches or breathing meditations.

After you've all finished, gather around for some healthy grub and chat. Skip the fancy hors d'oeuvres and sparkling drinks. Select simple, hearty fare that'll replenish what you've lost. This is when the real connections happen, when you're too exhilarated and energized to want to put up your usual corporate facade.

Overview:

- Structuring the session (warm-up, main activity, cool-down)
- Incorporating networking moments
- Planning post-activity socializing

Technology and Tools

Technology and tools for Sweatworking have their place, just not in your first session. Remember, the idea behind your first session is to remind them that we're not machines, we're flesh-and-blood creatures meant to move and sweat under the open sky.

Too much reliance on gadgets will have you staring at screens instead of the world and the people exercising with you in the first place. Before you know it, everyone will be so caught up in their data that they'll miss the scorching beauty of a person's smile while exercising, or the sunrise during the morning walk with colleagues.

Let them know, the real purpose of physical exertion isn't to generate pretty graphs on your smartphone from some software. It's to feel alive, to challenge yourself, to connect with your body and those in the world around you. There are AI programs that might keep you from throwing out your back during a squat. Hell, you can now buy socks that supposedly help you avoid busting an ankle on your run. However, most of the wellness products you've heard or read about haven't been vetted. Their goal is for you to buy the product.

If a few of your participants who are technology-obsessed are insistent, strap on those smart socks if they must. But don't forget to have them take them off once in a while and feel the earth beneath their feet. After all, the purpose of a giant sequoia isn't to provide shade for your fitness tracker, it's to provide shade for you when the world may seem upside down in your mind. And your purpose in moving your body should be equally simple and profound.

Overview:

- Foregoing the use of technology

Overcoming Common Challenges

When addressing varying fitness levels, the strong will lead, and the weaker will follow. That's nature's way. But remember, even the tortoise can outpace the hare if it's stubborn enough. Encourage your team to tap into their inner strengths by staying active and engaged throughout the first session. Take a breather if you must, walk slower, or do whatever needs to be done, but don't quit. That's why I love the outdoors best. The wilderness doesn't discriminate. It'll make you stronger no matter what the circumstances.

Make your first session the most impactful action you and your team take all day. If you do, that energy, promise, and confidence will resonate throughout the team for the rest of the day.

As you dive into the Sweatworking session, it's essential to remember that maintaining boundaries is just as important as pushing your limits. While you encourage camaraderie and networking, respect each other's personal space and comfort levels. During exercises, be mindful of your team's own physical boundaries and communicate openly with them about needing adjustments or modifications.

In the networking segment, feel free to have them share their professional insights and goals, but also be considerate of others' time and interests.

To ensure consistent participation for future sessions, try this: Make a pact with each other. Promise yourself and the group you'll return, again and again, to test yourself and be a force of nature within the team and your own life. Pitch the experiences and excitement of independence and unity that only come from pushing your limits in this world. In the long run, that's better than any corporate bonus, I guarantee it.

Potential injuries or health concerns are always a legitimate concern. You can't go through life trying to protect yourself from every little thing, and you shouldn't try. But having a plan is vital just in case. For the first session, keep in mind to know you and your team's limits, respect the land/area you're in and each other, hydrate properly, and have contingencies in place if something goes wrong that is more of a concern than a band-aid could handle.

Overview:

- Addressing varying fitness levels by creating an inclusive environment
- Managing professional boundaries by establishing clear expectations
- Creating accountability partnerships to ensure consistent participation
- Handling potential injuries or health concerns with safety protocols

Your Mantra: While in all your knowing, know yourself first

12

Mountains to Climb and Pitfalls

Throughout your life, you'll face formidable mountains, and while you may not conquer every peak, let the climbs themselves become your greatest triumphs. Sure, reaching summits is great, but the exhilaration is fleeting. You're up there for a few moments, perhaps sixty minutes tops on a good day. The true value lies in the challenges you overcome, the lessons you learn, and the memories you create along the way. It's in the striving, not just the arriving, that you'll find growth, meaning, and stories worth telling.

When I first began teaching master classes in functional fitness, I was able to form a collective tribe of journey-minded individuals who wanted to:

1. Be their best self, knowing the values of what that entails
2. Be in better shape and feel better than they ever have before
3. Age gracefully

I'm going to tell you something about passion that most fitness instructors wouldn't dare whisper because they'd lose clients. My class wasn't some sanitized workout for the comfort-seeking masses where everyone receives a participation trophy and raised fist of unity for just showing up. My students weren't looking for that, and neither should you. It was a demanding declaration of human potential where the passion to be your best self was number one on your bucket list.

Through the years, the word began to spread of my teaching methods and novel combination of physical and mental exercises. Why? Because I was the first to do this type of all-encompassing, functional training. National and international media came calling—USA Today, BBC News, The Washington Post—not because I was selling some watered-down fitness fantasy, but because I was offering a raw, uncompromising experience. Those 'one-timers' who'd show up, preened, and then disappear? They were tourists, not travelers. They didn't understand that fitness isn't just about looking good, it's about becoming something more than you were yesterday. Looking good was a by-product.

The tribe knew the truth, and so should you: Nothing worth achieving comes easy. Nothing. We didn't smile because something was pleasant. We smiled because we were demolishing our own limitations, one ambitious rep at a time, no matter what kind of shape each individual was in.

This wasn't exercise. This was a rebellion against mediocrity.

I wouldn't be true to my nature if I didn't point out the potential pitfalls of this Sweatworking trend. As with anything that gains popularity in society and the corporate world, there's a risk of it becoming co-opted, sanitized, and stripped of its authenticity, such as many of the current wellness trends today.

There's a fine line between encouraging physical activity and mandating it. The last thing I want is for Sweatworking to become another box to check, another obligation in already over-scheduled lives. The power of it lies in its voluntary nature and in the genuine enthusiasm of its participants.

You, a company, an organization, or whoever, need to be careful not to turn Sweatworking sessions into another form of forced fun, like those dreaded rah-rah team-building exercises that everyone secretly hates. The key is to offer opportunities, not mandates. To create an environment where physical activity and networking can naturally intersect, without trying to force connections or participation. You are offering a chance for your associates to escape stress and release stress, not create it for them.

Maintain Inclusivity

Another potential pitfall is the risk of exclusivity. Not everyone can climb mountains or run a 10k. Sweatworking initiatives must be diverse and inclusive, offering a range of activities that can accommodate different fitness levels and physical abilities.

You must be wary of creating a culture where physical ability becomes yet another measure of professional worth. The goal of Sweatworking should be to break down inner barriers, not erect new ones. One of the many virtues my 30+ years of mixed martial arts training has taught me is valuing righteousness and honor above physical prowess.

Additionally, some individuals may feel self-conscious about exercising in front of colleagues or professional contacts. It's important to emphasize health and well-being over appearance or performance.

Professional Boundaries

As mentioned in the last chapter, Sweatworking blurs the lines between personal and professional life, although it's important to maintain appropriate boundaries. While the informal nature of these activities can foster more authentic connections, it shouldn't come at the cost of professionalism.

Participants need to be mindful of maintaining a level of decorum appropriate to professional relationships, even in casual settings. The challenge lies in finding the right balance between genuineness and professional behavior, between casual interaction and appropriate boundaries.

Integration with Technology

As much as it pains me to say it, technology will likely play a role in the future of Sweatworking. We're already seeing apps and platforms that facilitate group fitness activities or outdoor adventures. These could be leveraged to connect professionals with similar interests, organize events, or track shared fitness goals.

But don't go thinking they're the be-all and end-all of your physical endeavors. Use them sparingly, such as apps and devices that facilitate on-the-go work, like voice-to-text software or wearable tech.

Bookmark this site: SeanBurch.com

The key with technology is to use tools like seasoning on a meal. Let them enhance your experience, not dominate it. The goal should always be to get people off their screens and into the world, moving their bodies and engaging with others face-to-face.

Technology has the power to connect us with other human beings in ways that were previously unimaginable. However, it also poses significant risks, fostering addictions and questionable behaviors among people, which can negatively impact our relationships and well-being.

Corporate Wellness Programs

Companies need to begin integrating Sweatworking into their corporate wellness calendar. This could take the form of:

- sponsored exercise classes
- company-wide physical challenges
- outdoor retreats that combine professional development with physical activity

The most forward-thinking companies will recognize that investing in the physical health and social connections of their employees pays dividends in terms of productivity, creativity, job satisfaction, and profit margins.

Conferences and Events

Imagine where it becomes standard in industry conferences for you not to be sitting in stuffy conference rooms just listening to endless presentations. Instead, picture all companies, and not just the elite with big budgets, holding events that incorporate physical activities—morning fitness sessions, group hikes, climbing wall excursions. There are activities interspersed with more traditional networking and learning opportunities that create a more holistic and engaging experience for you.

This approach wouldn't only make these events more enjoyable and memorable, but it would also foster deeper connections among attendees.

Educational Social Shift

Ultimately, the rise of this revolution would represent a broader cultural shift. It's a move away from the idea that your professional and personal life must be entirely separate. It's a recognition that you are a whole being, that your physical health, your social connections, and your professional development are all interconnected.

This shift challenges the notion that success must come at the cost of your health and/or your relationships. Instead, it suggests a more integrated approach to life and work, one that recognizes the value of physical activity and genuine human connection in all aspects of your life.

***

You are part of nature, not separate from it. Your body is designed to move, to strain, to overcome. Your mind flourishes when challenged and stimulated. Your spirit thrives on genuine connection with others.

Sweatworking creates growth opportunities that go beyond the superficial. You build strength, not just in your body, but in your character and your relationships. You develop resilience that serves you in all aspects of life. You forge connections that are based on shared experiences and mutual respect, not just shared business interests.

In a world that often seems intent on separating you from your true nature, Sweatworking offers a path back to something more sincere. It's a reminder that your professional growth doesn't have to come at the cost of your physical health or your need for genuine human connection. Instead, it suggests that these elements can reinforce and enhance each other.

Your Mantra: Change your body? Change your mind

13

All-Day Movement: Sitting is the New Smoking (But Less Cool)

Pushing yourself out of your comfort zone during a Sweatworking session is one thing, but feeling intimidated by the idea of exercising in front of others at the gym is a different challenge altogether. This has been recognized as 'gymtimidation.' Stupid sounding word? Absolutely, yet surprisingly, it's a common experience. The term was first coined by an advertising firm as an anxiety buzzword for a fitness gym ad campaign.

It seems labeling feelings gives our minds an excuse to rationalize them.

Once, during a Sweatworking session, I noticed two employees who seemed highly intrigued by the concepts that I was teaching. They were pacing back and forth, watching me, while I led their group from IBM through a comprehensive session that included exercise, motivational speaking, and breathing techniques. This was at a resort in Dongguan, China, where I was the Director of Wellness at the time. During the session, they discreetly positioned themselves near the group to listen in. However, as soon as I divided the participants into teams for the exercise components, they respectfully withdrew to observe from a distance. Their behavior suggested a strong interest in the instruction, yet a hesitancy to directly participate.

After the session concluded, I was approached by the two women who turned out to be middle managers at IBM. They were interested in discussing alternative strategies beyond Sweatworking that they could present to upper management to encourage employees to stay active during the workday. Essentially, they were looking for a discreet approach to promote physical activity without explicitly using the term 'exercise.'

Brilliant. I was happy to help.

People can experience anxiety about exercising in a public forum, and it's not just about being a beginner; it can affect anyone, regardless of their fitness level. The sources of group exercise anxiety can vary, including the fear of exercising in front of others, uncertainty about using equipment, and feeling like they don't belong with a particular group.

Research has found men are more likely to feel they don't belong in the gym, while women are more prone to feeling intimidated by other gym-goers. These feelings can stem from past negative experiences, self-consciousness about appearance or physical capabilities, or simply comparing yourself to more experienced participants exercising beside you.

I think part of the problem is that we've become a society where sitting around for long stretches is part of the deal. We've become sit-asses. It's not that we're lazy per se, it's just that many of our jobs and daily routines are now set up that way. As a result, your body starts to feel the effects of inactivity, and that leads to your mind not staying as sharp as it could be.

But you recognizing this can be the first step to making some positive changes.

Let's get started with real, honest-to-god movement integrated into you and your team's daily grind. So, how can you get your employees involved in a wellness program without them actually setting time aside during their day to do it?

Embrace these three actions:

1. Active workstation
2. Walking meeting
3. Microbreak

And not as some temporary corporate wellness petition, but as a radical act against the tyranny of the chair.

The Active Workstation: Your Desk-Bound Rebellion

Just imagine if instead of being chained to your desk like some white-collar convict, you're pedaling away on a bike while typing up your latest report. Or, you're strolling along on a workstation treadmill, your fingers moving across the keyboard as you put one foot in front of the other. It's not just about burning calories. It's about keeping your blood flowing, your synapses firing, and your spirit from withering away in the radiant-lit hellhole of the modern office.

A technician in a lab coat might tell you good health is all about increasing energy expenditure or regulating high blood pressure. And this is definitely true. But I also say it's about reclaiming your humanity, one step or pedal at a time. And if the executives upstairs give you grief, just remind them that exercise has been shown to maintain work productivity. That ought to resonate with them.

Height-Adjustable Desks

One of the most effective ways to introduce active workstations is by incorporating height-adjustable desks. These versatile pieces of furniture allow employees to smoothly transition between sitting and standing throughout the day. By enabling workers to adjust their posture regularly, these desks help reduce the negative health impacts associated with prolonged sitting.

Activity-Based Working Zones

Transforming the office layout to support activity-based working can greatly enhance the integration of active workstations. This approach involves designing various spaces within the office to cater to different work styles and tasks.

- Quiet zones: for focused, individual work
- Collaborative areas: equipped with movable furniture for team projects
- Standing meeting spaces: to encourage brief, energetic discussions

Treadmill and Cycling Workstations

For a more dynamic approach, companies can introduce treadmill or cycling workstations in designated areas. These stations are particularly useful for tasks that don't require intense concentration, such as phone calls or virtual meetings. It's important to strategically place these workstations to avoid disrupting colleagues who require a quieter environment.

Microbreaks: The Rebellious Rest

You may be thinking: "I can't spend all day on a treadmill desk. I lack coordination, and I've got important work to do." Well, even the most dedicated rebel such as yourself needs to take a breather now and then. That's where microbreaks come in.

These aren't your paycheck loafers' coffee breaks. We're talking short, frequent bursts of movement throughout the day. Stand up, stretch your arms over your head, do a few jumps in place—anything to shake off the cobwebs and remind your body it's not part of the furniture. And don't let anyone tell you it's a waste of time. These little moments of movement have been shown to improve concentration, enhance cognitive function, and increase productivity. Paradigm shifts aren't calculated, they're created.

Movement breaks can be seamlessly integrated into a busy work schedule through creative and strategic approaches. Here are several effective methods to add more physical activity to your workday:

Micro-Movement Strategies

- Set hourly timers for 5-minute movement breaks.
- Stand or walk during phone calls and meetings.
- Perform desk-based exercises like calf-raises, leg extensions, and shoulder stretches.
- Use waiting times for quick exercises.

Workplace Movement Hacks

- Take the stairs instead of the elevator.
- Walk to a colleague's office rather than emailing.
- Park further away from the office entrance.
- Use the farthest bathroom in the building.

Dynamic Break Ideas

- Conduct walking meetings around the office or outside.
- Do mini dance breaks while working (remember to close your blinds unless you don't mind someone filming you with their phone).
- Perform quick bodyweight exercises during short breaks.
- Use resistance bands or small exercise equipment at your desk.

Engagement Techniques

- Start office step-count challenges.
- Use a pedometer or mobile step-tracking app.
- Encourage co-workers to participate in movement activities.
- Set realistic movement goals that don't feel overwhelming.

Walking Meetings: Planning While on the Move

Take your meetings on the road. Instead of being trapped in some sterile conference room, breathing recycled air, and staring at your laptop and computer screens, you could be out in the world, feeling the sun on your face and the earth beneath your feet.

Not only does it get your blood pumping, but it's been shown to increase creative thinking. After all, how can you plot the success of the industrial-techno-consumer society if your brain is as stagnant as a watering hole full of mosquitoes on a humid day in August?

Every step you take is a middle finger to the system that's content to keep you docile and immobile. So get moving to reclaim a little bit of your wild, untamed self in this concrete maze we call civilization.

Overview:

- **Active workstations**: Incorporate standing desks, treadmill desks, or cycling desks into office environments to promote physical activity throughout the workday, potentially boosting both your cognitive performance and creativity.

- **Movement breaks**: Encourage regular movement breaks during long periods of seated work or study to help you maintain cognitive function and stimulate creative thinking.

- **Walking meetings**: Conduct meetings while walking, when appropriate, to combine physical activity with work-related discussions, potentially leading you to more creative problem-solving and idea generation.

Overcome Gym Anxiety

What if you can't institute active workstations, walking meetings, and movement techniques? Then the only solution is to go to a gym or start an 'unofficial' group exercise class.

How can you overcome this anxiety and make the gym a place where you feel empowered rather than intimidated? One of the best strategies is to start slowly. Ease into your gym routine by beginning with basic, low-intensity exercises and gradually increasing complexity as you build confidence.

Educating yourself about gym equipment and proper form can also be a game-changer.

Having a clear plan for your workouts reduces uncertainty and helps you focus on your goals rather than your surroundings. If possible, try visiting the gym during less crowded times to help ease into the environment.

Bringing a friend along can provide moral support and make the experience more enjoyable.

Joining or starting a group exercise class, if Sweatworking sessions aren't available at your company, can foster a sense of community and provide structured guidance, reducing anxiety about what to do.

Another effective approach is to seek professional help. Working with a personal trainer can guide you through exercises and build your confidence. They can help you understand how to use equipment properly and create a personalized workout plan that suits your needs.

Additionally, cultivating positive self-talk can be essential. Replace negative thoughts with affirmations, reminding yourself that everyone at the gym is focused on their own workout and not judging you. In fact, I dedicate an entire section of one of my workshops to self-talk because of its profound positive impact on personal growth and confidence.

It's essential to be patient with yourself and celebrate small victories along the way. With time and persistence, the gym can transform from a source of anxiety to a place of empowerment and self-development.

As in life, overcoming gym anxiety is a journey. By acknowledging your fears and taking proactive steps to address them, you're already on the path to a more confident and fulfilling wellness experience. Remember, every gym-goer started as a beginner, and the most important aspect of your fitness journey is your progress and well-being. So, take a deep breath, step into that gym, and start moving forward.

ALL-DAY MOVEMENT: SITTING IS THE NEW SMOKING (BUT LESS COOL)

Your Mantra: Every day is an opportunity to begin again—your rebirth

14

Sessions Activity Roulette: Beat Boredom

When I'm teaching a group, whether seasoned executives or beginners, I don't just sit back and watch them fumble. No sir. I navigate through their panoramas, keeping a keen eye out for areas of weakness to improve and strengths to use as motivational catalysts for them. What's beautiful about the imperfection or apprehension they feel is that it acts as the flash, igniting their inner transformation. Facing discomfort head-on, it's amazing how much stronger and more capable they become. They embrace that process to see where it takes them.

Don't get me wrong. I'm not out to break spirits and leave it at that. I'm talking about breaking down and building back up stronger than before. I'm there to strip away the artificial comforts of civilization and reveal the raw beauty within your soul. It's like polishing a piece of rough quartz until it gleams. When you push people beyond their own perceived limits, you give them a chance to discover their true strength. A strength they never knew they had.

Sweatworking sessions will rebuild and improve you, and make you realize you can achieve something greater than what you are today. And then, watch as you rise, phoenix-like, stronger and more resilient than before.

Take One World Trade Center, standing tall and proud in the megalopolis of New York City. After the old towers fell, they weren't just rebuilt. Something even more magnificent was created. That tower now reaches 1,776 (how about that number!) feet into the sky, a defiant punch raised against adversity. It's as unyielding as bedrock, laughing in the face of earthquakes and hurricanes. It exceeds human ambition while also being the tallest building in the USA. It's a symbol of America's resolve and courage to stand tall once again despite all odds against it.

Darwin was onto something when he noted the phrase 'survival of the fittest' in his book on the origin of species. Nature doesn't care about how comfortable you are; it's about adapting and growing. And who doesn't love a good underdog story, right? That is you. That is each and every one of us.

But here's the thing, why go it alone for your individual growth? You can make exercise a team effort. Choose activities that bring people together, and salute everyone for showing up consistently, giving their best efforts, and keeping a positive attitude. In group sessions, the leaders can step up and mentor those who might be struggling. Some people will need that extra support. But that's how you build grit and resilience. It's not about being perfect, it's about progress.

Now, if people aren't willing to step out of their comfort zones, whether that means ditching the buttered croissant for a healthier snack or leaving the office for a workout, what does that say about their commitment to growth? As a leader, it's worth paying attention to how your team members respond to challenges. Those willing to get a little uncomfortable often have a strong work ethic and a desire to succeed, both personally and professionally.

Time of Day

The sun rises, the sun sets. Pick a time, and then stick and commit for at least a few months. Morning sessions work the best to provide you and your team with energy, endorphins, and confidence. But feel free to play at uncommon times of the day. Night hikes to dawn bootcamps will show you who's serious about making a positive impact on themselves and the company for which they work. You must be willing to step up and believe. Time is just another obstacle to overcome.

Get clever and learn to weave physical activity into the fabric of your workday, like a chameleon blending into the landscape. Early morning sessions before the daily grind begins, or lunchtime workouts that replace the usual desk salad or meat hoagie, can be effective ways to incorporate Sweatworking without disrupting the flow of business. It's finding those pockets of time that are often wasted and transforming them into opportunities for connection and rejuvenation.

Consider the lunch hour, that sacred time when office workers emerge from their cubicles like prairie dogs from their burrows, blinking in the sunlight. Instead of wasting it on overpriced sandwiches and mindless small talk, why not use some time for a group bootcamp session or a brisk walk around the block? You'll return to your desk refreshed, reinvigorated, and possibly even enlightened by the conversations had while in motion.

Group Size

Keep the group size small if you can. Quality over quantity, always. Especially if you're going outside. Nature shouldn't feel like your conference room. Too many bodies drown out the whispers of the wind. Wherever gym or outdoor sessions are held, understand that nothing ruins a good wellness session like too many primate chatterboxes on steroids.

Networking Goals

Throw out your agenda. Real connections happen when you're moving, maybe a little scared, and facing a common challenge. If you're out there just to schmooze and tap phones to share your QR business card, you've missed the point entirely. Sweatworking isn't about checking boxes. Mother Earth, in all her colors and circumstances, doesn't care about your goals or your comfort. She just is. The goal is to strip away the bullshit and find out who you and your fellow employees really are. That's when you'll make real connections, not the fake ones over digital platforms, or cocktails and pigs in a blanket.

Low-Intensity Sweatworking Activities

Sweatworking sessions with low-intensity activities don't necessarily mean low impact; it means smart, sustainable resistance. This is why I highly recommend every program begin with this type of session, because it's the perfect provider of confidence to go bigger in your life. This isn't just exercise. This is reclaiming your human potential, and it's your rebellion against becoming a soft, passive lump. Light bodyweight movements with stretching, Pilates, or a brisk walk through an urban park can provide just enough physical challenge to get your blood pumping without rendering conversation impossible, and demonstrate that you can do this.

Walking Meetings (Chapter 19 Specific)

Imagine breaking free from those suffocating meeting rooms, where ideas go to die between the eye-searing strips of doom and exorbitant lattes. Walking meetings are your ticket to intellectual liberation. You're not just moving, you're thinking in motion. Each step gives you your rising, a chance to breathe in and out real air and provoke genuine conversation. As you stride alongside your compatriots, creativity flows like a river, unbound and unpredictable.

Yoga

Yoga is human machinery realigning itself. It's about reconnecting with your bodily primal strength that industrial society has tried to domesticate out of you. Stretch, bend, breathe. Remind yourself that your body is not just a transport mechanism for your brain, but a magnificent instrument of survival and beauty.

Group Cycling

Think of indoor cycling as training and preparation for a great escape. You're pedaling to build cardiovascular foundations from low impact to higher intensity. Every revolution of that wheel is your one-finger salute to the notion that fitness must be punishing. Burn some calories, build strength, and do it all while a community of wild spirits cheers each other on.

Moderate-Intensity Sweatworking Options

These Sweatworking options aren't just about burning calories, they're about burning through the soul-crushing mediocrity of your modern work life. It's a revolution disguised in running shorts and athletic shoes. Life is not a spectator sport, and work shouldn't be a prison. You're not just improving your health, you're staging a beautiful, sweaty revolt against the mundane.

Moderation, a concept often foreign to the corporate world, can be an essential element in the realm of Sweatworking when getting people to keep coming back session after session. The ideal activity will leave everyone invigorated, not incapacitated. Think of it as a slow, steady climb up a mesa rather than a frantic scramble up a sheer cliff face.

The beauty of moderate-intensity activities is that they still allow for your most precious of commodities in the corporate world: conversation. A bike ride along a city trail with intermittent, quick periods of going all out on the pedals provides ample opportunity for discussion without the risk of anyone keeling over from exhaustion. It's finding your balance between physical engagement and mental clarity.

Fun Runs

You're huffing and puffing through the burgs or downtown, dodging potholes and feral pigeons, all in the name of networking. The twist is you're actually enjoying it! Your lungs are expanding, your body is perspiring, and you're grinning like a fool because you've finally found a way to make small talk bearable. Find yourself part of a tribe of like-minded exercisers, and chase that runner's high. Who knows, you might even shed that spare tire you've been lugging around since your last promotion.

Then there's a 5K, half-marathon, or further distances. Don't consider them races at first, rather a declaration of human potential. You're not just training your body, you're training your spirit. The camaraderie of runners is a primal thing, more authentic than any boardroom powwow.

Group Fitness

Bootcamps and group classes? They're not torture, they're modern-day vision quests. You're transforming a collection of individual workers into a unified tribe of human potential. Each squat and each push-up is a ritual of collective empowerment. You're not just building muscle, you're dismantling the artificial barriers that separate you in your daily grind. And the shared challenges create bonds stronger than any conventional corporate team-building exercise ever could.

Picture you and a horde of office warriors, shouting and sweating in unison, united in your quest to undo the damage of endless meetings and take-out. Bootcamp is like a corporate team-building exercise, only more invigorating with high knees and frog jumps and fewer trust falls. And the best part? You're all in it together, taking on adversity and succeeding as one sweaty, panting mass of humanity.

Outdoor Activities

Ah, now we're talking! The great outdoors is always calling your name, and it's time to answer. Imagine swapping your boardroom for a canoe, or your laptop for a pair of trekking poles. Feel the sun on your face, the wind in your hair, and the sweet ache of muscles finally remembering what they're for. Outside, among the trees and rocks and rushing water, you'll find a different kind of connection, one that doesn't require a Wi-Fi signal or a LinkedIn profile.

Hiking and canoeing are activities and acts of ecological rebellion. You're reclaiming your humanity from the sterile world of screens and meetings. Every mountain trail you take is a negotiation with the unrefined, unfiltered universe. Every paddle stroke is a conversation with yourself or someone that is more profound than quarterly reports.

High-Intensity Sweatworking Choices

All right, now let's have a swig of truth serum and discuss high-intensity endeavors you may want to consider. We're talking about honest-to-goodness, dirt-under-your-fingernails, dig-deep, full-shirt of sweat exertion.

Hyperfitness Functional Workouts

My Hyperfitness program isn't a walk in the park. More like a joint march up a high-altitude peak, shooting for the summit. It's tough, but, damn, is it effective. Functional workouts will improve your overall fitness, build strength and muscle, increase cardiovascular health, support weight loss, promote mental health, and build community. You'll be panting and sweating like a pit bull in August, but by god, you'll feel alive and ready to take on the world! You'll be gaining strength and becoming a thunderstorm throwing lightning bolts.

High-Intensity Interval Training (HIIT) Workouts

These classes demand your all in short, fiery intervals, followed by just enough respite to catch your breath and stoke the flames of your heart rate. This isn't merely exercise, it's a mix of sweat and camaraderie, where you forge connections with fellow warriors in the shared struggle against your limits. Amidst the panting and laughter, your bonds will be sure to multiply, nourished by the adrenaline that courses through your veins. Plus, the time-efficient format means you can squeeze in a powerful workout while still leaving ample time for networking and a shower, making HIIT classes a perfect blend of fitness and professional engagement.

Sports Leagues

Participating in a sports league can be a step down from intensity, depending on the sport you choose. One of the best things about sports is that there are so many to choose from: soccer, swimming, tennis, pickleball, basketball, kickball, and the list goes on and on. It's a chance to recapture your misspent youth. Get out there and run around until you need a well-deserved break. But there's more to it than that. You'll find camaraderie and a little bit of that team spirit you had as a kid growing up playing outside. Remember that? This will help you forget about the soul-crushing monotony of modern life for a blessed hour or two.

Dance Classes

I'll admit, I don't do much dancing these days. But I certainly don't judge when it comes to people exercising. If dancing around to music makes you feel alive, then by all means, shake your body, and do it consistently for a half-hour to an hour. Hell, in college we sweated away our alcohol by slamdancing and headbanging. Dancing gets you moving, and motion creates emotion. Maybe you'll even attract a new friend from your moves, though I make no promises.

Remember, whatever you choose, do it with gusto. Do it with passion. Do it like your life depends on it. Because, in the end, it does.

Innovative Sweatworking Ideas

In the spirit of adventure and fellowship, let's explore some other invigorating Sweatworking ideas that not only promote your health but also foster connections. These will help you and your team find opportunities to grow and celebrate the beauty of collaboration amongst the wonders of nature and community.

Scavenger Hunts

Why not embrace the thrill of the hunt? Embark on a scavenger hunt where you and your team traverse the great outdoors or an urban setting, seeking hidden treasures and solving clever clues. This activity ignites the spirit of exploration and teamwork. What's better than sharing discovery and laughter under an open sky?

Obstacle Course Challenges

Forget a gym room or running on a piece of equipment where you go nowhere. Consider tackling an obstacle course challenge together. This activity encourages you to push your limits, conquer fears, and cheer each other on. The enjoyment and conquest shared in overcoming physical hurdles create a sense of unity and accomplishment that resonates long after the final obstacle is cleared.

Group Cooking Classes

Holding a group cooking class is a great idea after all that movement. Gather around a fire or in a cooking studio to craft meals from ingredients that still taste like the earth they came from. Forget processed junk; this is about real food. You come together to learn new culinary skills while preparing healthy recipes that nourish both body and spirit. This communal experience not only promotes healthy eating for you but also cultivates relationships as you all share in the joy of creating something delicious together. In the act of chopping, stirring, and tasting together, you rediscover what it means to be human, to be cooperative creatures bound by stories and sustenance.

Avoid Activities Requiring Revealing Attire

If you're participating in the Marathon des Sables, proper attire can mean the difference between life and death. In the world of Sweatworking, it can mean the difference between a productive networking session and an awkward encounter that haunts the next board meeting. Activities that require minimal clothing or skin-tight attire should be avoided, like a dentist with a bad breath problem. The goal is for you and your associates to build professional relationships, not to over-showcase physical attributes. Stick to activities where standard workout gear suffices, preserving both dignity and mystery.

Remember, in a fast-paced business environment, as on glacial terrain, it's often what's unseen that holds the most power. You want your colleagues to focus on your ideas, not your abs. Save the spandex and crop tops for your personal workouts. In the world of Sweatworking, modesty isn't just a virtue, it's a necessity.

Follow-up Social Interactions

The shared experience of physical exertion will be extended and deepened through planned social interactions after each session. A post-workout smoothie or a quick coffee provides the perfect opportunity for you to cool down and connect on a more personal level. These moments, free from the intensity of physical activity, allow for you to encounter deeper conversations and the curing of bonds forged in shared effort.

Think of it as the corporate equivalent of gathering around the fire pit after a long day's hike. It's in these moments of relaxation when the endorphins are still flowing and your barriers are down that real connections are made. Just be sure to choose venues that don't negate all the good work you've done. Swapping the treadmill for a bar stool defeats the purpose of Sweatworking.

Incorporating Wellness into Traditional Networking Events

These are some examples of how to wrestle some wellness into your networking events, by not turning every meet-and-greet conference and event into a cholesterol convention.

Walking Tour

We all know how hectic work can get: Juggling tasks, attending conferences, and sitting through back-to-back meetings can leave you feeling a bit drained. You can though escape those poorly upholstered chairs and bring some fresh air into your conversations. Instead of the usual boardroom chatter, take your discussions on a walking tour.

For instance, if you're at a conference in a city, why not explore a local museum together with your colleagues? Or if you find yourself in a serene, rural area, consider strolling through a beautiful park. Every town has its own unique story waiting to be uncovered. By walking through its streets and experiencing its culture firsthand, you open up a world of insights that can propel your company forward.

As you wander, you'll discover the rich history, diverse communities, and innovative businesses that make each place special. There's so much wisdom hidden in the nooks and crannies of your surroundings, stories that can inspire you and your team and prompt creativity.

If you're looking to add some variety to the Walking Tour or even to the corporate office routine, consider introducing step counters as a motivational tool. Desk workers don't get enough movement throughout the day, and this approach offers a simple way to incorporate more activity while still allowing everyone to focus on networking and collaboration.

Tip: You can name them 'Walk'n'Talks' or 'Moving Minutes.'

Healthy Foods & Beverages

Some conference spreads look like foods cooked up in a test tube. Let's change it up. Make sure you offer up some actual food—fruits, vegetables, and whole grains. That may shock some people at first, especially those used to chicken wings and chips, but they just might realize they feel better without a gut full of sugar, sodium, and grease.

Make sure you cater to all. Not everyone can partake of the usual fare. Label the food so folks with allergies don't end up in the emergency room.

Tip: Offer up brain food such as nuts and fruit and the like that can keep you and people energized without the jitters and crash of coffee and donuts.

Outdoor Venues and Events

I've had my share of challenging speaking experiences at certain venues, where the confines of a hotel conference room felt stifling and made me want to start hitting my head against the dividing room wall. I can only imagine how you might feel cooped up in those hotel ballrooms year after year.

Natural light and fresh air will do wonders for you. It beats fluorescent lights and recycled air any day. Try inspiring your team by trading those walls filled with artwork out of the corporate cliche collection for vineyard views or garden spaces. This is a key way to inspire some fresh thinking, or at least a few decent snapshots for your company's marketing page.

Tip: How about a kite-flying challenge as a team-building event? Host a kite-making and flying competition where teams create and fly their kites. This fosters creativity, teamwork, and nostalgia in an open-field setting. You'd get more honest interaction than any Human Knot or Eye Contact exercise.

Bottom Line

In the end, make sure you consider this: What's the point of all this action and movement if you can't swap stories and share a few laughs afterwards? The exercise and movement are just the opening acts.

The real magic happens when you kick back afterward with some good grub and cold drinks. Let the sweat dry, the smiles appear, and the bonds deepen. This is where deals get made, friendships blossom, productivity picks up, and the world feels a little less lonely and more together. And why should you ever feel lonely? The universe is inside you.

Your Mantra: Every day alive is a reason to be inspired

15

Juggling Chainsaws (aka Life)

I spent three years instructing several corporate chiefs through a weekly fitness regimen. I was still testing my Sweatworking applications with clients and groups at that time, but I was finally at the point where the process was becoming distilled to its purest form with the greatest results.

These men, all with seasoned boardroom bravado, quickly turned our sessions into a contest. After three months, it wasn't just about getting fit, it was about one-upping each other, puffing chests, and trading shots like boys on a playground. That's how we men bond after all—through insults and competition, and thinly veiled affection wrapped in mockery.

One of them, who'd been crushing the workouts, started griping. He couldn't understand why his weight had plateaued. For two months, he'd shed pounds like a snake shedding skin, but now? Stuck. Dead in the water. I saw the weak spot immediately. "What about the foods you eat?" I asked.

It turned out that, as the CEO of some mortgage empire, his days were filled with client dinners and late-night boozing sessions, three or four times a week. Bingo. There it was, the achilles' heel of every high-flying executive: indulgence disguised as networking.

So I gave him three instructions:

1. **Discipline at the dinner table**: Eat smaller portions, make smarter choices, and down fewer cocktails.
2. **Cook at home**: Spend more time eating meals with your family—real whole foods in real company and real time. Good for you and your family.
3. **Learn the art of grocery shopping**: I dragged him to the grocery store myself, pointing out what to buy and what to leave on the shelf.

And just like that, he turned the tide. Sometimes it's not about pushing harder, it's about knowing where to push.

Your Body Connection

Physical activity isn't just some isolated act. It can be the lifeblood that courses through your veins, intertwining with every aspect of your existence. Your body's a complex machine, and it needs more than just movement to keep it humming.

The cognitive and creative benefits of Sweatworking can be influenced by lifestyle factors like diet, sleep, and social engagement. The underlying mechanisms should be familiar to you from study after study: Stuff your face with real food, not any of that processed garbage. Let the crisp night air lull you into a deep, primal sleep. Surround yourself with fellow humans who challenge your mind and spirit. Yes, yes, and yes.

This intricate dance of lifestyle factors affects how our daily choices collide and conspire to shape our mental prowess and creative fire.

Sleep Patterns and Quality

Madness and slumber are in a waltz, and you can bet your last cocktail that one affects the other. Sleep is as necessary as water in the desert and just as often neglected by the fools who think they can outwit biology. You want to know what happens when you cheat sleep? Try hiking up a mountain or finishing an important work report with your mind fogged by a week of restless nights. Your legs stumble and shake, your eyes blur, and the world loses its sharpness.

Insufficient sleep contributes to irritability, anxiety, impaired concentration, and a higher likelihood of mental health disorders like depression. Sleep deprivation also slows reaction times and reduces alertness, increasing the risk of accidents. Poor and irregular sleep can also lead to you having an weakened immunity, metabolic problems, increased vulnerability to illness, and a shorter lifespan.

I know, I know, it's not your fault. It's civilization, with all its gadgets and glowing screens, that conspires to keep you awake, to rob you of the simple pleasure of a night's rest beneath the indifferent stars. And for what? A hypnotic, continuous stare at the idiot box, scrolling through the digital wasteland for hours on end, until you finally scroll yourself to sleep.

Consistent, restful sleep supports your immune function, tissue repair, and hormonal balance, and reduces the risk of chronic diseases such as heart disease, diabetes, and obesity. Good sleep also enhances your mood stability, cognitive performance, emotional resilience, and is essential for your memory consolidation, learning, and decision-making.

Dietary Patterns

There are clear relationships between dietary patterns and mental health. What you stuff in your mouth is a key to keeping your mind sharp and your spirits high.

Dig into the marrow of what you eat, and figure out which bits and pieces keep your brain humming like a well-oiled '76 Toyota FJ40. Identify specific nutrients and dietary components that may have protective or detrimental effects on mental health. Try and cook up a recipe for happiness, using Mother Nature's own ingredients.

I've always said a person's gut instinct is worth more than all the fancy gadgets in the world. Take the time to investigate your gut-brain axis and its role in your mental health and cognitive function. Your belly and your brain are yapping at each other constantly, and what you feed one affects the other.

Digital Social Engagement

We're all slaves to those glowing rectangles, aren't we? Staring at our phones like they hold the secrets of the universe. Well, sorry, but they don't. They're just fancy mirrors reflecting our own vapid existence back at us.

Do you think those virtual 'interactions' are the same as looking another human in the eye? Ha! We're deluding ourselves. There's a primal, visceral connection that happens when two flesh-and-blood creatures occupy the same physical space. When you're fully immersed, your body responds, your emotions kick in, and suddenly you're part of something way bigger than just you. But go ahead, keep pretending emoji reactions are just as meaningful.

And please, get me started on our precious social platforms. We're all so busy comparing ourselves to carefully curated highlight reels that we've forgotten how to actually live. Too busy chasing 'likes' and clickbait videos to notice the world crumbling around us.

Put down your damn phone and spend some quality time outside, every, single, day. Feel the sun on your face, the ground under your feet. Remember what it means to be human, to be alive on this miraculous planet. It's there inside you. You did it as a child. You remember when movement was done for sheer enjoyment don't you? If you do use technology, use it sparingly as a tool for self-improvement, not distraction.

Stress Management and Coping Strategies

I know you're stressed out. I was right there with you. After those few years of feeling mentally groundless, I effectively reconstructed my life by carefully redesigning my psyche and lifestyle through deliberate analysis and renewal back into functional wholeness. You can't let life grind you down. There are ways to keep your sanity in this world.

Mindfulness and Meditation

I thought mindfulness meditation was some new-age bullshit in my twenties, full of lotus postures and a lot of western world people saying, 'Namaste,' to give the perception that they were enlightened. The 'Namaste' component was true, but the rest wasn't. It's a research-proven way to reduce stress, anxiety, and even depression. It's like a mental enema, flushing out all the crap that's clogging up your brain. And it's not just for monks and yoga instructors. Even mountain whores and daily commuters trying to do the best we can in this world for ourselves and our family can benefit from a little mind-clearing.

Studies show mindfulness exercises can actually change your brain and biology, improving both mental and physical health. It's like rewiring your mind to be less of a neurotic mess. Hell, it might even boost your immune system and help you fight off the common cold.

Work-Life Balance: Don't Let the Big Cheeses Grind You Down

You think most corporate suits care about your well-being? Think again. If you live by a principle of mine, 'action, not words', then you know most, if not a majority of executives, are thinking of their own corporate bottom line, not yours. Some care sincerely about you and how you're doing, though it seems this is becoming more uncommon. It's human nature to be selfish, and that's fine. Though your work-life imbalance can become a cancer on your cognition, eating away at your attention, concentration, and memory. It's not just the Big Cheese making you feel like a miserable SOB, it's your brain turning to mush. Time to make an upgrade to Sweatworking. Now!

More Than Just Booze and Weed

I'm not saying to give up alcoholic beverages and puffing on the magic dragon, but there are other ways to take the edge off. Cognitive Behavioral Therapy (CBT) is like a mental jiu-jitsu, teaching you to grapple with your own bullshit thoughts. It's more effective than popping pills, and a hell of a lot cheaper than a shrink.

Acupuncture, despite sounding like some New Age hokum, might actually help with stress and insomnia. Getting poked with needles in just the right areas of one's body dates back to around 100 BCE, so that stands for something. And if you can stomach someone touching you, massage has been shown to help with anxiety and sleeplessness. Just try and forego having them sell you any magical crystals.

Environmental Factors

Urban living can be like a disease, a tumor on the human psyche. You pack yourself into steel and glass boxes, breathing others' exhaust fumes and listening to the endless drone of traffic. It's no wonder you're going mad. A recent study found that city folk need fewer mental health services when they have more exposure to urban green spaces. Well, no shit! A tree or two might remind us there's still a world beyond our smartphone screens.

Getting out into a park, the outdoors, and the wild doesn't just make you feel good; it rewires your brain. Researchers found that even a short walk in nature improved memory and mood in people with depression. There's a reason why big city parks like Central Park in New York City and Griffith Park in Los Angeles are tremendously popular. Imagine that, actual healing without pills or therapy, just by putting one foot in front of the other on a trail.

We seem to be too busy to notice enterprise is driving us batshit crazy. A 25-year study proves it—polluted air scrambles brains, and noise turns kids into nervous wrecks. I'm talking about psychotic experiences and despair. Anxiety's not just for those of us contemplating the vast emptiness of the cosmos anymore, it's becoming as common as fast food joints in our over-stimulated urban hellscapes.

And we call this progress? Get out, breathe deeply, and find some lucidity. Your mind, your company, and the whole world need us to stop being a bunch of soft-headed desk jockeys and get our heads right, and the world will thank us for it. That's the kind of exercise and networking that might just save our souls.

***

In the end, it's all about finding what works for you. Maybe it's meditation, maybe it's telling your boss to go to hell, or maybe it's just sitting on the summit of a Colorado 14er and screaming at the sky at the top of your lungs (which by the way is healthy for you). Do whatever keeps you from going postal in this insane world we've created.

The Earth doesn't need us, we need it. So take care of yourself, and by enjoying nature maybe we'll have a chance of not completely fucking everything up beyond repair. Get out there and find your own brand of positive craziness.

Your Mantra: Never stop learning

16

Brain in Motion = Couch in Defeat

I've stood in front of countless crowds, from executives leading large companies to everyday folks just trying to make it through the 9-to-5 grind. I've had a realization that's both sobering and eye-opening. Approximately 10-15% of adults who attend my keynote addresses internalize and apply insights to level up their lives. Though this figure rises to 75-85% among participants in hands-on workshops and interactive Sweatworking sessions, where collaborative problem-solving and practical exercises deepen engagement and skill retention.

Now, when it comes to those keynote speeches, I could blame my delivery, my hair, or even the phase of the moon. But let's be honest, that's not the real issue. The truth is, as you get older, you get comfortable. Too comfortable. You start building walls around yourself, brick by brick, year by year. Changing your life requires more than just a forty-minute motivational speech.

And then along comes something like COVID, throwing you for a loop, and suddenly those walls feel like a fortress you're afraid to leave. The pandemic messed with our heads and made us even more afraid of losing what we've got—our security, our families, our stuff. We've seen how quickly it can all vanish, and that's scary as hell.

I get it. You've got a family to think about, a mortgage to pay. It feels safer to stay put, even if you're not emotionally fulfilled. And while I understand that fear, I can't say I agree with giving in to it.

But here's the thing: Life isn't meant to be lived in a bubble-wrap cocoon. Living is messy, it's unpredictable, and that's what makes it beautiful. You've got to keep that spark of curiosity alive. Here's what I believe: You need to keep learning until the day you die. Not just surface-level stuff, but real, transformative learning. Pick up an instrument, learn a new language, or start your own Sweatworking group. Take a vacation somewhere that pushes you out of your comfort zone. And no tourist traps or luxury resorts, rather somewhere that doesn't have a gift shop on every corner. Do it all.

So, how do you go about doing this? You need to work on your brain. Keep challenging it, keep feeding it new information and new experiences. Because the moment you stop learning is the moment you start dying. At the end of the day, that's what makes life rich and meaningful. It's not about playing it safe, it's about squeezing every drop of experience and knowledge out of this wild ride you call life.

When you're taking your final bow, you want death to find you in the middle of a grand adventure, with dirt underneath your fingernails, your well-worn journal clutched in your hands, and a twinkle of mischief still in your eye.

Do you want to sharpen that dull blade you call a mind? Scientists have shown that physical activity boosts brain power. You don't need a bunch of electrodes stuck to your skull to figure that out. Just look at how our society has evolved. We've traded in our natural inclination for active, engaged living for the comfort of delivery dinners. It's easy to get caught up in this convenient lifestyle, but it comes at a cost.

Imagine spending time in a place where daily life is a constant challenge.

In many parts of the world where I've been privileged to carry out my expeditions, people have to labor just to find food or access basic healthcare. It's not easy, but it forces them to keep their minds sharp and bodies resilient. They're constantly problem-solving and adapting, because they have to, which is something we can learn from them. I'm not saying you must live in a third-world country to sharpen your wit. It's just that many of us are living in a fantasy world, full of expensive cars, expensive dinners, and ginormous houses, and yet still not satisfied. So obviously that's not the answer. By incorporating more physical activity and earnest face-to-face communication into your life, you can regain some of that mental edge, which in turn improves your overall well-being.

Your brain is like a muscle, and if you don't use it, it'll turn to pulp. But don't think you can outwit yourself by just doing jumping jacks in your living room. The real cognitive fireworks happen when you're involved in wellness on a daily basis. So, put down your phone, lace up your athletic shoes, and get the hell outside.

Let's delve into the intricate relationship between physical activity, cognitive function, and creative thinking, for optimizing our mental capabilities through Sweatworking.

Cognitive Benefits of Physical Activity

Being active does wonders for your brain. It helps with everything from focusing and remembering things to more complex thinking skills. But don't settle for a casual walk in a manicured park and think that's enough. It's a start, yes, but if you're looking to kindle some real creativity, you need to push yourself a bit. Get out into nature where the terrain is a little rougher or into a gym where the exercises challenge you. That's where the magic happens and your best ideas can start flowing.

Leveraging for Creative Problem-Solving

Movement-based brainstorming: Incorporating physical activity into Sweatworking sessions, such as having your employees walk while generating ideas, leads to more creative outcomes. When I'm out on a mountain, scrambling over rocks or up steep snowy slopes, or teaching a wellness class, that's when the real ideas start popping.

Exercise as cultivation: Engaging in physical activity during breaks from focused work on a creative problem provides valuable development time, potentially leading to insights and novel solutions. I've solved more problems while exercising and walking than I ever did sitting on my ass. It's as if the movement seeps into your bones and blood, rearranging your thoughts until something useful pops out.

Nature-based activities: Combining physical activity with exposure to natural environments (e.g., hiking, trail running) offers additional benefits for creativity, as nature exposure has been linked to enhanced creative thinking. There's no better way to clear the cobwebs from your brain than by facing the raw beauty of the outdoors. It'll strip away all your pretensions and leave you with nothing but the naked truth. Go experience your neighborhood with a walk today or some of our incomparable National Parks on your next vacation, and you'll see exactly what I mean.

Enhanced Executive Function

Construct a mental image of this: You're breathing heavily up a mountain trail, sweat trickling down your face like drops of determination. Your legs are in motion, your lungs are appreciating the air you're taking in, and you're pretty sure you just saw God in a tree. But while your body's going through its motions, your brain's throwing a goddamn party.

The technical term is called 'executive function,' though just think of it as if your head's wearing a suit and tie. These are your brain's gears—working memory, cognitive flexibility, and that stubborn little dictator called inhibitory control. Elaborate words for "remembering where you left your water bottle," "figuring out how to cross that raging Alaskan river without drowning," and "resisting the urge to push your hiking companion off a cliff after his or her last moronic comment." Turns out, science agrees with what your body's been screaming all along: Get off your ass and move. Exercise isn't just for athletes, it's a bootcamp for your neurons.

The real glory is that the more you enact this aerobic exercise, the sharper your mind gets. It's Mother Nature's cruel joke: Sure, I'll make you smarter, but first, you must learn to stay active. Lace up those running shoes, get outside or into a gym, and embrace movement of all kinds. Your body might rebel the first few times, but your brain will be doing back-flips, metaphorically speaking, of course.

Improved Attention and Processing Speed

Physical activity within a Sweatworking session is about waking up those dormant neurons. Science says the sweat-soaked among us see sharper, think faster, and outpace the cubicle zombies. Think of your brain as a vast desert landscape. Each step and breath you take is like a life-giving rainstorm washing over that parched earth. Suddenly, where there was only dust and silence, wildflowers bloom and rivers of quick thinking carve new pathways. This improved cognitive efficiency can translate into better performance in various real-world tasks that require your rapid decision-making and sustained focus. You'll be like a cheetah on the hunt—alert, focused, processing every rustle in the undergrowth with lightning speed.

In this age of screens and sedentary living, you've forgotten a fundamental truth: You are a creature of motion. Your ancestors didn't evolve these magnificent brains by sitting on their asses all day. They ran, climbed, explored, developed tools to use for planting and hunting, and in doing so, they honed their minds into the marvels of cognition you inherit today.

Memory Enhancement

When you naturally get your heart pumping and your sweat glands working overtime, you can feel that concurrently, and something magical happens in that skull of yours. The hippocampus, that's the part of your brain responsible for memory and not getting lost in the wilderness, actually grows. It's like your brain flipping the bird to old age and saying, "Not on my watch, MFs!"

One study involving 120 older adults found that aerobic exercise training led to an increase in the volume of the anterior hippocampus, resulting in significant improvements in spatial memory. These findings suggest that regular physical activity can be an effective strategy for combating age-related cognitive decline and potentially reducing the risk of neurodegenerative diseases.

It doesn't take much. Just forty minutes a day of Sweatworking sessions, putting one foot in front of the other (you can even include injury prevention stretching exercises), is enough to keep your mind sharp. Hell, even a year of this simple routine can turn back the clock on your brain by one to two years.

Neuroplasticity and Brain Health

Neuroplasticity is like the Grand Canyon of your mind, it's constantly evolving and expanding, shaped by the flowing river of your experiences. Getting active helps your brain stay flexible and make new connections.

Exercise helps produce a special protein called brain-derived neurotrophic factor, or BDNF for short. BDNF is a magic ingredient for your brain. When you're exercising, the transformation begins. BDNF ignites your brain connections, making them light up like fireflies. This amazing protein supports the survival of your brain cells, helps your synapses adapt and change, and even encourages the growth of new neurons.

When you're feeling low, just remember: Your brain is as adaptable as the untamed wild. It's ready to learn, ready to grow, ready for your dreams of new possibilities. All you need to do is get out there and move.

***

Fancy studies and meta-analyses might show some promising links between moving your body and firing up your cognitive gears, but you've got a trail ahead before you can claim victory over mental stagnation. Sure, you might be genetically predisposed to be more active, and yeah, you'll probably score better than others on those fancy cognitive tests the HR executives love so much. Factors such as age, baseline fitness level, genetic predisposition, and personal preferences for different types of exercise could all influence the extent to which you experience cognitive and creative benefits from physical activity.

But don't you dare use genetics as an excuse to stay glued to your screens. And forget using those fancy pills and snake oil supplements in place of movement. The U.S. federal guidelines for supplements are mainly aimed at ensuring the product is safe for consumption, not that it's effective. Most of the claims you see on supplement bottles are not supported by science, and therefore, their health claims are largely unregulated.

The fact is, movement, whether it's a stroll around the office perimeter or through town or an escape to the outdoors or a gym, is going to wake up that dormant lump of gray matter between your ears. It doesn't matter if you're a spring chicken or a greybeard, a marathon runner or a wheezing novice. Get off your ass and move.

I'm not saying you need to become some fitness-obsessed gym god. But find something that gets your blood pumping and your lungs working. The point is, stop making excuses and start moving. Your brain will thank you. This is why Sweatworking can change you and companies around the world. You are poised to redefine the future of corporate wellness and set a new standard for employee care and well-being that will inspire others to follow.

Your Mantra: Come back smarter and stronger

17

The Art of Doing Everything in Half the Time

The ceaseless ticking of a clock can be both a blessing and a curse in the grand portfolio of your existence. On one hand, it's a constant reminder of your mortality, a mechanical tyrant counting down the precious moments you have left on this earth. Yet, ironically, that same ticking can be a wake-up call, a provocative nudge to a complacent mind. The same as your bucket list that continues to grow every year, it startles and agitates, refusing to let you slumber through your life.

I find my deepest connection to the world in the silence of the mountains, far away from the things of humankind. The absence of that ticking allows me to tune into the timeless rhythms of nature. But in the disharmony of modern life, you need that mechanical heartbeat to remind you that your time is finite, that you must seize each moment to live fully, to love the earth and sun and animals, and to stand up against the craziness of your time.

So listen to that ticking, let it anger you, let it wake you up. This is where Sweatworking can hold precedence in your new modern world and help you better manage your time than any app could ever do.

Some of the sentences you will never hear in a conversation about exercise and networking on how to maximize time.

1. "I find the best way to break the ice at networking events is to challenge someone to a plank-off right in the middle of the hors d'oeuvres table."

2. "My networking strategy involves wearing a full Lycra body suit to the gym with my resume printed on it. It's all about maximizing visibility and minimizing drag."

3. "I only connect with people on LinkedIn if they can beat me in a 5k. It's a great way to build a team of high-achievers… and also ensure I always have someone to pace me."

4. "Instead of asking 'What do you do?' at networking events, I ask 'What's your one-rep max?' It cuts to the core of a person's strengths… literally."

5. "Instead of joining a fancy country club, I bought a llama and started a 'llama-working' group. We hike, discuss quarterly earnings, and occasionally get spat on. It's surprisingly effective for weeding out the weak."

Excuse Drop Today

Let's face it, "I don't have enough time," is an excuse we've all used at some point. Whether you're a busy professional, a parent juggling multiple responsibilities, or an entrepreneur chasing your dreams, time is always in short supply.

But the reality is that no one has enough time. You won't find anyone who says, "You know what? I've got all the time in the world to do everything I want." That's not how life works.

The next time you catch yourself saying, "I don't have enough time," remember that it's often just an excuse. It's a way of letting yourself off the hook from trying something new or pushing beyond your comfort zone.

The truth is, you have the same twenty-four hours as everyone else. It's how you choose to use them that matters. So, instead of letting time be an excuse, make it a challenge. Find ways to prioritize what's important, manage your time more effectively, and take small steps towards your goals every day.

Time Integration Advantages

- **Triple-Tasking Mastery**: Sweatworking allows you to accomplish three important tasks simultaneously—maintaining physical and mental wellness and making headway in your work, essentially cutting your time in half.

- **Enhanced Focus**: The increased blood flow and endorphin release during physical activity can sharpen concentration, allowing you to complete tasks more quickly and accurately in less time.

- **Creative Problem Solving**: Movement stimulates your creative thinking. Something as simple as a 10-minute walking meeting might lead to innovative solutions that wouldn't have surfaced in an hour of a traditional office meeting setting.

- **Natural Time Management**: The physical nature of Sweatworking creates natural time boundaries for you. A 30-minute workout of movement exercises becomes a perfectly timed brainstorming session.

- **Reduced Procrastination**: The energy boost from physical activity can help overcome the inertia that often leads to procrastination when you have more time to think about a particular task.

Sweatworking represents a fundamental change in how you approach productivity and time management. Today, you are awash with productivity tools where the simple act of choosing which project planner, note-taking app, or other software package is itself a task. Complementing physical activity with work tasks offers a more sincere and human tool for enhancing efficiency, creativity, and overall well-being. As you continue to seek ways to optimize your professional life and wellness, this method stands out as not only saving time but also contributing to a healthier, more balanced lifestyle.

Your Mantra: Aging is time's wake-up call

18

Dripping with Ambition: The Science Behind Your Sweat

"Never let them see you sweat." You may not remember that line, but many fellow GenXers sure do. That was a tagline attached to an ad campaign for *Dry Idea* deodorant back in the 1980s. They produced various commercials where character actors described how, in a professional work setting, you never let them see you sweat. Agreed. No one likes to be watching someone make a presentation or a speech, and then see that underneath their shirt or blouse their armpits are single-handedly solving the global water crisis.

However, with Sweatworking, the act of perspiring is not just tolerated, but celebrated as a badge of honor. It's a perverse sort of virtue, this notion that the more you sweat, the harder you're working, and thus the more admirable your toil.

Summers in Northern Virginia are sweltering, but I love pushing myself in my makeshift sweatbox, a building the size of a one-car garage, with no HVAC. After two hours of daily exercise training, I take pride in having to wring out my shirt of sweat multiple times during a workout. The more drenched I am, the more accomplished I feel. I've been doing this for 30+

years. Not every workout has been spectacular, but it's remained a constant in my life for as long as I've been an adult. It's a habit, just as brushing my teeth after a meal and going to sleep every evening. Positive habits produce positive results, no matter how you look at it.

This is your guarantee: You sweat, you'll feel better.

Sweating: The Natural Cooling System

Within the broad sweep of your bodily machinery, few mechanisms are as pervasive and vital as the humble act of sweating. This oft-maligned process, which can bring you discomfort and in some cases, embarrassment, is in truth a stalwart guardian of your health and vitality. It's not just a means to cool your body, but a path to invigorate the spirit and forge bonds with your fellow partakers in this wild and wondrous journey called Sweatworking.

Science of Sweat

Sweating is a damn intricate business. It involves more than getting dripping wet in the middle of a humid summer; no, it's a sophisticated scheme involving the release of fluids from those tiny pores in your skin. Sure, its main job is to keep your internal thermostat from overheating, but it's also got a few tricks up its sleeve—helping to flush out the waste, for one. It's a reminder that even in this mechanized world, your body still knows how to take care of itself if you just let it and guide it.

Thermoregulation: Keeping Cool Under Pressure

The primary function of sweating is thermoregulation, which is your body's ability to maintain its core temperature within a narrow range, typically around 98.6°F (37°C). When your internal temperature rises due to physical exertion, environmental heat, or fever, sweat glands release fluid onto the skin's surface. As this sweat evaporates, it cools the skin and the blood beneath, lowering your body's core temperature.

This cooling mechanism is remarkably efficient. During intense exercise or in hot environments, your body can produce up to two to four liters of sweat per hour. This allows you to engage in strenuous activities or survive in challenging climates without risking dangerous overheating.

During physical activity, your muscles generate heat as they contract. This heat production can rapidly increase your body temperature, potentially leading to heat exhaustion or even heat stroke if left unchecked. Sweating is your body's primary mechanism for dissipating this excess heat.

Composition of Sweat

While sweat is primarily composed of water (99%), it also contains small amounts of various substances, including:

- Electrolytes (sodium, chloride, potassium)
- Urea
- Lactate
- Amino acids
- Trace minerals

The precise composition of sweat can vary depending on factors such as diet, hydration status, and overall health.

Hydration and Performance

Sweating leads to fluid loss. Proper hydration before, during, and after exercise is essential to replace lost fluids and maintain performance.

Dehydration can significantly impair your exercise performance, leading to decreased endurance, reduced power output, and increased perceived exertion. It can also increase the risk of heat-related illnesses. Understanding individual sweat rates and developing appropriate hydration strategies is crucial for your optimal exercise performance and safety.

Health Benefits of Sweating

Natural Moisturizer

Contrary to popular belief, sweating can actually benefit your skin and can act as a natural moisturizer. When you sweat, it helps hydrate your skin from the inside out. The moisture from sweat can give your skin a healthy, dewy appearance, as well as help hydrate the outer layer of the skin, keeping it supple and reducing the appearance of fine lines and wrinkles. You can even refer to this as a 'post-workout glow.' This natural moisturizing effect can help keep your skin elastic and youthful-looking.

Skin Cleansing

Sweating opens up your pores, allowing for a natural cleansing process. As sweat flows out of the pores, it can help flush out dirt, oil, and other impurities that may have accumulated on the skin's surface. This cleansing action can contribute to clearer skin and may help reduce the occurrence of acne and other blemishes.

Detoxification

While the liver and kidneys are the primary organs responsible for detoxification, some research suggests that sweating may play a role in eliminating certain toxins from your body. A study published in the Archives of Environmental and Contamination Toxicology found that sweat contained higher concentrations of certain heavy metals compared to urine, suggesting that sweating could be an effective method for eliminating these substances from the body.

Some research has indicated that bisphenol A (BPA) and phthalates, chemicals found in many plastics, can be detected in sweat. A study published in the Journal of Environmental and Public Health found that these chemicals were present in the sweat of some individuals, suggesting that sweating could be a means of eliminating these endocrine-disrupting compounds from the body.

Antimicrobial Properties

Sweat contains a natural antibiotic called dermcidin. This peptide helps fight off various types of bacteria and fungi, including E. coli and Staphylococcus aureus. By producing dermcidin, your sweat glands contribute to the body's first line of defense against harmful microorganisms. In plain English, sweating helps defend your body from harm's way.

Enhanced Circulation

The process of sweating is often associated with increased blood flow, particularly during exercise. This improved circulation can help deliver oxygen and nutrients more efficiently to various parts of your body, including immune cells. Better-nourished immune cells are more effective at identifying and neutralizing potential threats.

Heat Shock Proteins

When you sweat due to heat exposure or exercise, your body produces heat shock proteins. These proteins play a crucial role in protecting your cells from stress and may enhance overall immune function.

Cardiovascular Health

Improved Heart Function

Regular exercise that induces sweating can strengthen the most important muscle in your body, your heart muscle. It improves its pumping efficiency and reduces the risk of cardiovascular diseases. The American Heart Association recommends at least 150 minutes of moderate-intensity aerobic activity or 75 minutes of vigorous-intensity aerobic activity per week for optimal heart health. To make it simpler, I advocate that you do some kind of exercise every single day.

Blood Pressure Regulation

Sweating during exercise can help lower blood pressure. As you exercise and sweat, your blood vessels dilate, reducing the resistance to blood flow. This can lead to both short-term and long-term improvements in blood pressure control.

Cholesterol Management

Regular physical activity that induces sweating can help improve your cholesterol levels by increasing HDL (good) cholesterol and reducing LDL (bad) cholesterol. This balance is crucial for you to maintain cardiovascular health and reduce the risk of heart disease.

Mood Enhancement

Endorphin Release

Physical activities that induce sweating stimulate the release of endorphins, often referred to as 'feel-good' hormones. These natural chemicals can create for you a sense of euphoria and well-being, commonly known as a 'runner's high.' Ask a runner about this, they deservedly love to talk about it.

Improved Sleep Quality

Regular physical activity that induces sweating can lead to improved sleep quality. The physical exertion and subsequent cooling of the body help regulate your body's circadian rhythm, making it easier to fall asleep and stay asleep throughout the night. Better sleep for you, in turn, contributes to improved mood, reduced stress, and better overall mental health.

Pain Relief and Muscle Recovery

Natural Pain Management

The release of endorphins during sweating can act as a natural pain reliever. This can be particularly beneficial if you're dealing with chronic pain conditions.

Muscle Relaxation

Heat exposure that induces sweating can help relax your tense muscles. Many people find relief from muscle aches and pains after a session in a sauna or a hot yoga class.

Improved Flexibility

Sweating in a warm environment can increase your muscle flexibility and range of motion. Athletes typically incorporate heat exposure for muscles, tendons, and ligaments within their warm-up routines.

Kidney Stone Prevention

Sweating causes the body to require more fluids, which increases water intake. This increased fluid consumption can help dilute your urine and prevent the formation of kidney stones. Moreover, the loss of salt through sweat may also play a role in reducing the risk of certain types of kidney stones. As mentioned, proper hydration is crucial when you're engaging in activities that induce heavy sweating to prevent dehydration and maintain this potential benefit.

Sweat Rate and Fitness Level

As you become more physically fit, your body becomes more efficient at sweating. Trained athletes often start sweating earlier in their workouts and produce more sweat than less fit individuals. This adaptation allows them to cool their bodies more effectively during intense exercise.

It's important to note that the amount of sweat produced doesn't necessarily correlate with the intensity of your workout or the number of calories you're burning. Factors such as temperature, humidity, and individual physiology play significant roles in your sweat production.

Sweat contains not only water but also electrolytes, primarily sodium and chloride. During prolonged or intense exercise, especially in hot conditions, significant electrolyte losses can occur through sweat. This can lead to electrolyte imbalances, which may cause you muscle cramps, fatigue, and impaired performance.

If you're a recreational exerciser of Sweatworking, a balanced diet is sufficient to replace electrolytes lost through sweat. However, if you are an endurance athlete or exercising in hot conditions apart from Sweatworking sessions, you may need to consider electrolyte replacement strategies, such as sports drinks or electrolyte supplements.

Skin Health

While sweating can benefit skin health and is good for flushing your pipes, it can also present challenges, particularly if you are prone to certain skin conditions. Sweating keeps you alive, but can turn your face into a disaster zone.

- **Acne**: If excessive sweating causes you acne, it's important to cleanse your skin properly before and after sweating and avoid wearing tight, non-breathable clothing during workouts.

- **Heat Rash**: Also known as prickly heat, this condition can occur when sweat ducts become blocked. Wearing loose, breathable clothing and showering promptly after sweating can help you prevent heat rash.

- **Fungal Infections**: Warm, moist environments created by sweat can promote the growth of fungi. Changing out of sweaty clothes promptly and keeping skin dry can help you prevent fungal infections.

Sweating and Mental Health

Stress Reduction

Exercise-induced sweating is one of the most effective natural stress relievers. Physical activity stimulates the production of endorphins, your body's natural mood elevators. These chemicals can create feelings of happiness and euphoria, often referred to as previously mentioned, 'runner's high.'

Sweating helps reduce levels of stress hormones like cortisol while increasing the production of norepinephrine, a chemical that helps your brain deal with stress more effectively. To put this more simply: Sweat=Less Stress.

The act of focusing on physical exertion can also serve as a form of moving meditation, allowing you to temporarily disconnect from daily stressors and clear your mind.

Anxiety and Depression Management

Regular exercise that induces sweating has been shown as an effective tool in managing symptoms of agitation and melancholy. The combination of physical exertion, endorphin release, and the sense of accomplishment with completing a workout can significantly improve your mood and reduce symptoms of these mental health conditions.

A study published in the Journal of Clinical Psychiatry found that regular exercise was comparable to antidepressant medication in treating depression. Pop a pill or exercise. Which one has more beneficial results for you in the long run?

Improved Cognitive Function

Sweating through exercise has been linked to improved cognitive function, including better memory, increased focus, and enhanced problem-solving skills. The increased blood flow to your brain during exercise can promote the growth of new brain cells and improve your overall brain performance. A study published in the Journal of Applied Physiology found that even brief bouts of exercise can improve your brain function and working memory.

Increased Self-Esteem

Engaging in regular exercise that induces sweating can boost your self-esteem and body image. As you see improvements in your physical fitness and appearance, you will experience increased confidence and a more positive self-image.

Social Contact

Many sweat-inducing activities, such as Sweatworking sessions, group fitness classes, or team sports, provide opportunities for social interaction. This social component can help you combat feelings of isolation and loneliness, contributing to better overall mental health.

Your Mantra: Consistency over perfection

19

Curb Your Enthusiasm: Let's Walk and Talk Before We Burst

Every day, no matter where I am in this world, I go for a walk after a meal. It's usually twice a day within a six-hour time period. As I've aged, I've discovered that intermittent fasting aligns perfectly with my body and lifestyle. The beauty of life lies in its diversity. What works for me might not work for you, and that's what makes your individual journey so unique and fascinating.

Taking a walk after a meal offers a moment to appreciate your life's simple pleasures. Your mind might be thinking, "Why leave the comfort of my plush couch for a walk after a hard day at work?" Trust me, a stroll can work wonders for both your physical and mental well-being.

First off, it's a great way to **balance your blood sugar**. You see, when you eat, your body converts that food into glucose, and if you just sit around, it can lead to a spike in blood sugar levels. But by getting moving, you're telling your muscles to use that glucose for energy, which helps keep those levels in check. It's like nudging your body gently back into balance.

Next, walking after meals can **improve digestion**. It's a bit like giving your stomach a friendly massage, helping food move through your system more smoothly. A good digestive system is like having a superpower, especially when it means you can save the day (or at least your pants) during those urgent bathroom breaks.

Then there's the **circulation boost.** Walking gets your blood flowing, which means more oxygen to your brain and muscles. You'll feel more invigorated, ready to tackle whatever the day or evening throws at you.

And don't forget about **weight management.** Research shows that walking briskly after meals can be more effective for shedding those extra pounds than sitting immediately back down in your office chair or on your couch for a digital streaming binge.

It's also a great way to **clear your mind** and **boost your mood**. Exercise releases those feel-good hormones like endorphins and dopamine, making you feel more balanced and happy.

Well, how are you supposed to jot down notes on your phone when you're pulsating with action like a human being on a mission from God? You're not. The real question is why aren't you out there kicking up dust every day, sucking in that sweet air, and wrangling with the glorious beast and unbridled beauty of life that God provides for you?

It's simple. Instead of sitting on an ever-expanding posterior in an office, you take your meeting outside. As you walk, you talk. Let the rhythm of your footsteps become the backdrop to your discussion, the changing scenery sparking new ideas and perspectives.

The physical act of moving forward will propel the conversation forward as well, cutting out the unnecessary fluff and getting to the heart of the matter. Each step you take will be a mutiny against the sedentary lifestyle that's creeping into your life like an unwelcome weed.

And that colleague who loves to drone on and on? That person will run out of breath eventually. The meeting that usually drags on for hours? It's amazing how quickly decisions can be made when there's a finish line in sight.

Now, I'm not saying you need to go for a few miles to reap all the benefits. Just a short, brisk walk will do when you begin this healthy habit. Aim for about ten minutes to start, and see how it feels. If you're at work, finish your lunch early and use those last minutes to take a walk around your office or down the street and back. The key is to make it a habit. Trust me, it's something you'll enjoy doing every day.

Even if you decide this whole Sweatworking thing isn't for you, if you take one thing with you from my ramblings, let it be this: Walk. Just walk. By your lonesome, or with a colleague from the office. Hell, drag your whole damn team along if you have to. Walk before you punch the clock, after you swallow your lunch, after another day of the work grind.

Go for walks on a daily basis, and I guarantee you'll be thanking me in your dreams, singing the praises of this book to the high heavens. You're welcome. Another of your superpowers has been officially activated.

Program #1

Schedule three walking meetings for twenty minutes each at these particular times of the day:

- **Dawn Patrol:** Keep your caffeine-fuzzy carcass out of that prison chair 30 minutes before clocking in by getting a move on. Your brain's still malleable, not yet beaten into submission by artificial lighting and endless emails. A brisk 20-minute jaunt will jump-start those synapses and flood your system with enough endorphins to make even the most mind-numbing meeting tolerable.

- **Digestive Ramble:** After you've shoveled down whatever passes for sustenance in that soul-crushing cafeteria or takeout box, hit the pavement. A post-lunch stroll will keep that meal from turning you into a slack-jawed, possibly drooling mess come 2 PM. You might even stumble upon an idea that's worth your dreams in gold while you're out there.

- **Escape Plan**: Before you flee your rectangular office bunker, take one last lap around the block. Use these precious minutes to plot your evening liberation from the commercial enterprise. Let the taste of freedom fuel your steps as you scheme ways to avoid becoming the soulless automaton some of your employers so desperately want you to be. Also, park your car a good ten minutes away from the office.

Program #2

A Midday Circuit: Take a thirty-minute walk around the office perimeter, your artificial boundary, or your manufactured landscape. Even here, between concrete and cultivation, the wild can be calling. You may hear a bird chirp or see a squirrel scramble across your path. Each step is a small act against a corporate apparatus that wants to reduce you to a billable unit.

Purpose

- Break the fluorescent trance
- Breathe unfiltered air
- Speak unfiltered thoughts
- Challenge the mechanical rhythm of productivity

What Really Happens

- Conversations emerge naturally
- Hierarchies dissolve on uneven ground
- Ideas will start like unexpected desert wildflowers
- You reconnect with your human potential

Cautionary: If this walk is not sanctioned as a Sweatworking session by your Human Resources Department, consider it a momentary escape from institutional control. Walk hard. Walk free.

Mantra: When you're walking, that's when life happens to you

20

Zen and the Art of Not Losing Your Cool at Work

I remember well the year when meditation and mindfulness became a part of my life—2001. It was during a mountaineering expedition on Shishapangma, the 14th-highest mountain in the world, located in Tibet. I was about to tackle my first 8000m peak, and the excitement was mixed with a bit of fear about this daunting challenge ahead of me.

I'd read months earlier about how there were Tibetan monks known for their ability to raise their body temperature through meditation, specifically using a technique called Tummo (inner fire). The monks who practice Tummo meditation are typically from Tibetan Buddhist traditions and reside in remote monasteries in the Himalayan region, including parts of Northern India and Tibet.

This practice involves deep meditation, breathing techniques, and visualization to generate heat, allowing them to withstand extremely cold conditions. These monks often live where temperatures can be very low, and they have been observed to dry wet sheets draped over them in freezing conditions, demonstrating their ability to generate significant body heat.

As I delved into the idea that monks could achieve this extraordinary physiological response, I felt a deep connection to the profound impact of meditation on our bodies. It was as if I were witnessing the incredible power of the human mind to shape our physical experiences. I was drawn in, eager to explore this connection for myself. And if it didn't work out, I figured, no harm done, it was worth a try.

We arrived at Advanced Base Camp (ABC), and that's when things got rough. I fell ill after eating at a local shanty the day before. My climbing partner, Dan Mazur, had this philosophy of eating at local places, no matter how rough they looked. He believed it was a way to toughen up the stomach for the adventure ahead so you wouldn't get sick. This particular shack was off a muddy road, about half a day's drive from Zhangmu, the border town between Nepal and China. It was one of those 'hidden gems' that only the locals knew about.

This was my first 8000m peak attempt, and I wanted to prove myself to Dan. So, I joined him in trying all sorts of local food, even when the food looked sketchy. Looking back, it was a bit reckless, but it taught me a valuable lesson. From that day on, I've made it a point to immerse myself in local cultures whenever I travel. I prefer to eat at local spots, not just for the food and to fortify my stomach with microbes to protect it from stomach ailments, but for the stories and connections I make with the people, and it also helps the local economy. It's become a part of who I am.

I was hit with a wave of illness the very next day. It was so severe that I found myself scribbling what I thought might be my final words to my family and girlfriend in my journal. But with a combination of Cipro, meditation, and three days of not leaving my tent or sleeping bag except for throwing up and bouts of diarrhea, I slowly began to recover. Meditation became my lifeline during those three days lying alone, helping me navigate the intense stomach pain and providing a sense of calm and presence in the midst of it all. It was a moment of vulnerability, but also a testament to the power of mindfulness in the darkest of times.

As the ascent of Shishapangma unfolded, with the arduous process of acclimatization and establishing high-altitude camps, I found solace in the rare moments of respite at Base Camp. During these interludes, I'd retreat into a world of my own making. With eyes closed, I'd vividly envision the moment of reaching the summit, savoring the imagined rush of accomplishment, and then, along with Dan, safely descending.

In these quiet moments of visualization (another technique I ardently teach in my workshops), I'd also employ mindfulness and meditation techniques, focusing on my breath to calm my mind and anchor myself in the present. This practice became a powerful tool for connecting with my inner self, cultivating a sense of tranquility amongst the intense physical and mental challenges of high-altitude mountaineering.

These meditative sessions served as a psychological balm, preparing me for the demanding days I knew were ahead on the mountain. They allowed me to find equilibrium between the excitement of the climb and the need for mental composure, focus, and strength.

After a month of acclimatizing and climbing the mountain, Dan and I found ourselves alone on the summit at 8:30pm, with darkness enveloping us. We were well past the time when most would have turned back. Just six hours earlier, we had paused to catch our breath in the thin air, our lungs burning with each labored inhale. Dan turned to me with a question that hung in the air as he asked me between short-winded breaths: "Is it worth it… to keep going?"

I was too exhausted to form words, so I simply nodded, my eyes locking onto his. He nodded back, and at that moment, we both knew we were in this together to the end. The silence that followed was a testament to our unspoken understanding, a partnership forged in the harsh conditions of the mountain. It wasn't until we stood on the windswept summit, one of the highest points on Earth, that we finally broke our silence.

Breathing For A Session

Before a Sweatworking session, take a moment to breathe like you're taking in clean air from an uninhabited island, not the stale recycled oxygen of where you may be at that moment. Mindfulness is about being present. It's about opening yourself up to vulnerability, which for many people is difficult. It scares some people, while others think they may lose their sharpness or become less competitive.

Your purpose is to use mindfulness and meditation as a way to harness energy in constructive ways.

During collaborative moments before, during, or after a Sweatworking session, strip away the bureaucratic bullshit. The business politics, the twice-weekly management meetings, favoritism, set hours—steer clear of that. Communicate like you mean it. And it isn't just about waiting to speak; it's about truly hearing another human being when words leave their mouth, just as you'd listen to your loved ones when they say, "I love you." It's about choosing your words carefully when forming sentences, rather than resorting to mindless chatter to fill the air and avoid awkward pauses.

After a Sweatworking session, reflect like you're watching a gorgeous sunset over a Pacific Ocean coastline. Self-awareness doesn't have to be navel-gazing and lotus postures, it's understanding your place in the ecosystem of life and human relationships. You're not just a single entity in some corporate compound, but a living, breathing human being capable of experiencing magical occurrences. Mindfulness is being truly, tantalizingly awake.

Overview:

- Before a Sweatworking session, breathe deeply and focus on the present moment.
- During the session, use mindfulness to communicate honestly and listen deeply, avoiding office politics and empty talk.
- After the session, reflect with self-awareness and appreciate your connection to others.

Mindful Listening

Today, I'd like you to put down your smartphone. That luminous rectangle is not more important than the living, breathing person standing in front of you, even if it's just you staring at yourself in the mirror. When someone speaks, be present, not just physically occupying space, but mentally engaged. Your brain might be racing at six hundred words per minute, but try and slow down and absorb what's being said.

Smartphones have given us a handy excuse to stop looking each other in the eye.

True listening is an act of defiance against our distracted, surface-level culture. It means you look someone in the eye, shut off the internal noise, and receive their words like it's the last time you will ever hear a person speak, completely, without interruption.

Don't fake attention with nervous nodding or neglected eye contact. Your colleagues aren't here to entertain your divided attention. They're here for the same reasons you are. They're human beings trying to communicate in a world that's forgotten how to genuinely connect.

Overview:

- Keep your phone put away and focus your attention fully on the session leader, minimizing distractions.
- Observe your internal thoughts and reactions without judgment while actively listening to others without interrupting or planning your response.
- Be aware of both verbal content and non-verbal cues like body language and tone of voice.

Mindfulness During Sweatworking Sessions

Incorporating mindfulness into Sweatworking sessions is a lifesaver for you and the potentially lethargic and tired situations of those participating. It's a survival skill for keeping you focused in this automated world of constant distraction.

When you're sweating it out, don't just move like some programmed robot. Breathe. Really breathe. Focus on each inhale and exhale. Your mind will most likely wander, thinking about dinner plans, grocery lists, problems at work, the soul-crushing minutiae of modern existence, but just recognize these thoughts, and then drag that wandering consciousness back to the present moment.

The beauty? This practice actually rewires your brain. Those fight-or-flight impulses that keep you perpetually wound tight? They start to lose their grip. Your frontal lobes—the part that makes us human, not just reactive robots—become more engaged. You're developing mental mobility as crucial as physical mobility. It's about staying sharp in a world designed to dull your senses.

Now breathe. Move. Be alive.

Overview:

- Begin sessions with a 'minute-to-arrive' practice, allowing participants to center themselves (i.e. be completely present).
- Foster device-free meetings to promote full presence and engagement.
- Implement brief mindfulness exercises at the start of meetings, such as guided breathing or intention-setting.

Emotional Awareness

It's time to cultivate some emotional awareness in your office. First, you've got to tune into yourself. Feel that rage when a meeting turns upside down? Embrace it. That spark of joy when the end-of-year bonuses come in? Cherish it. Your emotions are the last savage wilderness in a seemingly more domesticated world. Constantly try to promote and cultivate your emotional attentiveness in the workplace.

This isn't some new-age nonsense, it's survival. In a world ostensibly intent on paving over every last scrap of humanity, your feelings are the last line of defense. So champion this cause like your soul depends on it, because it does.

The beating heart of you and your tribe? That's your cadence. So nurture it, preach it, live it. Before the ocean of indifference swallows you whole.

Overview:

- Regularly check in with your own emotions throughout the day.
- Practice non-reactivity when faced with challenging situations or difficult colleagues.
- Use mindful breathing to regulate emotions during tense moments.

Mindful Transitions

Between tasks and interactions, take a moment to implement your transitions to maintain the right headspace. Taking shifts between tasks isn't unfruitful self-help; it's preserving your frenzied inner self against the job madness that can potentially grind you down.

When you shift from one activity to another, don't just shuffle like some domesticated yak. Pause. Breathe. Let your mind reset itself. Your changeovers aren't administrative checkpoints. Each is a chance to shake off the routine and reconnect with something more authentic. Stretch. Write in your journal. Take a quick walk. Remind yourself that you're not a droid, but a human being with dreams and goals.

And try and do it with a sense of humor. Life's too short to take these moments too seriously. Wake up. Stay provocative. Keep shining your light in every direction.

Overview:

- Take a few deep breaths before entering a new meeting or conversation.
- Use short mindfulness exercises when switching between projects.
- Practice a brief body scan to release tension and refocus your attention.

To Leaders - Compassionate Communication

Fostering empathy and understanding in professional relationships isn't about holding hands and singing kumbaya. It's about understanding your fellow associates and team members, even when they're driving you up the wall.

My dear friend and colleague, Richard Owen, who passed away in 2025, constantly taught and displayed this quality, and his relationships in business reflected it. He wasn't just another Executive VP. He had a knack for connecting with people, for seeing beyond the balance sheets and operational performance reports.

Owen didn't just preach about empathy; he lived it. He'd look you in the eye and listen to what you were saying, even if you may have been spouting complete horseshit. Your employees want to be seen, heard, and understood, and Owen did just that. And you know what? People responded. They'd follow him into the depths of bureaucratic hell because they knew he gave a damn.

I'm not saying you should go soft. This is still the world of business we're talking about. But maybe, just maybe, if you took a page out of Owen's mindset and tried to engage and listen to your colleagues better instead of miscommunicating, you might get to the corporate mountain top. Hell, you might even enjoy coming to work.

So if you are a leader, the next time you're about to tear into some poor sap for messing up a report, take a breath. Channel your inner Owen. Try to see the world through your colleague's eyes for a moment. You might be surprised at what you learn.

Overview:

- Practice loving-kindness meditation to help cultivate compassion for yourself and your colleagues and what they are going through daily.
- Use mindful speech, which is to choose words carefully and speak with intent.
- Respond to others with empathy and non-judgment as much as possible, i.e., channel your inner Owen.

Mindful Workspace

When you craft a physical space with purpose, you'll discover tranquility as you observe your immediate surroundings. This is pure, inherent awareness. It's like standing on an ocean shore at dawn, where the geology speaks louder than any self-help manual. Your environment isn't just scenery, it's a living, breathing entity that can calm or agitate your spirit.

As I've mentioned before, mindfulness is not about sitting cross-legged and humming. It's about seeing, truly seeing, the unfiltered landscape around you. Be enmeshed in nature—feel it, walk through it, listen to it.

Every carefully placed object, every cleared surface, every intentional space and picture frame that you observe is a middle finger to the cluttered, jumbled world that wants to keep you distracted and docile. Create a space that breathes. That speaks. That doesn't apologize for existing. And when you do, you'll feel that immediate, electric calm wash over you.

Wilderness begins at home. And enlightened sanity? It's a radical act of insurgency against our chaotic world.

Overview:

- Declutter your workspace and keep exercise areas tidy to reduce visual clutter.
- Introduce natural elements like plants to foster a sense of peace.
- Use small objects or affirmations as reminders to stay present and focused.

Single-Tasking

Yes, Sweatworking is a multi-tasking gem. But when you're focusing on mindfulness, or an exercise, or a project at work, this is where monotasking and providing your undivided attention can really shine. The modern workplace is a cesspool of distraction, a monument to our techno-consumer society's addiction to doing everything at once. Here's how to reclaim your focus and sanity.

Forget multitasking. That would be like splitting a single beam of light into many directions. Each beam becomes weaker and less effective. Instead, carve out your work like a solitary trek through a National Park without your phone—be deliberate, focused, and unapologetically present.

Limit your digital tourists by turning off those demonic email alerts and phone notifications. They're nothing but industrial interruptions designed to fragment your consciousness.

Compress your time by creating tight deadlines. Give yourself less time than you think you need. Nothing focuses the mind like the threat of an imminent deadline.

Be present with mindful attention. Be here. Catch your mind wandering and drag it back to the task at hand.

Single-task. Focus. Be steadfast in your concentration.

Overview:

- Practice single-tasking instead of multi-programming whenever possible.
- Focus intently for set periods with mindful breaks. My go-to is forty minutes of time-focused work and then a five-minute break.
- Minimize distractions by turning your smartphone screen down, closing unnecessary tabs, and silencing notifications.

***

It is not death that is tragic, but existing without ever truly living. This can be avoided in the workplace by incorporating mindfulness practices into your professional life. This will enhance the quality of your interactions, reduce stress, and create a more positive and productive work environment.

Developing mindfulness is a gradual process, so be patient and consistent in your practice. This is not the immediate satisfaction that we've all become accustomed to.

Keep Reminding Yourself: You must put in the time and effort to experience any life-changing result.

Your Mantra: Nothing can bring you peace but yourself

21

Conference Case Analysis With Solutions

I provided a keynote speech one late afternoon in Texas a few years back for a large national association that deals in financial planning and counseling. I had them running in place, breathing with their diaphragm, clapping, and shouting out their goals to the high heavens. During the standing ovation, it was apparent that the audience was switched on to their higher energy self. Nothing could have made me happier.

Before heading off to the airport the next morning, I decided to attend the conference's planned event, 'structured breakfast networking.' I noticed that the majority of the attendees now displayed colorless, dispirited faces while reaching for their morning joe. What the hell happened? Well, the attendees were experiencing a 'networking opportunity' as an overtly disguised invitation for complimentary refreshments and stilted conversations.

You're a hard worker, just trying to get ahead, yet encouraged (okay, forced) to attend a conference or organized event where you're not motivated to be. You may be nursing a mild hangover from last night's shenanigans, and now you're expected to drag yourself out of bed. Why? Because on the ballot for that morning was what the organizers referred to as 'structured breakfast networking.' Terrific, you now schmooze with a bunch of strangers or supposed new contacts over a sad buffet of pastries that'll send their blood sugar through the roof before crashing spectacularly.

You've got these poor souls, trying to make something of themselves, dressed to the nines in their business best, shuffling down to some stuffy conference banquet hall. They're clutching their coffee like it's a lifeline, trying to muster up enough energy to care about Bob from company XYZ, who's in HR, and dying to tell you about his latest AI coding innovation and newsletter.

The whole morning reeked of forced fun and corporate buzzwords. 'Synergy' anyone? Being productive and learning from and meeting people was the point of these sessions correct? Look, I get it. The association was trying to create opportunities for people to connect. But there's a better way than this cardboard food fest.

This breakfast meeting was just another way for corporate behemoths to copy and paste long-past traditional networking strategies as a means to sink their claws more deeply into your soul. They're stealing your mornings, the most sacred time of day when the world is still quiet and full of possibility. Instead of being outside, having a brisk walk with a group, watching the sunrise paint the city's buildings with fire, you're trapped in a windowless room, pretending to care about business forecasts, people spewing polite nonsense, and bagels that can bounce off the floor.

And let's mention again the food they provided. Soggy eggs, unhealthy carb-loaded bagels, overcooked bacon, and some fruit precut from many hours ago. Is this what passes for sustenance in our world? Where's the no-sugar-added Greek yogurt, the mesquite honey, the all-natural peanut butter on whole grain bread that'll stick to your ribs and fuel a day of honest work?

I wanted to scream, "They're soul-sucking your life!" The real world is out there, beyond the tinted windows and name badges. The conference was doing a disservice to its attendees with the follow-the-norm routines that zap their lives right from under them.

The next time you're invited to one of these breakfast abominations in any setting, do yourself a favor. Decline for the sake of your sanity. Head outside and take an energetic walk instead. If you're near a park, even better. Breathe in the air, feel the sun on your face, and remember what it means to be truly alive. Do this and speak out until more active and engaging Sweatworking type sessions become an option at your company, event, or conference. Because I guarantee you, no amount of networking over rubbery omelets will ever compare to the raw, honest connection you'll find with yourself and fellow humans when you're facing the elements of the natural world.

My wish for the attendees at that conference was that those bureaucratic gatekeepers had the decency to include crafting some genuine movement and food pairing options, like those I've prepared below. The goal—prevent you and your fellow attendees from lulling into a corporate-induced coma and provide you with an energetic kick in the pants.

Sunrise Yoga and Smoothie Bar

A yoga flow session to energize, followed by a smoothie bar featuring fresh fruits, yogurt, and granola toppings.

Group Nature Walk with Fresh Fruit Platters

A scenic nature walk or urban trail exploration, ending with a spread of seasonal fruit platters and yogurt parfaits.

Stretch and Breathe with Overnight Oats

A guided stretching and breathing exercise session, followed by a breakfast of overnight oats with various toppings like nuts, fruits, and seeds.

Team Scavenger Hunt and Bagel Station

An interactive scavenger hunt utilizing the whole venue or hotel, then offer a bagel station with fresh whole-grain options and healthy spreads.

Morning Tai Chi and Yogurt Parfaits

An introduction to the meditational movements of Tai Chi, followed by grab-and-go yogurt parfaits layered with granola and fresh berries.

Bootcamp Workout and Protein-Packed Breakfast

A bootcamp-style workout session with bodyweight exercises, then after, serve protein-rich options like hard-boiled eggs, turkey bacon, and vegetable omelets.

Interactive Movement Games with Fresh Smoothies

Engage in team-building movement games like Simon Says or puzzle relay races, followed by freshly blended fruit and vegetable smoothies.

Guided Walking Meditation and Whole-Grain Pastries

A walking meditation session to clear minds, followed by whole-grain mini muffins, toast, or English muffins with low-fat and no-added sugar spreads.

Your Mantra: Death is certain. Life is not

22

SB 1 Minute Mindfulness

One minute to alleviate your stress? This sounds like a scene straight out of *There's Something About Mary*, reminiscent of the 7-minute abs pitch. No, since this actually works.

You're feeling overwhelmed at work because upper management has placed another task on your to-do list. Last night's insensitive conversation with your significant other left you with a restless night's sleep that has carried over into the next day. The discomfort of feeling bloated only adds to your distress. Your anxiety level is at an eleven, and with just a minute to spare, you desperately need a moment to reset.

Here's what you do.

Sit in your office chair, in your parked car, on a park bench, i.e., whenever stress hits you.

Close your eyes.

Soften your face by relaxing your facial muscles.

Do the following exercise by breathing in and out through your nose.

1:1:1:1 (1 sec Inhale; 1 sec Hold Breath; 1 sec Exhale; 1 sec Hold Breath)
2:2:2:2
3:3:3:3
4:4:4:4
5:5:5:5

Count each number in your conscious mind as you breathe. When you've completed the one-second interval, move immediately to the two-second interval without skipping a beat.

As you get more comfortable doing this particular session, you may want to pick one of the following and focus only on that for one minute while you move through the seconds:

- The sensation of the breath.
- The rhythm of your breathing.
- The flow of air entering and exiting through your nostrils.
- The rise and fall of your chest and abdomen.

After you have completed the minute mindfulness session, take a moment to reconnect with your surroundings, then try and remain fully present as you dive back into your day with renewed focus.

Your Mantra: Lives remaining = 0. Get breathing

23

Your Venue Voodoo: The Essentials

I've taught group classes while hiking on the Appalachian Trail, on the side parking lots of gyms, in the backwoods behind a luxury resort, at a readiness center for the Army National Guard, at the FBI Center in Quantico for their special operations community, in air-conditioned rooms in summer, and in over-heated gyms across the country, among other places.

What I'm saying is, a Sweatworking session can be done anywhere. There are no excuses.

If you want to truly connect with yourself and your fellow humans at the highest levels, get outside. But, if you must stay inside, choose something that will energize your staff, not put them to sleep. Know your audience. Whether it's low-intensity workouts or challenging ones, variety and excitement are keys.

Remember, the goal isn't to make you or the group feel warm and fuzzy. It's to shake everyone up and wake them from their corporate slumber. Choose activities that will galvanize you first, and then the others. Make them question their cushy and temperature-controlled existence. This is where your thought processes can really expand.

Take your cohorts to a place where cell phones and tablets are useless. Stripped of technological crutches, you'll drive real conversation to occur.

I've kept this on repeat for a reason: No amount of Sweatworking indoors will ever replace the raw, honest connection forged by you all facing nature's challenges together. If you are searching for the ideal, heading outdoors would be it. In a wellness studio, you can't expect to wake anyone up to the real issues plaguing our world. Go deeper if allowed. Maximize the impact of a Sweatworking session by opening your office HQ's front door and taking it outside.

Outdoor Spaces

Try and forgo those manicured gardens and perfectly trimmed lawns. If you want a real outdoor venue, find a place that'll make you and your attendees question their life choices. A rugged canyon, a trail, sandy beach or shoreline, or a forest where the only Wi-Fi comes from the static electricity in your polyester pants. A clearing in the woods, a stretch of desert, or even an abandoned lot will do as well.

Let the canyons be your treadmill, the crags your weight rack. If you decide to hire a guide for your sessions, pick a seasoned professional who knows more about surviving for weeks in the outback than just proper squat form.

If you must hike or jog to the event site, this will separate the true nature lovers from the air-conditioned neophytes. And don't bring in cushions or mats. Sit on the grass to feel the ground and smell the earth.

If your location has a parking lot, and that's your only option, it will have to do. Something is always better than nothing.

Weather Considerations

If you're worried about a little rain or sun when you go outside, you've already lost the battle. The only caveats are thunderstorms, tornadoes, and hurricanes. All other weather conditions are non-negotiable. Embrace the elements. Let the wind mess up perfectly coiffed hairdos and the mud or rain dampen shoes. A word of advice: Keep your running shoes at your office. The point of being outdoors is to remind yourself and everyone that we're all part of this messy, unpredictable world, not separate from it. The more you do this, the more you will feel connected to Mother Earth.

The whole point of dragging your corporate butts outside is to wake you up and startle you out of your comfortable, claustrophobic boxed stupor. Risk making people a bit uncomfortable, rather than putting them to sleep with another soulless conference room meeting.

Indoor Capacity and Equipment

If you're holding a Sweatworking session indoors, your venue should be able to accommodate your group without turning it into a sardine can of sweaty business people. Choose a place with enough room for everyone to move without elbowing each other in the face.

As for equipment, keep it minimal. Fancy machines aren't necessary. If you want something more than just your bodyweight, bring along some jump ropes and resistance bands. They're light, portable, and won't insult whichever landscape you choose with their presence. If you go outside, your body weight alone will suffice for a workout, and you can also use natural elements like rocks or logs to create resistance for push and pull exercises.

Selecting Professional Trainers

When selecting a venue for Sweatworking events, the availability of professional trainers is an amenity that can significantly enhance your experience. Gyms or venues often provide access to a roster of trainers who can lead group workouts or offer personalized training sessions. Go to SeanBurch.com, where there's information to put you in contact with a seasoned professional in your area.

Some key benefits of having professional trainers run the sessions, if you so choose, include:

- **Expertise and Guidance**: Trainers can ensure proper form and technique, maximizing the effectiveness of workouts and minimizing the risk of injury.

- **Diverse Workout Options**: Professional trainers can offer a variety of exercise styles, from high-intensity interval training to tai chi, catering to different preferences and fitness levels.

- **Team Building**: Trainers can facilitate group exercises that promote teamwork and collaboration, fostering stronger connections among participants.

- **Customized Programs**: For more exclusive events, trainers can tailor workouts to suit the specific goals or themes of the networking session.

- **Health and Wellness Integration**: Professional trainers can provide valuable insights on fitness and wellness, adding an educational component to the networking experience.

Tip: Forget those perky, spandex-clad, and selfie-hound automatons. Pick a specialist who will challenge you and your associates but is also sincere and genuine in his or her interaction and teaching skills.

Optimal Timing for Sweatworking Event

The best choice for Mother Nature adventures is the crack of dawn. Strengthen yourself and your associates by having everyone drag themselves out of bed when the sky is still dark and the air crisp, if you all don't already do so to beat the lovely traffic. It's not necessarily the best time for some people, but it's the best option because it assures you get your exercise and wellness done before the workday begins. You want the appreciation of the beauty of watching a sunrise, instead of the 24/7 glow of a computer screen.

Or, plan it for high noon. Let everyone sweat under the sun and absorb some valuable Vitamin D. Just make it a short session. Anything longer than half an hour and you're dabbling with too much sun. This can be a detriment to your skin, overall body temperature, as well as other possible drawbacks.

When planning your outside session in the morning, don't limit it to an hour, unless it's before a workday during the week. If you're going to do this, especially at a conference or event, commit to it. Take two hours or even the whole morning if possible. The best way is by marching into nature and seeing how everyone fares when they can't check their phone every five minutes. Have everyone take turns leading portions of the hike.

Speaking of technology, ban all devices if possible—phones, tablets, smartwatches. Everyone needs to experience time as nature intended, measured by the arc of the sun and the growl of hungry stomachs from an energetic workout. What you bring instead is proper clothes and shoes, water, UV protection, a healthy snack, a pencil, and something small to write in.

Time in nature is about experiencing the eternal dance of life, growth, decline, and demise. Give them a chance to feel the pulse of the earth beneath their shoes. Your conversations and networking will flow like rivers.

Tip: If you come across a stream, stop and have the participants take off their shoes and socks and let them dip their feet in the water.

Work Schedules and Energy Levels

Optimal timing for Sweatworking should consider both work schedules and personal energy levels. Here's why:

- **Energy Levels**: Most people experience peak alertness and energy a few hours after starting work, typically around 11 AM to 12 PM for those who start at 9 AM. This period could be ideal for a Sweatworking session as you would be mentally sharp and physically energized.

- **Circadian Rhythms**: Your body's abilities peak in the afternoon and early evening, with optimal muscle function, strength, and endurance. This makes after-work, late afternoon, or early evening an excellent time for Sweatworking activities. Evening workouts can be appealing due to your body's natural ability to perform optimally during this time. Scheduling after work hours could capitalize on this performance peak while allowing you to decompress from the workday.

- **Work Schedule Flexibility**: Creating an effective work schedule that allows for Sweatworking is crucial for your productivity and time management. Consider employees' energy curves when scheduling such activities.

- **Avoiding Energy Dips**: Most people experience their lowest performance point around 3 PM. You should avoid scheduling Sweatworking during this time to ensure everybody is engaged and energetic, rather than feeling like a session is a chore.

- **Consideration for Different Chronotypes**: Not everyone has the same sleep and energy patterns. Some individuals may work better during the evenings rather than early mornings. By offering multiple Sweatworking options throughout the day you can accommodate different chronotypes.

- **Proper Hydration**: Sweat rate varies among individuals, with men typically sweating sooner and in higher volumes than women. Scheduling Sweatworking during cooler parts of the day or in climate-controlled environments will help manage the hydration needs of all attendees.

At Conferences & Events

For events and conferences, waive your by-the-minute agendas and schedules.

Morning sessions? Yes! there's something to be said for getting it over with before the crushing weight of the event day descends upon you, and provides you with the energy to face the conference head-on.

Late afternoon or early evening after a day of meetings and events can also be when the real magic happens. Your body temperature's up, your muscles are loose, and you've had all day to build up a healthy dose of rage at the machine for having to attend your umpteenth conference of the year.

You'll have more power, better reaction time, and be more attuned to talk with your fellow attendees before/during/after the session.

Duration of Indoor Sessions

Indoor Sweatworking sessions can vary in duration depending on the type of class, but generally range from 15 to 55 minutes. The key is to choose a length that challenges your group while still fitting into their conference schedule.

Here are some example guidelines:

- Low-Intensity Steady State (LISS) Cardio: 30 minutes or more

- High-Intensity Interval Training (HIIT): 15-30 minutes

- Functional Training: 45-90 minutes

- Quick Wellness Sessions: as short as 10 minutes for those with limited time. Provide as many session options for attendees as possible. These sessions work well if utilized in conferences and events periodically throughout the day.

Recovery Tools and Spa Services

Venues are slowly evolving to offer more than just a space for events. There are holistic wellness centers that cater to the physical and mental well-being of their clientele. This trend reflects a growing awareness of the importance of self-care and recovery in professional settings that incorporate various recovery tools to help attendees rejuvenate during or after intense networking sessions. These may include:

- Massage chairs for quick relaxation breaks.
- Compression therapy devices to aid muscle recovery.
- Foam rollers and stretching areas for self-myofascial release.
- Meditation pods with guided sessions for mental refreshment.

Spa Services

To elevate your Sweatworking experience, some venues partner with spa service providers or create in-house facilities. These services should be used sporadically, as the intention of Sweatworking is not to pamper yourself; it's to evolve. If you decide to go with spa services, or your audience demands it, offer only one of the following suggestions.

And make sure it's after a workout session.

- Express facials for a quick skin refresh.
- Hand and foot massages to relieve tension from long periods of standing or sitting.
- Aromatherapy stations to promote relaxation and focus.
- Hydration bars offering infused waters and electrolyte drinks.

Wellness Workshops

Hosting short wellness workshops is a different take on the Sweatworking experience. These are a few topic suggestions:

- Quick stress-relief techniques

- Proper posture and ergonomics for networking events
- Mindfulness practices for better professional interactions
- Nutritional tips for sustained energy during long events

Snacks, Refreshments, and Amenities

Do you want to plan a Sweatworking event with refreshments and amenities? There are several avenues of approach.

For Basic Sessions

Your Sweatworking session doesn't have to have a lavish display of food and beverages. It's more about the content that should matter. For a basic session, don't coddle your audience with cucumber water and organic kale chips. No catered lunches. And those who complain? Well, they're probably the ones who need this Sweatworking experience the most.

First, forget your fancy bottled water with microplastics. Use water that you fill with a reusable container such as a stainless steel water bottle made without BPA. Place the logo of the conference or a sponsor on the bottle. It's just another reminder for that participant to attend again next year.

For your snacks, keep them limited. Forego supplying too many fancy organic eats and smoothies. A PB & honey sandwich on 100% whole wheat bread using all-natural peanut butter (only peanuts as the ingredient) and honey; energy bars with only whole food ingredients; and/or vegetables for easy grazing, such as cucumber, squash, and celery sticks, which contain over 94% water to help with hydration. Don't offer food wrapped in shiny plastic that'll outlive your grandchildren. Choosing the right whole foods is the key to improving your metabolic health and helping balance your blood sugar.

The goal is to spark some genuine conversation, rather than how good the scented water and snacks are. That's just a reboot to the mindless drivel that can pass for networking these days.

Below are some options for a basic session to a more high-end event.

Healthy Snack Options

- Fresh fruit, non-added sugar yogurt sauce (provides fiber, carbs, and vitamins, probiotics)
- Nuts and seeds mix (pistachios, peanuts, pumpkin seeds—packed with vitamins and healthy fats)
- Low salt Jerky (high-protein, low-blood sugar impact)
- Cheese and vegetable platters for balanced nutrition

Snack Guidelines

- Low sugar content
- High protein options
- Easily portable
- Minimal mess
- Provides sustained energy

Portion Control

- Individual serving sizes
- Trail mix in small baggies
- Pre-portioned combinations

Hydration

- Water as the primary hydration option
- Herbal teas
- Infused water with fresh fruits

Your Mantra: Keep moving, keep evolving

24

Sweatworking Boundaries Guide: How Not to Get Fired

In the high mountains of the Himalayas, boundaries are fluid things, marked by volatile icefalls and shifting seracs. In the world of Sweatworking, however, boundaries must be as solid as the ancient peaks that dot the Appalachian Trail. The blurring of lines between professional and personal can be a dangerous thing, leading to misunderstandings and discomfort that can poison the well of your workplace relationships.

Having been raised to open doors for women yet also handle grocery shopping and cooking, I've noticed society's evolving views on traditional gender roles. The lines between what's considered appropriate for men and women have become increasingly blurred.

The way we relate to one another is shifting, and not always for the better. In the U.S., political polarization has reached historic highs, with the two major parties viewing each other more negatively than ever before. It's become so extreme that many people now choose to surround themselves only with those who share their political beliefs. But in a healthy democracy, disagreement is expected, even necessary. What's dangerous is the growing unwillingness to compromise. That erodes public trust, paralyzes progress, and ultimately threatens the very foundation of democracy. Next time you encounter someone with different views, consider having a conversation instead of a confrontation. You might be surprised at the common ground you'll find.

This is another avenue where Sweatworking can bind people together as opposed to ripping them apart. You are not perfect. No human being is. And no human being is right 100% of the time. That said, within your Sweatworking, common respect and maintaining professional boundaries are paramount.

Appropriate Physical Boundaries

Physical boundaries in Sweatworking are like the invisible line between predator and prey in the wild. Cross that line and one risks consequences. Respect for personal space is of foremost importance, even in activities that might involve close proximity or physical contact. A yoga class is not an invitation for unsolicited adjustments, and a group run is not the time to test someone's comfort with a casual touch.

Participants are not there to recreate a scene from *Dirty Dancing*. This is Sweatworking, not sweat-twerking. Everyone keeps their hands to themselves, maintains a respectful distance, and lets the shared experience of physical activity create the connection. After all, in the corporate world, as in the exercise world, it's often what's left unsaid (and untouched) that can speak the loudest.

Clear Emotional Boundaries

Emotional boundaries in Sweatworking are as important as a reliable compass or GPS in uncharted territory. The intensity of physical activity can sometimes lead to a false sense of intimacy, a mirage of closeness that evaporates in the harsh glare of the workplace. It's crucial to remember that Sweatworking is still, at its core, a professional interaction. Share enough to build rapport, but avoid delving into deeply personal topics or oversharing.

Sure, everyone might bond over the shared struggle of a particularly grueling workout, but that doesn't mean you should start relaying your deepest fears or family dramas. Keep it light, keep it professional, and have them save the heavy emotional lifting for their therapist or journal.

If a deeper relationship is meant to grow from your connection, let it develop gradually and with mutual intention. Real trust and rapport take time. Any shift toward a more personal dynamic should be a natural progression, built on respect and a shared willingness, and is not forced or one-sided.

Communicate Work-Related Boundaries

Just as a seasoned adventurer knows to establish clear guidelines with his team before embarking on a journey, so too must the sweatworker set clear work-related boundaries. Make it known that Sweatworking time is not for airing workplace grievances. This time is about building relationships and fostering teamwork, not about getting ahead or settling scores. Establish these boundaries early and firmly, like laying a strong foundation for a house.

If a colleague starts veering into work gossip, gently but firmly steer your colleague back to neutral territory. Give a reminder that this time is meant to be a break from the office grind.

Group Dynamics

In the dead of winter, survival can often depend on the strength of the team; the ability of individuals to come together for the common good in order for everyone to survive, as it was in the Imperial Trans-Antarctic Expedition, led by Sir Ernest Shackleton. His team aimed to cross Antarctica on foot but was thwarted when the ship *Endurance* became trapped and sank in the Weddell Sea, leaving 28 men stranded. Through Shackleton's leadership, which emphasized teamwork and collaboration, all crew members were ultimately rescued after enduring a perilous journey to Elephant Island and South Georgia.

Sweatworking, at its best, harnesses this same power of collective effort, transforming a group of dissimilar individuals into a cohesive unit bound by shared experience, mutual respect, and a common goal.

Foster Inclusivity Across Seniority Levels

For these group activities to truly flourish, they must be as inclusive as the expansive region of Antarctica itself, which cares not for the rank or status of those who traverse its land. Sweatworking offers a rare opportunity to level the playing field, strip away the trappings of corporate hierarchy, and reveal the human beneath. Promote participation across all levels of seniority, and watch as the lower-level employee and the C-Suite executive find common ground in the shared experience of a challenging workout. In the democracy of sweat, titles mean little and effort means everything.

Sweatworking is a world where the mail room clerk can high-five the CFO after a particularly grueling set of mountain climbers, and where the junior analyst can offer a word of motivation to the struggling VP during a group run and intermittent push-ups. These moments of shared humanity can do more to break down office barriers than a year's worth of egg-drop challenges, team board games, or trust falls. Just be sure to choose activities that don't inadvertently reinforce existing hierarchies. The last thing you want is for your session to turn into a display of alpha-dog dominance in place of mentoring or a reminder of who can afford the fanciest workout gear.

Etiquette Guidelines

In this world you're entering, decorum serves a similar function to professionalism and can provide a framework for interaction that ensures the experience is positive and productive for all involved.

Personal Hygiene and Equipment Care

You might think personal hygiene is self-explanatory, but trust me, from my years of experience, this topic needs to be included. Personal hygiene in Sweatworking is fundamental. No one wants to be downwind of a colleague who's skipped wearing deodorant or has thrown on week-old gym clothes. A tidy physical space reflects a righteous soul, especially when you're sharing close quarters and equipment.

Speaking of equipment, treat it with the same respect you'd show it if it were your very own. Every sweatworker should wipe down machines after use, return weights or bands to their proper place, and generally leave the space better than they found it.

Respecting Others' Space and Time

This should be a given, but unfortunately, I've seen otherwise. I'll stick with the program. During my mountain expeditions or while taking groups into the outdoors, personal space seems infinite. That's a major reason why I'll take a session outside in the first place. In a crowded gym or cycle studio, it's a precious commodity. Make it known to respect the bubble of those around them, giving them room to move and breathe without feeling crowded. That means no hovering over someone waiting for them to finish their routine, no invading someone's yoga mat space with your downward dog, and certainly no unsolicited spotting or form corrections unless explicitly asked. Leave that to the instructor, the mentors, and/or you implement the strategy.

And just as one wouldn't keep a fellow traveler waiting on a group tour of the Egyptian pyramids, call out those who are always late or who drag out the cool-down chat when others are ready to head back to the office. Punctuality isn't just a virtue, it's a necessity. Time is the business world's most valuable resource. Use it wisely and respect others' allocation of it. A person late to a group workout throws off the whole group dynamic and risks being left behind.

Noise Considerations

Being in nature and absorbing the silence is one of its most profound features, broken only by the whisper of wind or the occasional singing of a bird. In the world of Sweatworking, such silence can be rare depending on the location, but consideration for noise levels is necessary. The gym or room you're exercising in isn't someone's personal sound stage, and your colleagues aren't their captive audience. Not everyone appreciates or needs to hear phone conversations, alerts, or notifications. If someone absolutely must take a call, have them step outside. And as I've mentioned before, the ideal thing is to leave the phones behind or at least turn them off if at all possible. And for the love of all that's *Pumping Iron*, keep the grunting and groaning to a minimum. You're exercising, not giving birth to a cactus. If someone must vocalize their exertion, have them keep it to a level that doesn't shatter windows or startle small animals.

Balancing Work and Sweatworking

In mother nature, balance is everything. It's the delicate equilibrium between exertion and rest, between exposure and shelter. In the corporate world, the balance between work and Sweatworking is equally crucial, a tightrope walk between your professional development and personal well-being.

Setting Priorities

Just as someone who gets lost off a trail must prioritize water and shelter over less essential needs, so must you learn to prioritize. Sweatworking should enhance your professional life, not detract from it. It's a place of refreshment and rejuvenation. Set clear priorities. It's about finding that sweet spot where physical activity complements and enhances your productivity.

Managing Workload

Managing your workload in the age of Sweatworking requires foresight, planning, and a realistic assessment of your capabilities. Don't let the allure of a midday workout session cause you to fall behind on projects or miss deadlines. Instead, learn to integrate Sweatworking into your schedule in a way that energizes and motivates you. It's about working smarter, not harder, and using the boost from physical activity to enhance your focus and productivity when you return to your desk.

Maintaining Work-Life Balance

As previously mentioned in an earlier chapter, Sweatworking should be a tool for enhancing work-life balance, not another obligation that tips the scales toward all work and no play. Let Sweatworking be a source of refreshment and renewal in your professional life. Use it as a way to decompress, step away from the grind, and reconnect with your physical self and your colleagues on a human level.

Handling Potential Challenges

Even in the most carefully planned vacation, challenges arise. The same is true in the world of Sweatworking, where it can sometimes create prickly situations.

Preparing for Boundary Violations

On a high-altitude mountain expedition, you always keep an eye out for danger, be it a crevasse underfoot or an avalanche above. In Sweatworking, you must be equally vigilant for potential boundary violations. Prepare yourself mentally for how you'll handle situations that cross the line, whether it's a colleague who gets too handsy during partner stretches or a boss who uses wellness time to discuss work matters incessantly. Have a plan ready to deploy at the first sign of trouble. This might involve direct communication, seeking support from HR, or opting out of future sessions with problematic individuals.

Addressing Uncomfortable Situations

When uncomfortable situations arise, as they sometimes will in the sweaty, close-quarters world of exercise, address them with the same directness and clarity your HR cohorts are hired to do. Don't let discomfort fester. If someone's behavior is making you uneasy, speak up. Use clear, professional language to express your concerns. Silence can be dangerous. Your voice is your most powerful tool for maintaining a safe and respectful environment.

Your Mantra: Winning takes talent; to repeat takes character

25

Case Study - How SoulCycle Became the Boardroom on a Bike

In the modern American landscape, some temples aren't built in rocks and sand, they're carved out of strip malls and city blocks, filled with sweat, music, and the faint fragrance of eucalyptus. SoulCycle became one such sanctuary. No wilderness here, yet its meteoric rise can be traced to its unique formula: a fusion of intense wellness experiences and organic networking opportunities that reshaped what it means to 'do business.'

SoulCycle's studios became more than places to work out; they turned into hubs for cultivating meaningful relationships. Participants, especially women, found a space to challenge themselves physically while forging powerful professional and personal alliances. SoulCycle didn't just make riders stronger; it gave them a tribe. Deals were struck under disco balls and over handlebars, and trust was forged in forty-five minutes of sweat and struggle.

A Spark Ignites: Two Women, One Idea

Imagine New York City in the early 2000s, a place that never sleeps, a concrete panorama of ambition and anonymous crowds. Into this whirlwind arrived Julie Rice and Elizabeth Cutler. Both were new to the city and hungry for a wellness experience that went beyond machines and mirrors. Neither could find it.

By chance, a mutual acquaintance arranged a lunch. The connection between Rice and Cutler was immediate—they began finishing each other's sentences. By the end of the meal, they had scribbled the outline of their dream studio on a napkin: a fitness sanctuary where sweat, connection, and possibility coexisted.

As founders, Rice and Cutler defied the typical startup mold. Outsiders to the New York fitness scene, they saw their status not as a liability but as freedom. Both were new mothers with no prior business experience. They didn't pursue traditional venture capital. Instead, they trusted their intuition: people yearned for more than just exercise; they longed for connection, clarity, and inspiration.

In 2006, using their savings, they launched the first SoulCycle studio on the Upper West Side of Manhattan.

The SoulCycle Experience—Wellness as a Social Catalyst

Community Over Competition

The physical layout of SoulCycle studios, the signature dark rooms, motivating playlists, and enthusiastic instructors were crafted to foster a sense of belonging. Rather than competition, the atmosphere pulsed with collective energy. The studio became, in Rice and Cutler's words, a 'third place'—neither home nor work, but a space for self-care and socializing. Many returned not just for physical results, but because they knew their people would be there.

Empowering Women—From Fitness to the Boardroom

As SoulCycle grew, so did its female clientele. Estimates suggest as much as 86% of the company's leadership, instructors, and community consisted of women. They gathered not just for fitness, but for emotional release, inspiration, and the kind of camaraderie built in shared struggle and triumph. Class waitlists sometimes included celebrities, CEOs, financiers, and creative leaders—people who might never cross paths elsewhere.

SoulCycle Sweatworking - Why It Worked

The Science of Sweat-Soaked Networks

There's something elemental about shared physical challenge. Research shows that breaking a sweat together lowers barriers, builds trust, and accelerates relationship-building. At SoulCycle, everyone was on the same starting line, literally and metaphorically. Riders endured the grind and the glory as one. This was a powerful foundation for a lasting connection.

Unlike stilted networking events where small talk reigns, SoulCycle fostered openness. Riders showed up as they were. They found common ground in effort and encouragement. They cheered each other's personal bests and professional wins.

The Executive Alliance

PR and marketing execs, media leaders, and startup founders began holding intentional 'sweatworking' sessions—inviting clients, prospects, or colleagues to join them on the bike. The ride often served as a prelude to deeper conversations and future deals.

Startup Collaborations & Mentorship

Rice and Cutler shared in interviews that some of their earliest clients weren't just seeking fitness; they wanted business advice, guidance, and new opportunities. Many early investments and collaborations in New York's female startup ecosystem were sparked during or after a SoulCycle ride.

After class, as adrenaline faded, the lobby transformed into a lively networking hub. Business cards were exchanged as frequently as fitness tips. Ventures were discussed over smoothies. Partnerships were born from casual, post-sweat conversations. These informal moments led to mentorships, alliances, and collaborations that accelerated careers across industries, from finance to fashion to tech. SoulCycle, intentionally or not, became a platform where relationships were forged through vulnerability, commitment, and authenticity.

- **Adversity breeds trust:** When you're gasping on bike 17 next to a VC, you're equals, whether you like it or not.
- **Consistency builds kin:** See the same faces week after week? You start to care what happens, in and out of the studio.
- **The absence of walls:** No one hides behind a desk or a LinkedIn profile when sweat is dripping down your nose.
- **Trust through vulnerability:** A tough workout builds respect and openness faster and more honestly than cocktail hours ever could.
- **Open up post-workout:** When defenses are down and endorphins are high, some of the best ideas and partnerships emerge here.
- **Authentic relationships:** With no pretense or posturing, genuine friendships and collaborations grow.

SoulCycle's Broader Impact

By 2015, SoulCycle had grown into a nine-figure business. It had inspired the entire boutique fitness boom and transformed how Americans viewed group exercise. They proved that cultivating connection, rather than just competition, could result in both profit and meaning.

How Women Can Leverage Wellness for Professional Growth

- Join fitness communities that prioritize support and shared achievement.
- Use recurring workout commitments as opportunities to cultivate meaningful professional relationships.
- Embrace your vulnerability. Showing up sweaty and real can be more persuasive than a polished networking pitch.
- Create informal post-workout meetups to deepen conversations and explore collaborations.
- Appoint leaders or community managers (much like SoulCycle's instructors) to help facilitate introductions and draw out quieter

members.

The SoulCycle Blueprint for Sweatworking Success

Element	How SoulCycle Embodied It	Why It Worked for Networking
Shared Challenge	Tough rides, collective finish	Forges real bonds
Regular Touchpoints	Recurring classes & faces	Sparks repeat, deep conversations
Safe Environment	No-judgment, inclusive ethos	Encourages openness
Female Leadership	Women-led, women-filled	Inspires trust, mentorship

Through the vision of its two founders and the force of its community, SoulCycle proved that the most valuable connections aren't always made over cocktails or golf clubs. Whether on a bike or a mat, inside a studio or beyond, wellness has the power to unite, elevate, and ignite something bigger than ourselves.

Your Mantra: My effort fuels my growth

26

Genuine Relationships: Where Ghosting Goes to Die

Yep, that's correct. There's no 'authenticity' in the title here. I'm tired of that word being endlessly repeated and used by influencers, celebrities, athletes, companies, and in articles only to become clichéd and, ultimately, obsolete. It's time for a fresh perspective.

Essence of Genuineness

In our quest for meaningful connections, we often seek out individuals who embody certain admirable qualities. These traits go beyond mere authenticity, delving into the core of what makes a person truly genuine. The type of people I enjoy being around possesses a pattern of positive attributes:

- Honesty: Truthful and straightforward in their dealings
- Sincerity: Expresses genuine feelings without deceit
- Reliability: Consistently dependable and trustworthy
- Lack of Pretension: Modest and down-to-earth
- Naturalness: Displays natural, unaffected behavior

Beyond Legitimacy

Legitimacy certainly has its place, particularly in professional contexts. A legitimate company or individual that is officially recognized and endorsed often implies a level of trustworthiness and adherence to standards. This, however, doesn't fully encapsulate the warmth and depth you seek in personal relationships.

Power of Genuineness

At the heart of these qualities lies genuineness, a characteristic that encompasses being honest, innate, and true to oneself. A genuine person or action is:

1. Sincere in intent
2. Free from pretense or deceit
3. Reflective of one's true nature
4. Unadulterated by false or misleading elements

Genuineness often highlights the novel or natural qualities of a person, making it a powerful descriptor for those who live authentically and interact with others in a true, organic manner.

In your increasingly complex and sometimes artificial world, the value of genuineness cannot be overstated. It forms the foundation of trust, fosters deeper connections, and allows you more meaningful interactions in both personal and professional spheres. Sweatworking allows your originality to shine through.

Walking the Talk

Promoting the benefits of exercise while neglecting your own physical health should be seen as spurious. True advocates and influencers for fitness must embody the principles they espouse. While everyone's fitness journey is unique, if you passionately promote exercise, you should strive to align your actions and body with your words.

A good example is America's broken healthcare system and many personal care physicians who provide hurried and impersonal care, or who may advise patients to quit a certain health vice yet maintain their own. Imagine you're at your doctor's office, getting the full, "you really need to quit vaping," lecture. You nod, promise to do better, and head out feeling guilty. But as you walk to your car, who do you spot behind the building? Your doctor, puffing away with the nurses like it's a staff meeting at a vape convention. True story—one of my clients actually witnessed this.

Or how about other medical professionals who would rather quickly prescribe you medications and pop a pill instead of putting in the time needed to address certain mental and physical issues. Those persons face credibility issues. The most effective healthcare advocates lead by example, demonstrating the behaviors they recommend to others.

Genuineness in health and wellness involves more than just knowledge, it requires consistent effort to practice what you preach. While perfection isn't the goal, striving for alignment between one's advice and personal habits is.

So throw out 'authenticity,' and be 'genuine.' Be someone reliable, honest, and deliberate in your actions and words, whether you're exercising with a group or networking after a Sweatworking session. If you already encompass this, then welcome to the tribe.

I am reminded of the profound beauty and complexity of human relationships every time I communicate with an audience, a friend, or while on expeditions. As an example, while on my Volcanos+ world record expedition in late 2023, the connections I formed with Argentinians in a stone hut on the border of Argentina and Chile, exemplified the power of genuine interactions. In less than twenty-four hours after meeting, we became fast friends, and I promised them I'd learn Spanish, and they promised to learn English, so the next time we were to meet again in Argentina, we'd be able to speak and understand one another without translation. Since returning to the U.S., I haven't missed a single day of Spanish lessons. I am incredibly grateful for the profound impact they've had on me, and I sincerely hope I've contributed positively to their lives in return. This mutual exchange is precisely what genuine relationships are built upon.

That's the depth and attachment you should hope to have with the people in your sphere, both in the workplace and in your personal life. Seek those relationships and let them carry you forward to greater and more profound experiences.

Just as our beautiful earth requires a delicate balance of elements to thrive, your genuine relationships demand a foundation built upon sincerity, empathy, and mutual respect. These are not mere virtues but the very heart upon which meaningful connections are forged.

Sincerity, Empathy, and Mutual Respect

Your sincerity is the unyielding commitment to truthfulness. It is the first step toward building bridges of understanding between you and another person.

Empathy is your profound ability to see through the eyes of another, to feel the intensity of their joys and sorrows deeply. It bridges the gaps between you both, fostering a sense of unity and understanding that strengthens the bonds of your human connection.

Mutual respect involves acknowledging each other's autonomy and dignity. The recognition that you're both trailblazers on this mysterious journey called life.

In human interaction, these elements are as essential as water and sunlight. Without them, your relationships will tend to wither and die, leaving behind only the wasted remains of what could have been. But when cultivated, they'll prosper into trust and understanding, and where love and laughter can flourish.

Active Listening and Genuine Interest

Active listening is the art of you being fully present in the moment, of immersing yourself in the words and silences of another. It is not merely hearing but seeing, feeling, and understanding. When you listen actively, you signal to others that their thoughts and feelings are of value, that they are seen and heard in a world that often seems deaf to their voices.

Cultivating genuine interest in others not only fosters deeper relationships for you but also enriches your life with diverse perspectives and experiences. It's curiosity that should drive you to explore the depths of another's soul, to discover the hidden angles of their experiences and dreams. When you approach others with genuine interest, you create a space where they feel valued and respected.

Trust-Building With Honesty and Transparency

Honesty illuminates your path forward, while transparency ensures that every stage is visible and accountable, fostering trust and clarity in all interactions. By creating an environment of openness and accountability, you'll show others that you are willing to stand before them without pretense and take responsibility for your actions. This vulnerability is not a weakness but a strength, and it will build you bridges of trust that can withstand the turbulences in life.

Shared Purpose = Deep Bonds

In the wild, creatures often come together for a common cause—survival. Similarly, in the professional world, a shared purpose is the thread that weaves individuals into a cohesive unit. When you work with others towards a common goal, your differences become strengths rather than weaknesses. Shared purpose fosters deep bonds by aligning your aspirations with the organization's broader vision, creating a sense of belonging and contribution.

It's similar to a team of park rangers working together to protect a national park. Their collective goal is not just to preserve the land but to ensure that future generations can experience its beauty. This shared vision can inspire outstanding achievements, built on trust, respect, and mutual understanding.

Intellectual Humility

In the wilderness, humility allows you to learn from your mistakes and adapt to changing environments. In professional relationships, humility paves the way for open and honest discussions. It encourages you to consider alternative views, fostering a culture where everyone feels valued and heard.

Picture a team meeting where everyone is convinced his or her solution is the right one. We've all been there and seen that. Without intellectual humility, the discussion becomes a battle of egos. But with humility, the conversation shifts from "I'm right" to "Let's explore together." This openness to alternative perspectives not only helps you resolve conflicts but also leads to more innovative solutions.
If only all politicians followed this creed.

Balancing Healthy Competition and Collaboration

Competition can drive your innovation and motivation, but unchecked, it creates divides and discourages teamwork. The key is for you to balance competition with collaboration. In the wild, competition for resources is natural, but it's balanced by cooperation for survival. Similarly, in professional settings, you must ensure that competition does not overshadow the importance of working together with others toward a shared goal.

For example, what works is when a research team whose scientists and engineers are urged to compete in developing new technologies is also incentivized to collaborate and share their findings. This balance fosters a culture where success is not about winning over others but about achieving collective success. By shifting the focus from competition to cooperation, you will create a more supportive, innovative, and productive work environment.

Sustained Relationships in Career Growth

For some, the wilderness of Alaska may require patience and persistence to truly appreciate its beauty. Equally, building meaningful relationships in the sometimes daunting professional world demands your dedication and nurturing. Sustained relationships are not fleeting encounters, but rather enduring connections that foster trust, understanding, and mutual support. Your professional life is enriched by a steady sustenance of long-term relationships. These relationships provide a network of allies who can offer you guidance, encouragement, and opportunities for growth in the years to come.

In the professional world, it's easy for you to get lost in the noise of networking events and social media connections without something that brings you together in a shared experience. This is why Sweatworking shines. True success lies not in the quantity of contacts you have but in the quality of your relationships.

C-Suite Leaders: Prioritize building strong, lasting bonds with and between your colleagues and peers. You will be more likely to achieve success and inspire loyalty in your teams.

Nurturing Relationships Beyond Initial Engagement

Nurturing your relationships beyond the initial activity requires consistent effort, patience, and an understanding of the delicate balance between giving and receiving. A garden needs water, sunlight, and protection from the elements. Similarly, your professional relationships will need consistent communication, empathy, and mutual support.

It is the small, consistent actions you do that will often yield the greatest rewards. A phone call to check in, an offer to help with a project, or a recommendation to a valuable contact can all serve as nourishment for a growing relationship.

As I reflect on my own life and work, I realize that my most enduring connections have been those that I've nurtured over time. Whether through letters, photos, or shared adventures, these relationships have enriched my life and my work. In your professional life, cultivating long-term connections is not just a strategy for success, it is a way of living that brings depth, meaning, and joy to your career.

By valuing sustained relationships, transforming Sweatworking connections into business opportunities, and nurturing those relationships, you can build a foundation for career growth that's as robust and ever-changing as the world itself.

Your Contacts Challenge

So here's a challenge for you. Examine your professional network critically: Is it a vibrant group of diverse individuals, forged through authentic connections and shared principles, or merely a stagnant accumulation of forgotten contacts? If your network resembles the latter, it's time to reinvigorate and develop meaningful relationships that foster growth and opportunity.

Start by looking beyond your usual circles. Engage with people from different backgrounds, different industries, and different worldviews. Listen more than you talk. Be overtly curious. Be open to new ideas, new perspectives, and new ways of doing things.

***

In today's world, where information is abundant and attention is scarce, being genuine is your most valuable currency. Don't try to be someone you're not. Don't pretend to care about people or things you genuinely don't. No one likes being given the run-around. Instead, figure out what you truly care about, what you're truly passionate about, and let that guide your connections and your career.

Remember, the goal isn't to have the biggest network. It's to have the most meaningful one. It's to surround yourself with people who challenge you, who inspire you, who push you to be better and more successful both professionally and personally.

Your Mantra: Be different, not less

27

Plotting World Domination: Your Promotion Magic Formula

The goal behind a Sweatworking program is to lessen the traditional handshake and elevator pitch, and have you give way to a more dynamic, all-encompassing approach. This fusion of wellness and networking may be a new category and networking habit for you, but like any program you want to implement, whether it be for yourself or within your company, it requires careful promotion and strategizing to become a reality.

Promotion for a Sweatworking Event

Here's how you can conjure up interest in your Sweatworking event, using the tools of the digital age, the creation of promotional content, and establishing local partnerships.

Utilizing Social Media and Online Platforms

Social media, that behemoth of the digital world, is where your Sweatworking event can make a mark. Create an event page on Facebook detailing every aspect, from the date and time to the type of workout and networking opportunities. Use Instagram to share visuals—sneak peeks of the venue, snippets of the workout routine, or testimonials from past participants. X or a site similar, such as Reddit or Threads, can be your megaphone for updates and engaging polls that keep potential attendees intrigued.

Leverage platforms like Meetup and Eventbrite to reach a broader audience. Meetup can connect you with groups already interested in fitness, wellness, and networking, while Eventbrite offers a smooth ticketing system and targeted advertising options. Consistency is key. Use relevant hashtags across all platforms to create a buzz around your event.

Partnering with Local Businesses or Chambers of Commerce

In the heart of any community lies a network of local businesses and Chambers of Commerce, eager to support innovative initiatives. Approach gyms, health food stores, and outdoor gear shops to see if they'd be interested in co-promoting your event or partnering with your company. For example, a company could offer discounts to attendees or provide equipment.

Chambers of Commerce can also be invaluable allies. They often have extensive networks and can help spread the word about your event through their newsletters and local business directories. Consider offering them a speaking opportunity or a booth at your event in exchange for their support.

Creating Engaging Promotional Content

Promotional content is the fire that will ignite interest in your event. Create a virtual tour of the venue, showcasing the scenic views or state-of-the-art facilities. Produce a video that captures the energy of a Sweatworking session—laughter, unique exercises, and participants connecting. Share these on your social channels and event or company page to give potential attendees a glimpse into what they can expect.

Craft compelling narratives about past events if you or your company has had a few, highlighting the connections made and the recreation had. Share testimonials from satisfied participants to build credibility and excitement. The key to successful promotional content is your genuineness. Let the enthusiasm of you and your attendees shine through.

Promoting a Sweatworking event is about weaving together the threads of technology, community, and creativity. Each element must complement the others to create a dynamic program that draws people in.

Strategies for Sweatworking Events: Continued Success

What's not to love about a blend of sweat and strategy? The following is how you make such an event not just a novelty, but a meaningful experience that fosters genuine connections and mutual support among colleagues, and is an ongoing venture at your company.

Genuine Interest in Colleagues' Success

In southern Arizona, where my mother lives, I've learned that the most resilient plants are those that grow in harmony with their environment. Similarly, in the realm of Sweatworking, success hinges on showing genuine interest in you and your colleagues' achievements. It's not about merely exchanging contact information or discussing the latest industry trends; it's about understanding what drives you and them, the challenges you face, and how you can help.

Imagine you're on a hike with a colleague, the sun beating down on your backs as you climb a steep trail. You ask about his or her goals, not just in the context of the company, but in life. Listen intently to your coworker's shared aspirations, and offer words of encouragement. This builds a bond that transcends the confines of a conference room.

Offering Value and Support to Others

During a Sweatworking session, cultivate inner growth and share that positivity with others. Whether insights from your own experiences or connecting someone with a valuable resource, your actions should be guided by a desire to help others succeed. Sharing creates community.

Consider organizing a group wellness session where everyone works together towards a common goal, like the ones I've recommended in previous chapters. Perhaps it's a charity run or a team-building obstacle course. After the event, follow up with your colleagues to see how they're progressing, offering advice or assistance where needed.

Maintaining Consistent Communication and Follow-Up

Consistent communication is key before, during, and after a Sweatworking session. It's not enough to meet them once and then disappear into the abyss of work life. You must follow up, check in regularly, and continue to nurture those relationships.

After each Sweatworking session, send a group email or message to thank everyone for participating. Share photos or stories from the day, and invite feedback on how to improve future sessions. This ongoing dialogue keeps the momentum going at your company, ensuring that the connections made during Sweatworking continue to grow and flourish both in Sweatworking and during company work hours.

By showing genuine interest in your colleagues' success, offering value and support, and maintaining consistent communication, you can turn what might seem like an out-of-the-box program into a powerful tool for building lasting professional relationships and company success, both financially and psychologically. Stand up for the view that even in the most unconventional settings, you can all find meaningful connections that enrich your lives and work.

Mantra: You can either give in to the world or change it

28

Sweat, Tears, & Logos: Branding While Breaking a Sweat

The concept feels as alien to me as a bustling New York City street might to a Mongolian herder. Yet, after years of reluctantly and sporadically attempting to share my brand, hoping people would listen, believe, and take action toward self-improvement, I've come to appreciate its significance in today's world where the boundary between self-promotion and self-expression is so blurry it's hard to tell where one ends and the other begins.

You see this all the time with companies. They'll only show you the shiny, polished layers of their onion, the parts they want you to see, while keeping everything else hidden. The good stuff, the messy stuff, the real stuff? That rarely makes it to the surface. And honestly, it's a reminder of how much we all wrestle with balancing authenticity and image in today's world.

Creating a Positive Public Perception

Creating a positive public perception is like navigating uncharted mountains, challenging and unpredictable. At first, I believed it was as simple as being authentic and speaking candidly, and no B.S. That philosophy still resonates with me, but I've come to realize that genuineness alone doesn't always yield the results I envisioned. Perhaps I underestimated the subtle art of understanding what truly captures people's attention and inspires them to act.

I've always preferred letting my actions speak louder than words, avoiding over self-promotion. Yet, actions alone don't always connect with others in the way we hope. People will surprise you in what they gravitate toward in narratives, visuals, and emotional resonance. It's not about abandoning values or ethics but rather about learning how to communicate with them effectively.

Even if the world doesn't immediately embrace your efforts, like a crowdfunding campaign I ran for a short film I was making to try and help nomads in Nepal, stay true to your principles. The lack of recognition doesn't diminish the value of your work. Instead, it's an opportunity to refine how you share your story, ensuring it resonates with the right audience while remaining genuine to who you are.

I've been told relentlessly by agents, production companies, and TV shows that branding requires a strategic approach, where every step is deliberate and every word is chosen with care, whether you truly believe those words or not. It's about crafting a narrative that resonates with others, true or not, much like the way a well-told story around a campfire can captivate an audience. I've always felt that was a strategy to try and guess what people were looking for as opposed to just doing what you believe is important, meaningful, and real, i.e., your moral code. I don't believe in tricking people for your own ambitions.

One thing for certain is that tactical communication is key. It must be clear, consistent, and genuine, lest it sound like the hollow echo in a canyon. Yes, yes, and yes. But never sign on to anything that doesn't resonate with your values and ethics. I know, it's becoming more of a stretch for some people, but our society needs to get back to ideals and principles of the self that carry some inner weight and expansiveness.

Differentiation and Market Positioning

Follow the creed of identifying what makes you or your company unique. Take a deep study of your strengths, your passions, and your values. Use these to carve out a niche that is distinctly yours.

Market positioning is the art of placing yourself in the minds of others, so they see you or your company as an authority in your field. It's a delicate balance between standing out and fitting in, but still singular in notion and path. It must be what works for you and what you can live with and value each day. For me, it's like finding the perfect spot to pitch a tent in the wilderness that leaves a satisfying view while being on level ground.

Balancing Self-Promotion and Self-Expression

Self-promotion can feel like shouting into the void, hoping someone will hear you. This is why I have such contempt for social platforms and decided to write this book on subjects for which I have deep passions. I want to get individuals and companies back to more authentic communication and also to be healthier through Sweatworking programs.

Self-expression is different; it's the quiet confidence of knowing who you are and what you stand for. The challenge lies in balancing these two. You must promote yourself enough to be seen, with a larger audience or within your company, yet remain true to your essence. It reminds me of when I was on the *National Geographic Show*, 'Ultimate Survival Alaska.' When my team and I were navigating a river in our inflatable packrafts, sometimes we needed to paddle hard to reach the shore, but other times we had to let the current carry us.

It's about being a voice in the corporate wilderness, clear and strong, yet humble and genuine. In this way, your branding becomes not just a strategy, but a way of being.

Leveraging for Branding

When you're using a novel approach such as Sweatworking to help gain better employees or network through forging connections with others through physical activities such as hiking, running, or even a spirited game of basketball, you're entering a realm where the boundaries between work and play blur. Within the sweat and toil lies an opportunity to craft a brand that is as rugged and veritable as your own landscape.

Showcasing Personality and Values

Sweatworking offers a unique canvas to paint your personality and values. It's not just about the miles you run or the weights you lift, it's about the true character stories you tell, the laughter you share, and the challenges you overcome together. As you push through exhaustion, your true personality emerges. This authenticity is the bedrock upon which a strong brand is built. In this non-traditional setting, you can reveal your genuine self, your passions, your quirks, and your unwavering commitment to your craft. Companies should use this as a tool not only for their present employees but to attract employees who desire a company that cares about their overall wellness.

Building a Memorable Brand Image

Sweat and exertion allow you and your employees to create memories that linger long after the workout is over. These shared experiences become the fabric of you or your company's brand, weaving together tales of resilience, camaraderie, and triumph. It's about how you do it, your style, and your unwavering optimism.

Demonstration of Vital Skills: Teamwork, Perseverance, and Leadership

The reason I am a believer in Sweatworking is that the concept is not a networking gimmick. These sessions are a proving ground for essential skills for a company and individual: teamwork, perseverance, and leadership. As you navigate physical obstacles, whether they be steep trails or sprints, you demonstrate your mental fortitude to collaborate, adapt, and inspire others. These qualities are the pillars of strong branding, showcasing your capacity to lead, motivate, and overcome challenges.

Integrating Sweatworking into Your Brand

Your brand is not just about what you do, but also about who you are. When I think of Sweatworking for companies, I envision a fusion of physical exertion and professional ambition that aligns wellness activities with the values and goals that define a company's brand. For instance, if your brand is built on the principles of resilience and perseverance, then your Sweatworking activities should reflect those qualities.

Every time you lace up your running shoes or hit the gym, you're not only building your physical strength, you're also reinforcing the narrative of your brand. It's about being consistent in your message and actions, ensuring that every sweat drop aligns with the values you stand for.

Crafting Your Individual Story

Your personal wellness story is a powerful tool in building your brand. It's the physical transformations you've undergone and the emotional and mental journeys that have shaped you. Share your struggles, your setbacks, and your successes. Genuineness is key here.

When you share your personal story, you're not only a storyteller, you're inviting others into your world. You're showing them that behind the facade of your brand, there's a real person who works for a real company, with real challenges and real triumphs. This is what makes your brand memorable and impactful.

Leveraging Social Platforms

As mentioned, I'm not a social platform hound. Anyone who has followed my history knows this. I prefer to live the life I preach as opposed to living it online. You've seen what people can do when they leverage social platforms to tell their story. Many of those may be fake or not 100% true, but their message is still getting across.

In the end, it's whether or not it's right for you. Your personal brand is just that, personal. You're the one who needs to live with yourself every day, not the human beings checking out your posts.

Consider these examples:

- Imagine posting a photo of yourself at the summit of a mountain, sweat-drenched and triumphant, with a caption that reflects your brand's

message of resilience.
- Create a series of videos documenting your training regimen by yourself, or better yet, with a few company employees, highlighting not just the physical challenges but also the mental toughness required to push through them.

This isn't just about sharing your wellness journey. It's crafting a narrative that resonates with yourself first and foremost, and then with your audience.

Creating a Cohesive Narrative

Your professional story and your wellness journey shouldn't be separate entities; they should be intertwining threads of your brand. If you eat a dozen donuts every day, that will display who you are, physically and emotionally. When you incorporate Sweatworking into your professional narrative, you're showing the world that your brand is not just about what you do and what matters to you (i.e., wellness and connection), but also about how you do it.

Example:

- If you're a business consultant, your Sweatworking activities could reflect your ability to push boundaries and achieve goals under pressure. You might share how your marathon training has taught you discipline and perseverance, qualities that you bring to your consulting work. Your fitness attributes showcase the qualities that make you a valuable professional.

Your Niche and Unique Value Proposition

Every person these days seems to be trying to find their niche for their own brand. That's a good thing because I truly believe every person on earth has a story to tell. Whether or not your story is an interesting one is up to you. You dig deep enough, you'll uncover rare minerals and gems.

It's a crowded landscape. But that's okay, as long as you stay true to your ethos. It's crucial to identify your personal slot and unique value proposition. What sets you apart from others? Figure out a way to use the genius of Sweatworking as a catalyst for telling your story. You have one. Find it.

Once you've identified your niche, use it to craft a unique value proposition that resonates with you. This could be anything from showcasing your motivation to helping others during Sweatworking sessions, to creating your own sessions, exercising, and influencing your team members in your company. That's what you call leadership. The key is to ensure that your daily activities align with your brand's overall mission and values.

Consistent Messaging Across Sweatworking Activities

Consistency is the backbone of any successful brand. But first, you must believe in yourself. This means ensuring that every activity, every social post, and every story you share reflects your brand's core values and messaging.

Imagine your company or personal brand as your dream home. Every activity, every post, and every story is a building block that either adds to the building of your home or disrupts it. Consistency ensures that your message remains clear and powerful, building upward through all aspects of your life, including your Sweatworking activities.

Measuring Impact on Your Brand

A network is not only about who you know, but who knows you. As you engage in Sweatworking, observe how your professional circle expands. Are you meeting new faces at the gym, conferences, or during group runs? Are these encounters leading to meaningful exchanges, or merely fleeting hellos? The true measure of growth lies not in the quantity of connections but in their quality.

Ask yourself:

- Are these new relationships enriching my professional life, or merely padding my contact list?
- Are these sessions building my company and team's confidence or driving a wedge between the healthy and the unfit?

Keep in mind that with social platforms. A 'like' doesn't mean horseshit in the overall scheme of anything. You're looking for something much deeper and connective.

Evaluating New Opportunities from Connections

Nature teaches us that opportunities often arise from unexpected places. As you sweat alongside potential clients or collaborators, pay attention to the conversations that unfold. Are they discussing projects or ideas that align with your passions and skills? Do these interactions lead to tangible opportunities—a new project, a speaking engagement, or perhaps a partnership? The value of Sweatworking lies in its ability to foster genuine connections that can blossom into professional opportunities.

Feedback and Impact on Brand Perception

Feedback is the cloud that shapes how our brands flow. This is especially pertinent for mid-level managers and executive leaders of companies. Seek out those who have encountered you through Sweatworking and ask for their honest impressions. How do they perceive you? Do they see a dedicated professional, a captivating leader, or perhaps a passionate advocate for your field? Their insights can help refine your or your company's brand, ensuring it accurately reflects your values and strengths.

This type of feedback is a trickier process because many people may be hesitant to actually tell you the truth in fear of retaliation somehow. I know plenty of leaders who give off the persona of wanting to know how their employees feel, but deep down they're not ingesting the feedback or processing it for their employees' self-improvement, but rather building up bigger divides between themselves and the team they lead.

You've been warned.

Setting Goals for Networking Through Wellness Activities

Goals are like the trails we blaze in the wilderness. They guide us through the unknown. As you embark on this journey of Sweatworking, define what you hope to achieve.

For brands, do you aim to expand your network or build your employee base by a certain number each month? Are you seeking to secure a specific number of collaborations or projects through these connections? Setting clear objectives will help you navigate the landscape of Sweatworking with purpose.

Tracking New Connections and Opportunities

When I'm trying to achieve a first ascent of a mountain, landmarks are crucial for navigation. There have been plenty of times when I've gotten lost on the way down a mountain if the winds were high and the clouds were dark. It was due to poor decisions on my part while trying to summit a peak without taking the necessary precautions with my navigation on the ascent.

Similarly, tracking your progress in Sweatworking is essential. Keep a log of new connections made and opportunities that arise. Note the activities that yield the most fruitful interactions. Is it during group fitness classes, meditation sessions, or perhaps post-workout socials? By monitoring these details, you can refine your approach.

In the end, integrating Sweatworking into a personal or company brand is not just about overall wellness and communication; it's about genuineness, adaptability, and the unwavering commitment to your values. It's living a life that is as authentic as the wilderness itself. Our brands go beyond what we create; they are who we are. What better way to express that than through the sweat of our brows?

Genuineness is what will set you free and apart, allowing your true self to shine like a beacon in the darkness. This is your path to enlightenment.

Mantra: Your brand is your own truth expressed consistently

29

The Future of Productivity: Your Wellness Is The New ROI

As you gaze out into the future, the landscape of your workplace dynamics should unfold like a mountain sunrise, full of promise and possibility. The alternative is a growing, catastrophic cancer for you, me, and society as a whole.

A Forewarning

Virtual Reality and Augmented Reality Integration

You're standing in a virtual conference hall, your avatar decked out in your finest digital attire. The air around you hums with the energy of countless professionals, all gathered in this ethereal space. Virtual reality has transformed the way you connect, breaking down the barriers of physical distance and creating immersive networking experiences that rival even the most extravagant real-world events.

You turn your head, and suddenly, floating before your eyes is the profile of a potential collaborator. Is it a real, or just another bot? Augmented reality has integrated information into your field of view, allowing you to see beyond the surface and into the depths of each person's professional journey. All their particulars are displayed in a mix of data and outward, surface-level humanity. And corporations are turning your curiosity into profit. You're not just giving away your clicks, you're selling off pieces of yourself and your soul.

AI-Powered Networking

As you navigate this digital landscape, an invisible hand guides you towards the most relevant connections. AI algorithms work to match you with kindred spirits in the professional realm. These matchmaking wonders analyze your interests, goals, and past interactions with the precision of a master stalker.

And when the conversation lulls, fear not. Chatbots, those tenacious digital assistants, stand ready to oil the gears of interaction. They introduce you to new faces, follow up on promising leads, and ensure that no opportunity for connection slips through the cracks. It's networking on autopilot, with your thought process eliminated.

Gamification of Networking Activities

Networking has also become a game, and you are a player in this grand tournament of professional growth. Your personal interactive challenges await at every turn, allowing you to stay within your comfort zone and into the arena of opportunity. Complete a task, earn a badge, climb the leaderboard. It's a constant dance of achievement and recognition from the comfort of your domicile, alone, and with no communion.

But it's not all just fun and games. These networking challenges are designed to hone your skills for you. As you navigate through skill-based networking games, you're not just collecting points, you're collecting valuable virtual experiences and virtual connections that you hope will serve you well in the cutthroat world of business.

The boundaries between work and play, between reality and virtual, have now blurred into totality. You stand on the precipice of a new era, where you're told every interaction is an opportunity, every connection a potential goldmine of collaboration and growth. Where everyone you meet can be utilized and exploited for your own professional goals.

Cross-Cultural Networking Opportunities

The digital age has also thrown open the gates to international connections. You can reach out and touch someone halfway around the world without even leaving your pajamas or temperature-controlled room. But you had better develop some cultural intelligence. You'll have to learn to read the room, even when that room's on the other side of the planet.

Multilingual Networking Platforms

You think language is a barrier? Ha! You've got AI-powered translation tools that can turn your backwoods drawl into sophisticated Mandarin faster than you can say, "WTF." There are also virtual language exchange networking events popping up like prairie dogs for your virtual love and participation.

Time Zone-Friendly Networking Solutions

The sun never sets on your global empire of networking. There are serial networking options that let you connect with folks while they're sleeping and vice versa. It's cyber time travel that will provide more LinkedIn requests. It's a non-stop virtual party, and everyone's invited.

The distinction between work and play is vanishing. Your personal life and professional life are merging like two streams into one mighty river of connections. There is no personal life. There is no time to take a step back and breathe. Your life is leaving your control and being replaced by computer-generated intelligence.

Preparing for the Future of Professional Networking

Did that glimpse into the future of professional networking excite you? For some, perhaps yes, but for others, me included, it's a definitive NO. It's coming at you faster than a freight train, and promising a crazy, virtual ride. Cross-cultural connections, AI translators, time-bending communication. It's all part of what can become the new frontier of professional networking.

Surrounded by all this innovation lies a cautionary tale, a reminder that progress often comes at a cost. As you embrace these new modes of interaction, you're already experiencing and losing sight of what truly matters: genuine human connection.

Unless you rise and take a stand, for yourself and against the relentless corporate juggernaut of traditional networking and day-to-day professionalism, nothing will change. Sweatworking is your first bold step forward. The world is unwittingly hungry for a revolution of the human spirit, and it begins with you. Dare to dream bigger. Act with greater courage. Become more than you ever thought possible. The power to transform your life is already within you. I believe in you, and deep down, you do too. Now is the moment to unleash it.

Your Company's Perspectives

I also hope that your workplace of tomorrow will shed the sterile confines of cubicles, embracing instead energetic spaces that nurture connection and community, where collaboration blooms like irises, and where the very essence of your work is not just about productivity, but about fostering a sense of belonging and shared purpose. A future where you don't labour in isolation but thrive in environments that inspire, that provoke, and that remind you of the beauty in your collective endeavors.

Companies will beckon their employees to leave the confines of their desks, embracing the freedom of diverse exercise classes and communal wellness sessions. Obligatory microbreaks will become grand opportunities for camaraderie. The somber, sedentary workspaces of yesteryear will give way to lively and active workstations, where the confines between labor and well-being dissolve like mist at dawn. The sedate rituals of traditional meetings yield to the invigorating rhythms of walking discussions or brainstorming sessions, where creativity and collaboration run dominant.

Sweatworking is the signpost pointing to the future of your human connection in an increasingly disconnected world. It is unfiltered humanity, sweat dripping, muscles straining, egos left breathless for air on the exercise floor.

C-Suite Executive: Your traditional networking can smoothly merge with Sweatworking and become more structured and intentional. It involves your company offering tailored programs designed specifically to foster professional connections while molding physiques and minds, and corporate wellness initiatives that integrate team-building exercises into Sweatworking events. The positive results from financial and productivity standpoints will exceed your board's wildest expectations.

Global Perspectives

In the future, Sweatworking can take on different complexions, shaped by cultural norms and socio-economic realities. In the United States, it can be a high-energy affair—cycle classes turned networking hubs or bootcamps where deals are sealed between push-ups, squat jumps, and dynamic stretching. The American obsession with productivity finds its perfect partner in Sweatworking.

In Brazil, Sweatworking would embrace the nation's vibrant culture and love for movement. Samba-inspired fitness classes double as networking events, blending rhythm with rapport-building.

India could offer yet another perspective. With its deep-rooted traditions in yoga and meditation, Sweatworking can take a more introspective turn. Professional connections are shaped not through competition but through collective mindfulness practices that emphasize balance and harmony, a stark contrast to the cutthroat ethos often associated with Western networking.

Despite these differences, one common thread should bind all these iterations: the universal human need for connection. Whether it's through synchronized squats in São Paulo or sun salutations in Mumbai, Sweatworking taps into something primal. A reminder that we are social creatures at heart.

***

Embrace the opportunity for a brave new world with your eyes wide open.

Sweat not just for your success but for something deeper—for humanity overall. For the bonds that will make you stronger, more than you could ever do alone. For your wellness.

I can't help but feel a twinge of hope within my usual cynicism. Perhaps there is still room for genuineness in this hyperconnected age. Even within the dissonance of modern life, you will uncover transcendent connections where your heart, though beating alone, synchronizes in perfect harmony with the rest of humanity.

The world will not change for you. You must change yourself.

Your Mantra: Your health is your wealth

30

One Breath To Your Freedom

Y ou have more control over your life than you realize. Your feelings, what you're thinking, your perception. All of that is changeable.

A single breath is all you need to prove it. The power of a conscious breath helps you shift your internal landscape to help you recognize your agency over your thoughts and emotions. It's a fascinating and incredibly valuable power for you.

Your Instant Freedom Moment Exercise

Wherever you are, whatever you feel—stressed, angry, tired, or frustrated—stop.

Breathe in deeply for 5 seconds.
Exhale slowly through your mouth until the air is expelled.

Reset. Refresh. Feel free.

The Internal Mirror

Think about it: Your breath is always with you, a steady anchor to the present moment from the day of your birth until the day of your death. Yet, how often do you truly notice it? A conscious inhalation and exhalation can act like an internal mirror. It draws your attention inward, away from the external noise and the constant stream of thoughts. In that brief pause, you can become aware of the subtle sensations within your body. The rise and fall of your chest or abdomen, the coolness of the air entering your nostrils, and the gentle warmth of the exhale. This direct experience of your physical self, unburdened by judgment or analysis, can be a powerful reminder of your embodied presence. It's a moment of pure being, stripped of the stories you tell yourself.

Self-Realization: Moment of Support

As you become more attuned to your breath, you might start to notice the subtle ways your emotional state influences it. When you're anxious, your breath might be shallow and rapid. When you're relaxed, it tends to be deeper and slower. This direct correlation can lead to a profound self-realization: Your internal state and physical experiences are intimately connected, and the breath is a tangible bridge between them. This understanding can be the first crack in the perception of being at the mercy of your feelings. You begin to see that you have a tool—your breath—that you can consciously use to influence your internal state.

Presence in Your Anchor

Your mind is often thinking between the past and the future, caught in cycles of contemplation and worry. The conscious breath is a powerful anchor to the present moment. By focusing your attention on the sensation of breathing, you gently guide our awareness away from those mental wanderings and back to the here and now. This isn't about suppressing thoughts or feelings, but rather about acknowledging them without getting carried away. Each inhale and exhale is a fresh start, a return to the immediacy of your experience. In this moment of presence, the intensity of your thoughts and emotions can often lessen. You gain a bit of distance, a clearer perspective, simply by being grounded in the physical reality of your breath.

Your Control: Inner vs. Outer Landscapes

Through the consistent practice of mindful breathing, you begin to discern what lies within your sphere of influence and what doesn't. You can't control the traffic jam, the weather, or other people's actions. However, you can control your response to these external events. The breath becomes a tangible example of this inner control. You can choose to breathe deeply and calmly even amid chaos. This direct experience of influencing your internal state through your breath can then extend to your thoughts and emotions. You start to recognize that while you can't always dictate what thoughts arise, you can choose how you engage with them. You can learn to observe them without judgment, to let them pass without getting swept away. The breath becomes a microcosm of your inner agency, a constant reminder of the power we hold within, even when the external world feels overwhelming.

***

That single, conscious breath is not a magic wand, but rather a powerful invitation. It's an invitation to turn inward, to connect with your physical self, to recognize your inherent agency, to find grounding in the present, and to discern the boundaries of your control. It's a subtle act with the potential for profound and lasting change in how you perceive yourself and your relationship to your inner and outer worlds.

Your Mantra: Breathe deep, return home

31

The Hero Is You. The Time Is Now

Your Manifesto

You've reached the finish line. But this ain't the end. This is where your real adventure begins. It's a whole way of life, a way of looking at things, a defiant middle finger to the soul-crushing monotony that'll swallow you whole if you let it. You've discovered what Sweatworking is—a powerful merging of movement, connection, and purpose that will transform your life in ways you've never imagined. It's not just exercise or networking; it's a lifestyle, a mindset, and a rebellion against the ordinary.

You're standing at a fork in the trail. To one side, you have the soft, predictable rut of the same old crap—the lazy slide into nothing, the slow rot of fear and the blues, the steady march toward declining health and a body that's given up the ghost. On the other side? There's another path, the one that leads to growing, to feeling alive, to your transformation. The choice is yours. But if you stand there gawking like a tourist, you'll never experience the underbelly. You've got to make your move, and you've got to make it now, before time, disease, and technology swallow you whole.

THE HERO IS YOU. THE TIME IS NOW

Sweatworking is going to help:

- **Boost your career** by building meaningful relationships and sharpening your focus.
- **Strengthen your home life** through increased energy, confidence, and emotional resilience.
- **Overcome fear and depression** by releasing endorphins and rewiring your mindset.
- **Break free from complacency** by embracing challenge and movement.
- **Prevent future diseases** by prioritizing your health and vitality.
- **Feel and look younger** as you reclaim your body and spirit.

The clock's ticking for you and every one of us, and it can't be rewound. Each sunrise you squander on your backside is a day your edge dulls, a day those aches and pains whisper a little louder. If you keep waiting, you'll find yourself shackled by the very mindset you've cultivated. Those ruts you've worn in the landscape of your life? They only get deeper with each passing season.

But the spark in the flint is that if you decide to kick the complacency in the teeth, your whole narrative flips. You morph from a bystander into the protagonist, the one who roars at mediocrity, who rolls up your sleeves and wrestles life into a better shape, who feels the honest sweat on your brow and the genuine connection in your heart, and who ultimately, by god, prevails.

Sweatworking. What a word. Sounds like something cooked up by a marketing committee in a windowless conference room. But don't let the word fool you. This isn't another self-help fad. This is your secret weapon in the daily brawl for survival—at work, at home, and in the battered outpost of your own skull. In the real world, you need more than caffeine and corporate jargon to get by. You need energy, focus, and a tribe that's got your back. Sweatworking gives you all three—if you're willing to bleed a little for it.

As I've relayed in this book, forget the soft-sell. Let's startle the corporate world awake. You're not schmoozing in spandex or trading QR codes between push-ups. It's about forging real connections, the kind that only come when you're breathless and your carefully constructed mask has slipped off with the sweat. It's about building a body that can take a life punch and a mind that won't fold at the first sign of trouble. You want to be more present at home? Try dragging your carcass through a sunrise run, then see if the day's petty annoyances can touch you. You want to shake off fear and depression? Flood your brain with endorphins, rewire your circuits, and breathe your way to enlightenment.

Complacency is your enemy. The modern world wants you docile, fat, and glued to a glowing screen. Sweatworking is a rebellion against that slow death. You want to dodge the diseases waiting for you down the line? You want to look and feel younger, not just for the mirror but for the sheer hell of being alive? Then move. Work. Sweat. There's no magic pills to consume, just the steady, relentless transformation of a body and mind that refuses to quit.

But here's the hard truth I learned from my Norwegian grandfather on his deathbed—none of this matters if you don't believe in yourself. If you don't act. Of course, your journey starts with doubt, with fear gnawing at your insides. The difference is, you don't let fear drive. Listen to your rebel voice—the one that says "not today, not me, not this life." That rebel is real. It's the blue flames raging from within that keep you from settling for mediocrity. It's time to burn.

Your Next Steps: Make It Count

Your next steps are simple but powerful:

- Commit to your Sweatworking routine today.
- Reach out and build your Sweatworking community.
- Face your fears head-on with movement and connection.
- Celebrate every small victory as a step toward your ultimate transformation.

Every moment you wait is a moment lost. The future you want, the healthier, happier, more vibrant you, is within reach. But only if you act now. Create your history. Don't wait for it to occur.

Sweatworking is your proving ground, your training ground. This is where you build the strength, the connections, and the wild, stubborn mindset to become unstoppable. Imagine waking up each morning with enough white light in your heart energy to illuminate the office and still have plenty of radiance left over for the people you love. You will walk through the world with confidence, where your health is your own, your relationships are alive, and your spirit is untamed.

This isn't a fantasy. It's a reality waiting for you to grab it by the throat. But it won't come easily. Thank god, because nothing of value ever does. You have to act. You have to commit. The world doesn't need more spectators, more influencers, more content creators posting their favorite meals and faux sunny dispositions. It needs mavericks. It needs iconoclasts.

You're wondering if you're ready? If you can actually go through with this formidable change? Good. Doubt means you're awake. You, I, and every other person with a pulse feel the weight of uncertainty before they break through the shackles of complacency. Start small? Hell, start anywhere—but start. One sweat-drenched session, one raw conversation, one act against the soft, sedentary rot of modern life. Celebrate it by howling at the moon, then build on it like a pirate hoarding treasures. Momentum isn't some corporate buzzword, it's the grit under your boots as you march toward the edge of what's possible. Fear? Turn it into fuel. Complacency? Burn it down. Potential? Drag it kicking and screaming into the light of action.

This world's choking on its own exhaust fumes, shackled to screens and synthetic dreams. Sweatworking isn't self-help, it's a vulgar hand gesture to the air-conditioned cubicles and convenience that can turn you into a sloth. You want power? Earn it with your furnace of energy. Connection? Forge it in the space of shared struggle. Purpose? Carve it out of the wilderness of your resolve.

Your journey doesn't have to be some solo pilgrimage. It can be a wildfire that's a prescribed burn. Every step you take spreads a blaze within those around you—your family, your comrades, your poor associates still asleep at the wheel. Be the blessed signal, the lighthouse on a far distant shore. Show them how to gut the status quo with calloused hands and a spine of iron. Transformation? It's not handed out in pamphlets and virtual assistants. It's seized through effort and ethos, one beautiful breath at a time.

Commit like your life depends on it, because it does. Find the others out there who'd rather bleed effort than drown in comfort. Face your fear head-on, then spit its eye. Celebrate every victory, even the ones that come wrapped in failure.

Your story's not some prefab corporate policy manual. It's a live wire crackling with untamed energy. You've got the tools? Use 'em. The rebel inside you isn't some whispered fantasy, it's the primal scream of a creature refusing to be domesticated. The future's not waiting. It's clawing its way into existence through your actions. Perfect moment? There's no such thing. There's only now. Sweatwork your way into the annals of the unbroken, and watch the world bend to your grit.

The planet's on fire, and the clock's ticking. We need your power. We need your fury. Your passion. Your refusal to kneel. You're no hero? Bullshit. Heroes are forged within the souls who act, not dream. The time for action isn't coming, it's here. So spread your arms out wide, scream with the gods, and then get to work.

Your Mantra: The hero is you. The time is now.

Author's Note on Appendices

The Appendices are your blueprint for dynamic Sweatworking sessions. While an experienced instructor is always an advantage, I understand that not every session leader will be a wellness veteran. That's why I've crafted detailed guidelines designed to empower anyone leading a session. It's essentially a year's worth of mentorship condensed into these pages.

Revisit these tools often. They cover every facet of a successful Sweatworking experience: from optimizing session structure and offering engaging activity variations to sparking meaningful conversation starters, ensuring crucial safety tips are front and center, outlining essential equipment needs, mastering time management, and providing creative post-session follow-up ideas.

I've also included detailed appendices tailored specifically for professional instructors who teach wellness classes. These supplementary materials offer practical tools and insights designed to enhance participant engagement in movement-based networking sessions. They provide structure, guidance, and strategies to foster deeper connections through shared physical experience.

I encourage you to explore this material for both inspiration and practical guidance on how to integrate Sweatworking into your daily routines and broader company culture. Whether you're considering in-house wellness programs, external partnerships, or reimagining how your teams connect and collaborate, this comprehensive framework offers the tools and insights to help you move forward. It's designed to support you

AUTHOR'S NOTE ON APPENDICES

in transforming wellness initiatives into meaningful opportunities for connection, growth, and organizational vitality.

For More Information About Hiring Your Professional Instructor or Exercises, Go to: SeanBurch.com

Appendix A: Sweatworking Sessions - Adrenaline Outdoors

Hike & Huddle: Group Hiking with Team-Building Activities

Hike & Huddle is more than just a trek through nature, it's an odyssey that ignites camaraderie, sharpens communication, and promotes physical vitality. It's a journey where the beauty of the outdoors converges with the spirit of teamwork. In this setting, participants forge lasting bonds, discover leadership within themselves, and cultivate resilience. By blending the adventure of hiking with dynamic team-building exercises, we create a haven where individuals emerge feeling revitalized, connected, and inspired, ready to tackle life's challenges with renewed vigor and a deeper appreciation for the natural world.
Hiking with a group instead of solo makes your energy linger long after the session is complete.

Duration: Approximately 2-3 hours, depending on the trail length and activities.

Equipment Needed:

- Comfortable hiking shoes
- Clothing layers depending on the outside temperature

- Water and snacks
- First aid kit
- Trekking poles
- Optional: GPS devices or maps for navigation challenges

Hiking Segment

- Warm-Up Hike: Begin with a gentle hike to warm up the muscles and get participants moving.
- Team Navigation Challenge: Divide participants into teams and provide them with a map or GPS device. Challenge them to navigate through a section of the trail, promoting teamwork and problem-solving.

Team-Building Activities: Checkpoint Challenges

Problem-Solving Tasks: At designated checkpoints, teams must solve puzzles or complete tasks that require collaboration and creativity.

Trivia: Incorporate trivia questions related to nature, fitness, or teamwork to keep participants engaged and informed.

Creative Tasks: Encourage teams to create short skits or songs about their hiking experience, fostering creativity and camaraderie.

Leader Rotation: Rotate leadership roles within each team at different checkpoints. This helps develop leadership skills and encourages participants to step out of their comfort zones.

Silent Hike: Incorporate a silent segment where participants must communicate non-verbally, enhancing observation and listening skills by tuning in to their natural surroundings.

Reflection Sessions: After reaching a scenic spot, hold a group discussion on teamwork, challenges faced, and lessons learned. This encourages reflection and self-awareness. You can improve this by taking out a small journal you've been given or have brought with you. Instruct the participants to scribble down their feelings and reorganize any negative thoughts into positive declarations.

Physical Fitness Drills

- Hill Climbs: At intervals, have teams sprint, jog, or walk up hills to boost cardiovascular fitness and strength.
- Trail Strength Exercises: Incorporate bodyweight exercises like squats, body hangs, core work, and push-ups at designated stops to maintain muscle engagement.
- Balance Challenges: Use natural obstacles like logs or rocks for balance exercises, improving agility and coordination.

Beach Bootcamp: Sand-Based Workouts with Networking Games

Beach Bootcamp is where the challenges of sand-based workouts are tempered by the camaraderie of networking games. This session combines the thrill of physical exertion with the warmth of shared experience, creating connections that weave together the structure of community.

Class Structure

Warm-Up (10 minutes)

- Barefoot Jogging: Start with slow jogging on the sand to warm up the muscles, followed by backward jogging to loosen up the legs and hips.
- High Knees: Run or step in place, bringing knees up high to get the heart rate up and prepare for the workout.

Sand-Based Workouts (30 minutes)

- Sandbell Deadlift: Use a sand-filled bucket as a kettlebell. Perform deadlifts to engage the core and legs.
- Sandbell Swing: Swing the bucket up to shoulder level, focusing on explosive power from the hips and glutes.
- Push-ups: Perform push-ups on the sand, which increases difficulty due to the soft surface and uneven terrain.
- Air-squat jumps: Excellent for lower body strength, these are even more challenging on sand.

Networking Games (20 minutes)

- Fitness Relay: Divide the group into teams. Each team member must complete a different exercise (e.g., burpees, broad jumps, plank hold) before passing a baton to the next team member.
- Beach Scavenger Hunt: Create a list of items or locations on the beach. At each location, teams must perform a specific exercise before moving on.

Cool Down and Bonding (10 minutes)

- Team Yoga Challenge: Divide the group into teams and have them create and hold a group yoga pose for a set time. This enhances flexibility and teamwork.
- Networking Circle: Have participants stand in a circle and share one thing they learned or enjoyed about the workout. This encourages bonding and community building. No whining. Positive comments only.

Motivational Tips

- Demonstrate Proper Form: Ensure participants understand how to perform exercises safely and effectively.
- Modify Exercises: Encourage participants to modify exercises based on their fitness level to prevent injury and build confidence.
- Emphasize Muscle Groups: Explain the benefits of each exercise to help participants connect with their muscles and stay motivated.

Park Circuit & Pitch: Outdoor Circuit Training with Elevator Pitch

Park Circuit & Pitch is a class that combines the tasks of circuit training with elevator pitch practice. This is where the rugged terrain of physical challenge meets the open vista of the mind. We forge a community of confidants, each pushing their limits. It's a realm where personal growth develops, supported by the fellowship of shared effort and the thrill of mastering the art of communication and persuasiveness.

Class Structure

Warm-Up (5-10 minutes)

- Dynamic stretching to prepare participants for the workout.
- Light cardio, such as jogging in place or full-range jumping jacks.

Circuit Training (20 minutes)

Station 1: Upper Body

- Push-Up Variations: Standard push-ups, diamond push-ups, decline or incline push-ups using a park bench. 10-15 reps
- Tricep Dips: Using a park bench. 10-15 reps

Station 2: Lower Body

- Bodyweight Squats: Focus on proper form. 15-20 reps
- Side-lunges: Alternate legs. 8-12 reps per leg

Station 3: Cardio

- Sprints: Short 10-meter sprints. 3-5 reps
- Burpees: Provide modified versions for beginners. 8-15 reps

Station 4: Core

- Full Sit-ups: Engage core muscles. 30-60 seconds
- Russian Twists: Use a light weight or medicine ball. 10-15 reps

Elevator Pitch Practice (10 minutes)

- Participants will practice delivering a 30-second elevator pitch.
- Encourage creativity and confidence in their speaking.
- Preparation: Provide participants with a prompt or topic for their pitch.
- Delivery: Participants practice their pitches while moving between stations.
- Feedback: Encourage peer feedback and support.

Cool-Down (5 minutes)

- Static stretches that focus on major muscle groups.
- Final motivational speech to reinforce the importance of both physical fitness and effective communication.

Motivational Elements

- Community Building: Encourage participants to support each other

during the workout and pitch practice.
- **Goal Setting**: Help participants set personal fitness and communication goals.
- **Inspirational Quotes**: Share motivational quotes throughout the class to keep participants engaged and motivated.

Trail Run & Teamwork: Group Trail Running with Collaborative Challenges

Get out there, you wild souls, and let nature course through your veins! *Trail Run & Teamwork* is more than just a challenge, it's a celebration of the satisfaction that comes from pounding the trails with colleagues by your side. Your lungs will burn, your legs will pump, and sweat will stream down your face, but you'll find it's all worth it for that radiant grin. This isn't just about building endurance or strength, it's about forging bonds that last more than a fleeting moment and finding adventure in every step. Lace up those shoes, breathe in that crisp air, and let the wildness of the world ignite your spirit.

Class Overview
   Duration: 60 minutes
   Objective: To challenge participants physically while promoting teamwork and camaraderie.
   Equipment: Trail running shoes, water, and a first-aid kit.
   Location: Local trails with varied terrain.

Warm-Up (10 minutes)

- **Dynamic Stretching**: Incorporate leg swings, arm circles, and torso

twists to prepare muscles for running.
- Team Jog: Begin with a light jog to warm up the cardiovascular system and get participants moving together.

Trail Running Segment (20 minutes)

- Terrain Variety: Incorporate hills, inclines, and declines to challenge participants and improve trail running skills.
- Pace Setting: Encourage participants to maintain a steady pace, with faster runners supporting slower ones.

Collaborative Challenges (20 minutes)

Challenge 1: Team Relay Hill Sprints

- Divide the group into teams of 3-4.
- Each team member runs up a designated hill and back down before tagging the next team member.
- The team with the fastest combined time wins.

Challenge 2: Partner Navigation

- Pair participants up to navigate through a marked section of the trail.
- One partner acts as the navigator, guiding the other through obstacles and turns.
- Switch roles halfway through.

Challenge 3: Group Obstacle Course

- Set up an obstacle course with natural elements like logs, rocks, and streams.
- Participants must work together to overcome obstacles, using teamwork and communication.

Cool Down and Stretching (10 minutes)

- Static Stretching: Focus on stretching major muscle groups used during running, such as hamstrings, quadriceps, and calves.
- Team Reflection: Encourage participants to share their experiences and what they learned about teamwork and perseverance.

Key Exercises and Drills

- Hill Sprints: Short bursts of intense running uphill to improve explosive power and endurance.
- Log Jumps: Jumping over logs to enhance agility and coordination.
- Stream Crossings: Practicing balance and stability by crossing streams or narrow paths.

Motivational Elements

- Teamwork Awards: Recognize teams that demonstrate exceptional teamwork and support.
- Personal Challenges: Encourage participants to set personal goals and celebrate achievements.
- Social Sharing: Encourage participants to share their experiences on social media using a class hashtag.

Paddle & Strategy: Stand-up Paddleboarding with Floating Idea Sessions

Embark on a wild adventure with *Paddle & Strategy*, where the thrill of stand-up paddleboarding meets the meditative calm of planned floating sessions. This session is tailored for those who crave a workout that not only tests their physical mettle but also sharpens their mental acuity. As you glide across the water, you'll find your balance honed, your core strengthened, and your heart pounding with renewed vivacity. But it's not just about individual prowess; this session weaves in the camaraderie of teamwork and the cunning of strategy.

Class Overview
Duration: 90 minutes
Format: The class will be divided into three segments: warm-up and paddling technique, strategy sessions, and a high-intensity workout.
Equipment: Stand-up paddleboards, paddles, life jackets, and a floating obstacle course.

Segment 1: Warm-Up and Paddling Technique (15 minutes)

- Paddling Technique: Begin with a brief on-land session to review basic paddling strokes and board handling.
- Warm-Up Paddle: Participants will paddle at a leisurely pace to warm up their muscles and get comfortable on the boards.

Segment 2: Strategy Sessions (30 minutes)

- Floating Obstacle Course: Set up a floating obstacle course that participants must navigate through while maintaining balance and focus.

Team Challenges: Divide participants into teams to complete challenges such as:

- Paddle Relay: Teams paddle to a designated point, perform a specific task (e.g., squat or push-up exercise), and return.
- Board Balance: Participants must balance on their boards while teammates try to distract them with fun challenges.

Segment 3: High-Intensity Workout (35 minutes)

SUP Squats: Paddle air squats on the board to engage legs and core.

- Reps: 10-15, 3 sets.
- Modification: Use a paddle for added resistance.

Plank Jumps: Start in a plank position on the board, then jump up and land softly.

- Reps: 10-15, 3 sets.

SUP Burpees: Modified burpees on the board, focusing on quick transitions.

- Reps: 10-15, 3 sets.

Paddle Sprints: Short sprints between markers to boost cardiovascular endurance.

- Reps: 5-7 sprints, with 30-second rest intervals.

Core Twists: Stand on the board and twist your torso while holding the paddle.

- Reps: 15-20 each side, 3 sets.

Cool Down and Reflection (10 minutes)

- Stretching: Focus on stretching major muscle groups used during the workout.
- Reflection: Encourage participants to reflect on their experience, highlighting teamwork, strategy and potential networking links.

Appendix B: Sweatworking Sessions - Strength and Camaraderie

Lift & Lead - Weight Training Circuits with Leadership Exercises

Lift & Lead forges a community of leaders who not only strengthen their bodies but also sharpen their minds. Together, we'll blaze trails of adaptability, ignite the fire of leadership, and kindle a sense of belonging that echoes long after the session has ended. We don't just build muscle, we craft leaders who stand tall and lift each other up.

Class Structure

Warm-Up (5 minutes): High-energy music and dynamic warm-up to get participants moving and engaged.

Weight Training Circuits (30 minutes): A series of strength-building exercises in a circuit format, incorporating leadership elements.

Leadership Exercises (15 minutes): Activities designed to enhance leadership skills and teamwork.

Cool Down and Reflection (5 minutes): Stretching and a moment for participants to reflect on their experience and network.

Weight Training Circuits

Circuit 1: Strength and Teamwork

- Squats: Emphasize proper form and encourage participants to support each other.
- Bench Press: Focus on teamwork by having pairs assist with spotting.
- Pull-Ups: Use resistance bands for assistance and promote peer encouragement.

Circuit 2: Agility and Communication

- Burpees (Various): Incorporate verbal cues for timing and coordination.
- Mountain Climbers (Various): Encourage participants to motivate their neighbors.
- Box Jumps: Use visual cues to enhance communication and timing.

Circuit 3: Endurance and Resilience

- Plank Hold: Challenge participants to hold the plank while sharing motivational phrases.
- Dumbbell Swings: Focus on consistent effort and perseverance.
- Rowing Machine Intervals: Emphasize the importance of pacing and teamwork.

Leadership Exercises

Trust Walk: Divide participants into pairs. One person is blindfolded, and the other guides him/her through a short exercise obstacle course fusing only verbal instructions. This activity builds trust and communication skills.

Mission Statement: Have participants write down their personal wellness goals and why the goals are important. Then, ask them to share these goals with a partner or the group, emphasizing the value of accountability and support.

Motivational Techniques

- Speak to the Why: Explain how each exercise contributes to overall fitness and leadership goals.
- Create a Sense of Community: Encourage high-fives, teamwork, and mutual support throughout the class.
- Mind-to-Muscle Connection: Emphasize the importance of focusing on the muscle groups being worked during each exercise.

Extended Leadership Exercises

Leadership Pizza: This activity helps participants visualize and assess their leadership qualities.

Instructions:
1. Ask each participant to list essential leadership traits.
2. Have them draw a pizza, dividing it into slices representing these traits.
3. The size of each slice should reflect the perceived importance of that trait.
4. Participants present their 'pizzas' to the group, explaining their

choices.

5. Each person identifies areas for improvement.

Benefits:

- Encourages self-reflection
- Promotes open discussion about leadership qualities
- Helps identify areas for personal growth
- Provides a visual representation of leadership skills

Duration: 45-60 minutes

Circles of Influence: This exercise helps team members identify where they can have the most impact and helps them use their skills effectively.

Instructions:

1. Provide participants with a large sheet of paper and markers.
2. Ask them to draw three concentric circles.
3. In the innermost circle, they write things they have direct control over.
4. In the middle circle, they list things they can influence.
5. In the outer circle, they note things they're concerned about but have little control over.
6. Participants share their circles and discuss how to focus energy on areas of control and influence.

Benefits:

- Encourages pro-activity and responsibility
- Helps identify areas where individuals can make the most impact
- Promotes reflection on personal and team effectiveness
- Facilitates discussion on prioritization and resource allocation

Duration: 30-120 minutes

Hyperfitness© Links - Functional Workouts with Paired Exercise

The wild beauty of *Hyperfitness* allows this session to not be just a workout; it's a communal odyssey that binds a group together in the pursuit of strength and camaraderie. In these functional-style workouts, you'll find we're not just pushing our limits, but also lifting each other up. The intensity is matched only by the support of shared triumphs. It's a celebration of human connection and resilience, where every exercise movement and moment is a testament to the power of unity and the discovery of what your body is capable of doing.

Class Structure

Warm-Up (5-10 minutes): Begin with a dynamic warm-up that includes light cardio and mobility exercises to prepare participants for the workout.

Workouts (40 minutes): The main segment will feature a series of exercises that alternate between strength, cardio, and synchronized movements.

Cool Down (10 minutes): Finish with a stretching session to help participants recover and relax.

Exercises and Drills

Lift Run Jump
Exercise: Bodyweight push-ups, Sprints, Frog Jumps

How It Works: Continuous movement ensuring maximum effect. Alternating rounds of various styles of bodyweight push-ups followed by a 100-meter run and frog jumps.

Medicine Ball Baby
Exercise: Medicine Ball Squat Jumps 10 reps, Runs 20 yards, Side-to-side jumps for 30 yards
How It Works: Squat jumps using medicine ball from chest to straight overhead; Fast feet over line front to back to 20 yard sprint; Side-to-side jumps forward while holding a medicine ball at stomach level. Do each drill for 2 minutes without stopping. Repeat series 5 times with less than a minute rest in between sets.

High Five
Exercise: 15 Jump Squats and 15 Overhead Dumbbell Presses repeated for 5 sets.
How It Works: Partners alternate exercises, waiting for each other to complete their reps before starting the next exercise. After both complete their reps, they do 10 high-five push-ups together.

Wheelbarrows
Exercise: With a partner: a half-mile treadmill run set at 2 degrees, followed by 10 wheelbarrow push-ups (partner holds feet, hollow hold), 15 tricep push-ups on knees with a clap wall balls (partner holds plank), and complete as many air squats as your age (while partner does an isometric squat).
How It Works: Partners support each other through holding the other's feet off the ground while the partner completes push-ups. Modify to knees push-ups if necessary.

The Rhythm Maker
Exercise: Jump Rope 25 yards forward, Frog Jumps 10 reps, Knee-high Claps for 30 yards.
How It Works: With a 1 or 2 lb rope, jump rope by straight hopping

for 25 yards; Frog jumps with palms touching ground; Knee-highs with underneath hamstring clap. Perform drill for 30 yards out and back. Repeat series for 5 minutes with no rest. Two rounds. Initiate self-mantras during second round.

Additional Hyperfitness Exercises - *Hyperfitness: 12 Weeks to Conquering Your Inner Everest and Getting into the Best Shape of Your Life (Penguin Random House)*

1. Speed skater drills with optional weight vest or medicine ball
2. Tricep crusher with push-press and crunch
3. Medicine ball push-up with leg lift
4. Bosu burpee with Bosu press
5. Squat body bar throw straight overhead to self-catch and include left/right knee up
6. Scale the whale
7. Rock climbers
8. Standing barbell squat incline press with one arm
9. Pop-ups with jumping jack
10. Cable lat pull downs while knees on Bosu (vary hand positions each set)

Motivational Tips

- Emphasize Teamwork: Encourage participants to support and motivate each other throughout the workout.
- Demonstrate Proper Form: Ensure participants understand and execute exercises safely and effectively.
- Explain the Benefits: Highlight how each exercise contributes to overall fitness and well-being.
- Music and Energy: Use upbeat music to maintain a high-energy

atmosphere and keep participants engaged.

TRX Team Building - Suspension Training with Group Solving Tasks

TRX Team Building training meets the spirit of group problem-solving. In this creative session, we find a realm where teamwork, communication, and motivation are not merely ideals, but living, breathing entities that thrive under the challenge of a communal adventure. We don't merely exercise, we forge bonds, sharpen our wits, and emerge stronger.

Note: To teach this class, TRX Suspension Trainers must either be available at the gym, event, or purchased individually by your company or class participants.

Class Overview
The objective is to create a dynamic environment where participants work together to achieve fitness goals while building trust and camaraderie.

Class Structure

Warm-Up (10 minutes): TRX exercises focusing on mobility and core engagement.

Team Building Challenges (30 minutes): Incorporate TRX exercises with problem-solving tasks.

Cool Down and Reflection (10 minutes): Stretching and group discussion.

Specific Exercises and Drills

Warm-Up Exercises

- TRX Squat Rows: Engage legs and back while maintaining core stability.
- TRX Alternating Forward Lunge with T Fly: Targets legs and shoulders.
- TRX Standing Rollouts: Focuses on core strength and stability.

Team Building Challenges

TRX Partner Squats with Communication Task

- Participants pair up, with one holding the TRX straps and the other providing verbal cues to maintain form.
- The goal is to complete a set of squats while ensuring proper form through effective communication.

TRX Relay Row Challenge

- Divide the group into teams of three.
- Each team member performs a TRX row for a set number of reps before passing the straps to the next team member.
- The twist: Each member must complete a mini obstacle course before passing the straps.

TRX Puzzle Challenge

- Divide the group into teams and provide a puzzle that requires

collaboration to solve.
- Each puzzle piece is attached to a TRX exercise (e.g., TRX push-ups, rows).
- Teams must complete the exercises to unlock the puzzle pieces.

Cool Down and Reflection

- TRX Chest Stretch: Focus on flexibility and relaxation.
- TRX Figure 4 Stretch: Targets hips and lower back.
- Group Discussion: Reflect on teamwork, communication, and the benefits of working together.

Motivational Tips

- Encourage Participation: Emphasize the importance of teamwork and mutual support.
- Modify Exercises: Offer variations to accommodate different fitness levels.
- Celebrate Successes: Acknowledge achievements and progress throughout the class.
- Use Music and Movement: Create an energetic atmosphere that fosters engagement and motivation.

Kettlebell Communal - Kettlebell Workouts with Networking Breaks

This is where the intensity of kettlebell workouts converges with the dynamic energy of communal connection. *Kettlebell Communal* is more than just a wellness session, it's a sanctuary where individuals forge bonds and challenge their limits together. As we swing and lift, our bodies are strengthened—strong, resilient, and unyielding. Yet, amidst the physical trials, we find moments to pause, to breathe, and to weave in professional dialogue. We find strength not just in our muscles, but in the pacts we form with one another.

Class Structure

Warm-Up (5 minutes): Dynamic stretching and light cardio to get everyone moving and energized.

Kettlebell Workout Segments (30 minutes): Alternating between kettlebell exercises and networking breaks

Networking Breaks (5 minutes each): Participants will have the opportunity to introduce themselves and discuss common interests.

Cool Down and Final Networking (10 minutes): Stretching exercises followed by a final networking session that may be more in-depth.

Kettlebell Exercises and Drills

- Kettlebell Swing: A foundational exercise that works the hips and legs. Emphasize proper form by focusing on the hip hinge and explosive power.

- Goblet Squat: Targets the legs and glutes. Perform with a dynamic pulse for added challenge.
- Double Kettlebell Front Squat: Engages the entire lower body and requires core stability. Great for building strength and endurance.
- Kettlebell Clean and Press: A multi-joint exercise that works the entire body. Focus on controlled movements and proper form.
- Turkish Getup: A full-body exercise that improves coordination and strength. Start with lighter weights and progress as comfort allows.

Networking Breaks

During these breaks, participants will be encouraged to share their professional backgrounds, discuss current projects, and explore potential collaborations. This relaxed environment, enhanced by the endorphins from exercise, fosters open communication and meaningful connections.

Example Class Flow

Introduction and Warm-Up (5 minutes)

- Introduce participants and briefly explain the class structure.
- Perform dynamic stretching and light cardio.

Kettlebell Segment 1 (10 minutes)

- Kettlebell Swings (3 sets of 30 seconds with 15 seconds rest).
- Goblet Squats (3 sets of 30 seconds with 15 seconds rest).

Networking Break 1 (5 minutes)

- Participants quickly introduce themselves and share their professional backgrounds.

Kettlebell Segment 2 (10 minutes)

- Double Kettlebell Front Squats (3 sets of 30 seconds with 15 seconds rest).
- Kettlebell Clean and Press (3 sets of 30 seconds with 15 seconds rest).

Networking Break 2 (5 minutes)

- Quickly discuss one current project that interests them and why.

Kettlebell Segment 3 (10 minutes)

- Turkish Getup (3 sets of 30 seconds with 15 seconds rest).
- Kettlebell Swings with Alternating Arms (3 sets of 30 seconds with 15 seconds rest).

Cool Down and Final Networking (10 minutes)

- Stretching exercises focusing on major muscle groups.
- Final networking session and a chance to more solidify connections made during the class.

Power Yoga Alliance - Strength-Focused Yoga with Partner Poses

This isn't just some tame, solitary stretch fest, but a dynamic combo of strength and connection, where you and your partner become an unstoppable duo, challenging each other, supporting each other, and forging alliances that go far beyond the mat. By merging the timeless wisdom of traditional yoga with the added resistance and support of a partner, you're not just building core strength and balance, you're crafting a partnership that's as steadfast as long-lost friends. This isn't just about physical fitness; it's about trust, communication, and the kind of connection that makes life richer and more meaningful. This session will ignite your spirit one pose at a time.

Class Structure

Warm-Up (5-10 minutes)

- Begin with a dynamic warm-up that includes light cardio and mobility exercises to prepare the body for the upcoming poses. This can include jogging in place, jumping jacks, and dynamic stretching.

Partner Poses (35 minutes)

- Double Tree Pose: Stand side by side, raise one leg, and place the foot on the inner thigh. Interlace arms for support and balance. This pose enhances balance and concentration while providing mutual support.
- Double Boat Pose: Sit facing each other with legs bent, hold hands on the outside of your legs, and press soles together. Lift one leg at a time, extending it while engaging your core for stability and strength.
- Partner Warrior II: Stand back to back with arms extended and clasped.

Turn one foot outward and bend the corresponding knee. This pose builds strength and balance while promoting teamwork.
- Seated Spinal Twist: Sit cross-legged with backs touching. Twist to one side, using your partner's knee for leverage, then switch sides. This pose stretches the back, chest, and abdominal muscles.

Core Strengthening Exercises (15 minutes)

- Partner Side-Plank: Start in a side-plank position with your partner behind you for support. Lift your higher leg off the ground. Hold for 30 seconds to a minute, engaging your core and building strength.
- Partner Leg Lifts: Lie on your back with your partner standing behind you holding on to your feet. Lift your legs towards your partner, who provides resistance by gently pushing down on your feet at the center, and at left and right angles. This exercise targets the core and leg muscles.

Cool Down and Stretching (5-10 minutes)

- End the class with a series of static stretches, focusing on major muscle groups. Use partner support to deepen stretches and enhance flexibility.

Motivational Elements

- Teamwork and Trust: Encourage participants to support each other throughout the class, fostering a sense of community and trust.
- Variety and Challenge: Incorporate a mix of poses and exercises to keep the class engaging and challenging.
- Positive Reinforcement: Offer encouragement and positive feedback

to motivate participants and celebrate their achievements.

Appendix C: Sweatworking Sessions - Hyper-Connected

HIIT & Hi's - High-Intensity Interval Training with Quick Introductions

HIIT & Hi's weaves together the fierce intensity of short, explosive workouts with comradeship and community. It's not just about sculpting your physique or igniting your metabolism. This is where the rugged individualism of HIIT meets the enjoyment of a challenging shared experience, creating a landscape of camaraderie and expanding your social circle.

The 'Introduction' Component
In *HIIT & Hi's*, we incorporate quick introductions and interactions between participants. Before each HIIT segment, you'll have the opportunity to meet someone new and share a few words about yourself. This element adds a fun and engaging social aspect to the class, helping you build connections with your fellow fitness enthusiasts before you begin the session.

Class Structure

Warm-Up (5 minutes): A dynamic warm-up to get your heart rate up and prepare your muscles for the intense workout ahead.

HIIT Segments (30 minutes): These will include a variety of exercises such as burpees, jump squats, rock climbers, skaters, and plank jacks. Each segment will be followed by a brief rest period.

Handshakes (Throughout the Class): Before each HIIT segment, you'll be encouraged to introduce yourself to someone new and share a quick handshake. This is your chance to make new acquaintances and feel supported throughout the workout.

Cool Down and Stretching (5-10 minutes): A gentle cool-down session to help your body recover and prevent soreness.

Benefits

- Physical Benefits: Improves cardiovascular health, boosts metabolism, and enhances muscular endurance.
- Social Benefits: Fosters a sense of community, reduces stress, and increases motivation through social interaction.
- Mental Benefits: Enhances focus, boosts mood, and provides a sense of accomplishment.

Tips for Participants

- Arrive Early: Get to class a few minutes early to meet your fellow participants and get settled.
- Be Open-Minded: Don't be shy; introduce yourself and enjoy the social aspect of the class.
- Listen to Your Body: Rest when needed during the workout, and enter the class properly hydrated.

Kickbox & Connect - Kickboxing Class with Partner Drills

Kickbox & Connect is a kickboxing class that combines high-energy workouts with partner drills. We ignite a sense of collective community that transcends mere exercise. It's a shared journey where individuals of all fitness levels can come together, challenge themselves, and find inspiration in the mutual energy of the group. It's a session where physical exertion meets emotional connection, creating a vibrant support and growth that weaves us all together.

Class Structure

Warm-Up (10 minutes): Begin with a dynamic warm-up that includes light cardio to prepare the muscles for the workout ahead.

Kickboxing Techniques (20 minutes): Introduce basic kickboxing techniques such as jabs, hooks, kicks, and combinations. Emphasize proper form and technique to ensure safety and effectiveness.

Partner Drills (25 minutes)

- Isolation Sparring: Focus on specific strikes like jabs or kicks, allowing participants to practice timing and defense.
- Foot Drill (Pocket Drill): Participants practice tap sparring with feet no more than two feet apart, enhancing distance, timing, and defense skills.
- Pad Work: Use focus mitts or kicking shields for alternating strikes, improving coordination and reaction time.

Strength Training (15 minutes): Incorporate strength exercises using bodyweight or light dumbbells to enhance muscle power and endurance.

Cool Down and Stretching (10 minutes): End the class with a relaxing cool-down session, focusing on stretching to prevent soreness and promote flexibility.

Motivational Elements

- Music: Use high-energy music to keep participants motivated and engaged throughout the class.
- Community Building: Encourage participants to support and motivate each other during partner drills.
- Instructor Interaction: Provide personalized feedback and encouragement to help participants reach their full potential.
- Explain the Why: Share the benefits of each exercise, such as improved cardiovascular health, increased strength, self-confidence skills, and enhanced coordination, to connect participants with their goals.

Safety and Modifications

- Safety Briefing: Begin each class with a safety briefing, emphasizing proper form and injury prevention.
- Modifications: Offer modifications for exercises to accommodate different fitness levels and abilities, ensuring everyone can participate.

Class Goals

- Physical Fitness: Improve cardiovascular health, increase strength, and enhance coordination.
- Mental Well-being: Foster a sense of community and connection among participants, promoting mental well-being through shared

physical activity that they can discuss during and after the class.
- Motivation: Encourage participants to push beyond their limits, celebrating small victories and progress along the way.

Tabata & Talk - Tabata-Style Workouts with Discussion Intervals

Join your fellow employees for a new experience, where the intensity of Tabata workouts meets the sociability of shared tales. In *Tabata & Talk*, we'll push our bodies to new limits, ignite our minds with lively discussions, and foster connections that will carry us far beyond the confines of our daily routines. Whether you're a seasoned weekend warrior or just setting out on your fitness journey, this is a place where we challenge ourselves and uplift each other to reach the uncharted territories of our potential.

What is Tabata
Tabata is a high-intensity interval training (HIIT) protocol that involves short bursts of all-out effort followed by brief periods of rest. It was developed by Japanese sports scientist Dr. Izumi Tabata and has been shown to improve cardiovascular fitness, increase speed, and enhance muscular endurance.

The Concept
In *Tabata & Talk*, you will alternate between intense Tabata workouts and discussion intervals. Here's a glimpse into what your workout sessions will look like:

Class Structure

Warm-Up (5-10 minutes): High-energy music and dynamic warm-up to get participants moving and engaged.

Tabata Workout Exercises (20-30 minutes): Each Tabata session will consist of 20 seconds of intense exercise followed by 10 seconds of rest. You repeat this cycle for 4 minutes, focusing on one exercise per session. One minute rest between new exercises.

- Burpees: Start in a standing position, drop down into a squat, kick your feet back into a plank position, do a push-up, then quickly return your feet to the squat position and stand up. Jump up in the air at the top.
- Jump Squats: Stand with your feet shoulder-width apart, lower your body into a squat, then explosively jump up into the air.
- Mountain Climbers: Start in a plank position and bring one knee up towards your chest, quickly alternating legs as if running. You can add a push-up after each rep to make the exercise more challenging.
- Plank Jumps: Begin in a plank position, then jump your feet between different positions within each second (e.g., shoulder-width apart, together, or in a wide stance).

Cool Down (10 minutes): Finish with a stretching session to help participants recover and relax.

Discussion Intervals

Between each Tabata session, you'll take one to two minutes to discuss a topic that inspires and motivates the group. These discussions might cover themes such as:

- Goal Setting: How to set achievable goals and stay motivated.
- Overcoming Obstacles: Strategies for dealing with challenges and setbacks.
- Positive Mindset: Techniques for maintaining a positive outlook in

daily life.

Benefits

- Physical Benefits: Improve cardiovascular health, increase strength and endurance, and enhance overall fitness.
- Mental Benefits: Develop resilience, build confidence, and cultivate a supportive community.
- Emotional Benefits: Enhance motivation, reduce stress, and foster a sense of accomplishment.

Plyometrics & Huddle - Jump Training with Problem-Solving

Here's a Sweatworking session that marries the explosive power of plyometrics with the thrill of communal problem-solving. This bold approach doesn't just boost your cardiovascular fitness and muscular strength, it also sparks collaboration, communication, and creative thinking among participants. It's a full-on experience that will challenge you, inspire you, and leave you feeling like you can conquer the world. Whether you're a seasoned athlete or want to take yourself to the next fitness level, this class is designed to help you grow both physically and mentally. So come ready to sweat, think, and connect with fellow adventurers who share your passion for life.

Key Components

Plyometric Training: (For more specific and dynamic exercises, buy the book, *Hyperfitness*, and use exercises from Trekker and Climber Programs).

High-Intensity Intervals: Engage in explosive movements like:

- Box Jumps: Jump onto a box or bench, focusing on quick turnover and explosive power.
- Burpees: Perform a squat, push-up, and jump.
- Ballistic push-ups: Do an explosive push-up where hands and feet leave the ground on each repetition, landing softly on the balls of your feet.
- Lateral Bounds: Jump sideways, emphasizing speed and agility.

Group Problem-Solving

Interactive Challenges: Throughout the class, participants will be presented with fun, physical challenges that require teamwork to solve. Examples include:

- Obstacle Course Decoding: Teams must decode a series of clues while navigating an obstacle course that includes plyometric exercises.
- Riddle Relay: Divide into teams and complete a puzzle while each member performs a specific plyometric exercise (e.g., jump squats, bounds) to earn puzzle pieces.
- Scavenger Hunt: Find and solve physical challenges around the room, such as jumping over hurdles to reach a hidden clue.

Mind-Body Connection

- Focus and Concentration: The combination of physical activity and mental challenges helps improve focus and concentration.
- Stress Relief: The social aspect and sense of accomplishment provide a natural stress-relief mechanism.

Class Structure

Warm-Up (10 minutes): Dynamic stretching focusing on leg swings, arm circles, and light cardio to prepare the body for plyometric exercises.

Plyometric Circuit (30 minutes): Rotate through stations with brief intervals for water breaks and problem-solving challenges.

- Station 1: Box Jumps (3 sets of 10 reps)
- Station 2: Burpees (3 sets of 10 reps)
- Station 3: Ballistic push-ups (3 sets of 15 reps)
- Station 4: Lateral Bounds (3 sets of 20 reps, alternating legs)

Problem-Solving Segments (20 minutes): Engage in team-based challenges that require physical movement and mental agility, such as the obstacle course decoding or puzzle relay.

Cool Down and Reflection (10 minutes): Perform static stretching, focusing on major muscle groups and taking a moment to reflect on the experience and accomplishments.

Benefits

- Physical Fitness: Improves cardiovascular health, increases muscular strength, and enhances agility.
- Mental Well-being: Boosts confidence, encourages teamwork, and provides stress relief.
- Social Connection: Fosters a sense of community and friendship among participants.

Dance Mixer - High-Energy Dance with Partner-Switching

The goal of this session is to kick up some dust and shake off the monotony of your daily routine. *Dance Mixer* is a ride that binds the thrill of dance with the invigorating rush of cardio, all while throwing in an engaging twist: partner switching. It's a chance to sweat, to dance, and to forge new friendships in the most unexpected ways. So, join the revelry, let loose, and dance your way into a fitter, more vibrant life.

Bonus: Memorizing a dance routine is like a brain exercise.

Class Overview
High-Energy Dance Routines: You'll be moving through a variety of dance styles, from hip-hop to pop and Latin rhythms. Each routine is carefully crafted to keep you engaged and energized throughout the class.

Cardio Intervals: Interspersed with the dance segments are cardio bursts that will push your endurance and burn calories. These intervals include activities like burpees, jump squats, and mountain climbers.

Partner Switching: The unique twist in this class is the partner-switching element. You'll be paired with a partner at the beginning of the class, but don't get too comfortable. Throughout the session, you'll switch partners several times, keeping the energy fresh and exciting. This not only adds a social element but also helps you stay focused and motivated.

Class Structure and Dance Drills

Warm-Up (5 minutes):

- Dynamic Stretching: Leg swings, arm circles, and torso twists to get you ready for movement.
- Cardio Primer: Light jogging in place or jumping jacks to elevate your heart rate.

Dance Segment 1: Hip-Hop (15 minutes):

- Basic Steps: Master simple hip-hop moves like the 'b-boy bounce' and 'chest pop'.
- Choreographed Routine: Learn a fun, energetic routine set to a popular hip-hop track.
- Partner Interaction: Incorporate partner moves like mirroring and call-and-response.

Cardio 1: Burpees (3 minutes): Perform a series of burpees with a focus on proper form and speed. For those who need modification, offer a step-back version instead of a full jump.

Dance Segment 2: Latin Fusion (15 minutes):

- Salsa Basics: Learn basic salsa steps like the 'forward and back' and 'side to side'.
- Choreographed Routine: Combine salsa with other Latin styles for a dynamic routine.
- Partner Switch: Switch partners and repeat the routine with your new partner.

Cardio 2: Jump Squats (3 minutes): Alternate between jump squats and regular squats to keep your heart rate up. For lower impact, focus on bodyweight squats without the jump.

Dance Segment 3: Pop Dance (15 minutes):

- Pop Moves: Master moves like the 'running man' and 'floss'.
- Choreographed Routine: Learn a high-energy pop routine with lots of arm movements and footwork.
- Final Partner Switch: Switch partners one last time and perform the routine together.

Cool Down (5 minutes):

- Static Stretching: Focus on stretching major muscle groups like hamstrings, quadriceps, and chest muscles.
- Final Energizer: End with a quick, upbeat dance segment to leave you feeling invigorated.
- Connect: Gather with the partners you were with during class for a refreshing and energizing networking discussion.

Benefits

- Improved Cardiovascular Health: Intervals will help increase your heart rate and improve your overall cardiovascular fitness.
- Weight Management: The combination of dance and cardio exercises will help burn calories and support weight management goals.
- Social Benefits: Partner switching encourages interaction and camaraderie among participants, making the class a fun and engaging experience.
- Coordination and Balance: The dance routines will help improve your coordination and balance, enhancing your overall physical fitness.
- Stress Relief: Dancing is a great way to reduce stress and boost mood. The upbeat music and energetic atmosphere will leave you feeling invigorated and refreshed.

Appendix D: Sweatworking Sessions - Sane in the Membrane

Mindful Meetings - Meditation and Gentle Movement with Discussions

Mindful Meetings is a journey that weaves together the threads of meditation, gentle movements, and communal dialogue, fostering a profound connection with the land within and around us. This gathering is designed to nurture mindfulness, build a community of kindred spirits, and elevate your overall sense of well-being. By blending the stillness of meditation, the fluidity of gentle movement, and the richness of meaningful discussions, *Mindful Meetings* offers a holistic path to fitness that harmonizes body, mind, and spirit, much like a desert landscape itself, where every element is intertwined in perfect balance.

Class Structure

Introduction and Welcome (5 minutes)

- Begin by welcoming participants and setting a calming atmosphere with soothing music and dimmed lighting.
- Encourage everyone to find a comfortable seated position on their mats or chairs.

Guided Meditation (15 minutes)

- Lead a guided meditation focusing on breath awareness and body relaxation.
- Use gentle, calming voice cues to help participants let go of tension and stress.

Gentle Movement (20 minutes)

Transition into gentle movements that promote flexibility and balance.

Exercises

- Neck Stretch: Slowly tilt your head to the side, bringing your ear towards your shoulder. Hold for a few breaths and then switch sides.
- Shoulder Rolls: Roll your shoulders forward and backward in a circular motion. Repeat several times.
- Seated Twist: Gently twist your torso to one side, keeping your feet planted on the ground. Hold for a few breaths and then switch sides.
- Leg Raises: Slowly lift one leg off the ground, keeping it straight. Hold for a few breaths and then lower it back down. Repeat with the other leg.

Group Discussions (20 minutes)

- After the movement segment, invite participants to form small groups.
- Provide thought-provoking questions or prompts related to mindfulness, self-care, or personal growth.
- Encourage active listening and respectful dialogue among group members.

Closing Meditation (10 minutes)

- Gather everyone back together for a final guided meditation.
- Focus on gratitude and setting aspirations for the day ahead.

Final Reflection and Farewell (5 minutes)

- Allow time for participants to reflect on their experience and share any insights or feelings they wish to express.
- End the class with a sense of community and connection.

Key Elements

- Mindfulness: Encourage participants to stay present and aware throughout the class.
- Community Building: Foster connections among participants through group discussions and shared experiences.
- Self-Care: Emphasize the importance of taking care of one's mental and physical well-being.

Pilates & Planning- Pilates Class with Project Planning

Liberate yourselves from monotony and embrace *Pilates & Planning*, a fusion that marries the invigorating core strength of Pilates with the strategic know-how of project planning. This class is not merely a physical workout, but one of mental clarity and productivity. It's a holistic approach that awakens the body, sharpens the mind, and ignites the spirit. As you leave this transformative experience, you'll feel empowered, motivated, and ready to conquer the world with renewed vigor and purpose.

Class Overview

Duration: 60 minutes

Structure: Alternating between Pilates exercises and project planning sessions.

Objective: To boost physical strength, flexibility, and mental focus.

Motivational Elements

- Community Building: Encourage participants to support each other in both fitness and project goals.
- Music: Use uplifting and appropriate music during Pilates segments to enhance motivation and energy.
- Project Planning: Provide tools and strategies for setting and achieving personal and professional goals.

Pilates Exercises

Warm-Up (5 minutes)

- Breathing Exercises: Focus on deep, controlled breathing to center the mind and prepare the body.
- Shoulder Rolls: Loosen up the shoulders to improve posture and reduce tension.

Core Strengthening (20 minutes)

- Ab Rolls: Perform and hold for 10 seconds to engage the core and improve stability.
- Leg Lifts: Alternate lifting legs while in a plank position to target the lower abs.

Flexibility and Balance (20 minutes)

- Single Leg Stretch: Lie on your back with your head and shoulders lifted, bring both knees to your chest, then extend one leg straight at about a 45-degree angle while holding the other knee with your hands, and alternate legs in a smooth, controlled motion.
- Side Bends: Sit sideways with your legs bent and feet stacked or staggered, then lift your pelvis and upper body to form a straight line, maintaining core engagement and control, before lowering back down in a smooth, controlled motion.
- Tree Pose: Stand on one leg with the other foot resting against the inner thigh, engage your core, keep your spine straight, and balance while maintaining a calm and focused posture.

Cool Down (5 minutes)

- Spine Stretch Forward: Sit with legs extended, then exhale to fold forward in a C-curve, rounding your spine vertebra by vertebra, before inhaling to return to a tall, upright position, enhancing spinal flexibility and core strength.
- Final Breathing: End with deep, calming breaths to center the mind.

Project Planning Interludes
Introduction to Project Planning (5 minutes)

- Introduce the concept of SMART goals (Specific, Measurable, Achievable, Relevant, Time-bound).
- Encourage participants to think about their personal or professional projects.

Goal Setting (10 minutes)

- Have participants write down their goals on sticky notes.
- Encourage them to share their goals with a partner or the group for accountability.

Strategy Session (10 minutes)

- Discuss strategies for overcoming obstacles and staying motivated.
- Provide tools for breaking down large projects into manageable tasks.

Wrap-Up (5 minutes)

- Review goals and strategies.
- Encourage participants to reflect on how their physical and mental well-being can support their project success.

Tai Chi Exchange - Slow-Paced Movements with Idea-Sharing

The union of body and mind. *Tai Chi Exchange* is where the gentle, meditative flow of Tai Chi meets the personal exchange of ideas. Here, we don't just cultivate physical balance and coordination, we nurture mental clarity and forge unity of community. It's a harbor for those who crave a wellness experience that melds the beauty of physical movement with intellectual stimulation.

Class Structure

Warm-Up (5 minutes): Gentle stretching and breathing exercises to prepare the body and mind.

Tai Chi Movements (20 minutes): Focus on slow, flowing movements that emphasize balance, coordination, and mindfulness.

Idea-Sharing Sessions (15 minutes): Participants share thoughts on wellness, mindfulness, or personal growth, fostering a supportive community.

Cool-Down (5 minutes): Guided meditation to relax and center the mind.

Specific Exercises and Drills
Tai Chi Movements

- Grasping the Sparrow's Tail: A foundational movement that emphasizes balance and coordination.
- Single Whip: Focuses on fluid transitions and control.
- Parting the Wild Horse's Mane: Enhances flexibility and balance.

Mindfulness Drills

- Walking Meditation: Participants walk slowly, focusing on each step, to cultivate mindfulness.
- Breathing Exercises: Deep, controlled breathing to enhance relaxation and focus.

Idea-Sharing Exercises

- Circle of Reflection: Participants sit in a circle and share thoughts on a chosen topic, such as gratitude or self-improvement.

- Mindful Listening: Focus on fully engaging with others' perspectives, fostering empathy and understanding.

Cueing Techniques

- Visual Cues: Demonstrate each Tai Chi movement clearly.
- Verbal Cues: Provide concise instructions and encouragement.
- Non-Verbal Cues: Use gestures to guide participants through movements and idea-sharing sessions.

Motivational Elements

- Community Building: Encourage participants to support each other in achieving their wellness goals.
- Personal Growth: Emphasize how the class can help improve mental clarity and overall well-being.
- Inspirational Quotes: Share motivational quotes during the idea-sharing sessions to inspire reflection and growth.

APPENDIX D: SWEATWORKING SESSIONS - SANE IN THE MEMBRANE

Stretch & Strategize - Flexibility Training with Business Strategy

Stretch your limbs and sharpen your minds. In this session of *Stretch & Strategize*, we'll mix the art of flexibility with the enterprise of business strategy. As you bend and twist, your body will find new ease, and your mind will become refined. Together, we'll intertwine the realms of physical agility and mental acuity.

Class Structure

Warm-Up (10 minutes): Begin with dynamic stretching to loosen muscles and prepare participants for the session. This includes leg swings, arm circles, and torso twists.

Flexibility Training Segments (30 minutes): Incorporate a variety of yoga and Pilates exercises to improve flexibility and balance. Each segment will be followed by a brief business strategy discussion.

Business Strategy Discussions (20 minutes): Interspersed throughout the class, strategy sessions will focus on topics like teamwork, innovation, and goal setting.

Cool Down and Final Discussion (10 minutes): End with static stretches and a final group discussion on applying learned strategies in business.

Specific Exercises and Drills
Flexibility Training Exercises

- Downward-Facing Dog (Adho Mukha Svanasana): Strengthens arms

and shoulders while stretching hamstrings and calves.
- Warrior Pose (Virabhadrasana): Improves balance and stretches hips and thighs.
- Seated Forward Fold (Paschimottanasana): Stretches back, shoulders, and hamstrings.
- Plank Pose (Phalakasana): Strengthens core and improves posture.

Business Strategy Discussions

- Teamwork and Collaboration: Discuss how yoga and group fitness promote teamwork and how these principles can be applied in business settings.
- Innovation and Adaptability: Explore how flexibility exercises can inspire creative problem-solving and adaptability in business.
- Goal Setting and Motivation: Use the physical challenges of the class to illustrate strategies for setting and achieving goals.

Drills to Enhance Engagement

- Partner Stretching: Participants work in pairs to assist each other in deeper stretches, fostering teamwork and trust.
- Mindfulness Exercises: Incorporate mindfulness techniques to enhance focus and mental clarity, applicable to both fitness and business strategies.

Motivational Techniques

- Encourage Participation: Emphasize the importance of listening to one's body and modifying exercises as needed.
- Visualizations: Use motivational visualizations to connect physical

challenges with business goals, such as imagining overcoming obstacles.
- Hands-on Adjustments: Provide personalized feedback to help participants improve form and engage more deeply with the exercises.

Barre Mastermind - Ballet-Inspired Workout with Creative Thinking

Barre Mastermind is where the refined beauty of ballet converges with the force of creative thinking. This class challenges both body and mind to forge a path of holistic wellness. Here, you cultivate not just physical strength and flexibility but also mental agility, inviting you to explore the vast expanse of your potential. As you move with purpose, you discover that the true beauty of this journey lies not just in the physical form but in the uncharted territories of the mind, where creativity and strength entwine like the branches of a tree.

Class Structure

Warm-Up (5 minutes)

- Begin with a dynamic warm-up that includes ballet-inspired movements such as pliés, tendus, and dégagés. This will prepare your muscles for the upcoming exercises and get your heart rate up.

Barre Segment (20 minutes)

- Plié Pulses: Stand with your feet shoulder-width apart and perform

deep pliés, focusing on engaging your core and maintaining proper posture.
- Leg Lifts: Hold onto the barre and lift one leg out to the side, keeping it straight. Alternate legs and focus on controlled movements.
- Arabesque Holds: Stand on one leg, with the other extended behind you. Hold for a few seconds, then switch legs. This exercise improves balance and strength.

Creative Thinking Exercises (15 minutes)

- Mindful Movement: Perform a series of slow, deliberate movements while focusing on your breath. This helps connect your body and mind.
- Word Association Game: As you move through exercises, call out words related to ballet or wellness. Participants must respond with a word associated with the previous one, promoting quick thinking and engagement.
- Pattern Recognition: Create a sequence of ballet-inspired steps and ask participants to repeat them. Gradually increase the complexity of the sequence to challenge memory and coordination.

Cool Down and Stretching (10 minutes)

- End the class with a relaxing cool-down session that includes static stretches for major muscle groups. This will help reduce muscle soreness and improve flexibility.

Specific Exercises and Drills

- Ballet-Inspired Jumps: Incorporate small jumps into your routine, focusing on quick takeoffs and landings. This enhances cardiovascular fitness and agility.
- Core Engagements: Use barre exercises like 'tiny pulses' against the

wall to engage your core muscles, improving posture and stability.
- Hip Circles: Stand with your feet together and draw large circles with your hips. This targets the glutes and improves flexibility.

Creative Thinking Drills

- Dance and Describe: Participants perform a short dance sequence and then describe it in one sentence. This encourages creativity and self-expression.
- Movement Storytelling: Divide the class into small groups and ask them to create a short dance story using ballet-inspired movements. This fosters teamwork and creative problem-solving.

Motivational Elements

- Positive Affirmations: Throughout the class, use affirmations to motivate participants, such as 'You are strong and capable.'
- Community Building: Encourage participants to support and cheer each other on, creating a sense of camaraderie.
- Reward System: Offer small rewards or recognition for participants who complete challenges or show significant improvement, providing an extra motivational boost and encouraging continued participation in future classes.

Appendix E: Sweatworking Sessions - Low-Impact Gentle Giants

Aqua Aerobics Alliance - Water-Based Exercises with Team Challenges

Aqua Aerobics Alliance unites the benefits of aquatic exercise with team challenges. This class is tailor-made for those free spirits seeking a workout that's as much about camaraderie as it is about getting the heart rate up. You'll find a tribe of like-minded souls, all united in their quest for a high-energy and low-impact workout that will energize you like rain on a hot, humid day.

Class Structure

Warm-Up (10 minutes): Gentle stretching and light cardio to prepare the body.

Water-Based Exercises (30 minutes): Engage in a mix of shallow and deep water exercises.

Team Challenges (20 minutes): Participate in relay races and other team-building activities.

APPENDIX E: SWEATWORKING SESSIONS - LOW-IMPACT GENTLE GIANTS

Cool Down (10 minutes): Stretching and relaxation techniques to conclude the class.

Key Components

Water-Based Exercises

- Shallow Water Aerobics: Engage in aerobic movements like jumping jacks, marching, and arm lifts in shallow water to improve cardiovascular health and muscle strength.
- Deep Water Power Moves: Use flotation devices to perform suspension exercises that mimic jogging, cross-country skiing, and bicycling, focusing on core strength and endurance.
- Water Resistance Training: Utilize pool noodles and water dumbbells for resistance exercises that target arms, legs, and core muscles.

Team Challenges

- Relay Races: Divide into teams and participate in water-based relay races, such as swimming laps or completing obstacle courses using pool equipment.
- Water Balloon Toss: A fun team-building activity where participants must toss water balloons to teammates, emphasizing coordination and trust.
- Pool Volleyball Challenge: Engage in a game of pool volleyball, promoting teamwork and strategy while maintaining a high level of physical activity.

Motivational Elements

- Music and Movement: Use upbeat music to energize the class and encourage participants to move beyond their comfort zones.
- Community Building: Foster a sense of community by encouraging participants to support and motivate each other throughout the class.
- Instructor Interaction: Provide clear instructions, demonstrations, and encouragement to ensure participants feel confident and motivated.

Benefits

- Low Impact: Ideal for those with joint issues or injuries, as water reduces impact on joints.
- Cardiovascular Improvement: Enhances heart health through aerobic exercises.
- Muscle Strength: Builds strength using water resistance.
- Teamwork and Camaraderie: Encourages bonding and teamwork through fun challenges.

Restorative Yoga & Gathering - Gentle Yoga with Group Discussions

Restorative Yoga & Gathering is where the gentle art of restorative yoga and the richness of shared dialogue converge to nourish both bodies and minds. This holistic journey invites you to breathe deeply, to let go of the burdens of your busy life, and to rediscover the tranquility that resides within you. Whether you seek to unwind the knots of stress, to awaken your flexibility, or simply to find solace in the company of like-minded souls, this gathering is designed to meet you exactly where you are.

Class Overview

Duration: 60 minutes
Intensity: Gentle and Restorative
Focus: Mindfulness, Relaxation, and Community Building

What to Expect

Arrival: Please arrive 10 minutes early to set up your space and get comfortable.

Equipment: All necessary yoga props should be provided, but feel free to bring your own if you prefer.

Attire: Wear comfortable clothing that allows for ease of movement.

Hydration: Stay hydrated throughout the class by drinking water that is available.

Key Components

Gentle Yoga Flow

Begin with a gentle yoga sequence tailored to ease tension, improve flexibility, and promote relaxation. This flow is accessible to all levels, ensuring everyone feels comfortable and supported.

Restorative Yoga

Follow the flow. Transition into restorative yoga poses. These poses use props to support your body, allowing you to fully relax and rejuvenate. This segment is designed to calm your nervous system and promote deep relaxation.

Group Discussions

Interspersed throughout the class, have discussions focused on mindfulness, self-care, and personal growth. These conversations are guided but open-ended, encouraging you to share your thoughts, listen to others, and build connections within the group.

Mindfulness Meditation

Conclude the class with a guided mindfulness meditation, helping you integrate the insights from your discussions and the calmness from your yoga practice.

Benefits

- Physical Relaxation: Reduce stress and tension through gentle stretches and restorative poses.
- Mental Clarity: Engage in meaningful discussions to gain new perspectives and insights.
- Community Building: Connect with like-minded individuals, fostering a sense of belonging and support.
- Emotional Well-being: Cultivate mindfulness and self-awareness to enhance your emotional resilience.

Walk & Workshop - Power Walking with Mobile Brainstorming

Walk & Workshop is a wellness session that combines the invigorating rhythm of power walking with the dynamic spark of mobile brainstorming sessions. This bold fusion will ignite your spirit and sharpen your mind, nurturing both the body's vitality and the soul's creativity. As you stride through the landscape, the world unfolds, and your mind, freed from the confines of static thinking, bursts forth with innovative ideas. It's a journey that celebrates the beauty of nature and the boundless potential of the human imagination.

Key Components

Power Walking

- Intensity and Duration: Your sessions begin with a dynamic warm-up, followed by a brisk 30-minute power walk. This segment is designed to boost cardiovascular health, improve circulation, and burn calories.
- Route Variety: Each class features a different scenic route, ensuring that you stay engaged and motivated by new surroundings.

Mobile Brainstorming Sessions

- Interactive Challenges: During the walk, incorporate short, interactive brainstorming sessions. These sessions are designed to stimulate creativity, problem-solving skills, and teamwork.
- Themed Discussions: Each class focuses on a specific theme, such as innovation, productivity, or personal growth. Participants are encouraged to share ideas and insights, fostering a supportive and collaborative environment.

Mindfulness and Reflection

- Cool Down and Reflection: After the walk, conclude with a short mindfulness session. This involves guided meditation and reflection on the ideas and insights gathered during the brainstorming sessions.
- Goal Setting: Participants are encouraged to set personal or professional goals based on the discussions, helping to integrate their learning into daily life.

Benefits

- Physical Health: Improves cardiovascular fitness, boosts metabolism,

and enhances overall physical well-being.
- Mental Clarity: Enhances creativity, problem-solving skills, and mental focus.
- Social Connection: Fosters a sense of community and teamwork among participants.
- Personal Growth: Encourages goal setting and personal development.

Foam Rolling Forum - Self-Myofascial Release with Idea-Sharing

Foam Rolling Forum is like a sunrise—warm, inviting, and full of promise. It's not just a Sweatworking session, but a gathering of kindred spirits united in a quest for flexibility and tension relief. You explore the art of self-myofascial release and share stories of triumph and learning from each other's life journeys. Every participant becomes a pioneer in the vast landscape of their well-being. This path invites all, regardless of their fitness journey, to join in the quest for a healthier, more vibrant life. By embracing this communal spirit, you turn the pursuit of wellness into a shared experience that enriches everyone.

Key Components

Introduction to Foam Rolling: Participants will learn the basics of foam rolling, including how to identify areas of tension and effectively use the roller to release knots and improve muscle flexibility.

Group Sharing and Discussion: Throughout the class, participants will have opportunities to share their favorite foam rolling techniques, discuss common challenges, and learn from each other's experiences.

APPENDIX E: SWEATWORKING SESSIONS - LOW-IMPACT GENTLE GIANTS

Guided Foam Rolling Session: The class will include a guided foam rolling session where participants will work through various muscle groups, focusing on areas such as the back, shoulders, and legs.

Innovative Techniques: Participants will be introduced to innovative techniques using different types of rollers and balls, such as tennis balls or therapy balls for targeted release in hard-to-reach areas.

Mind-Body Connection: The class emphasizes the importance of breathing and mindfulness during self-myofascial release, helping participants connect with their bodies and enhance their overall relaxation and focus.

Benefits

- Improved Flexibility: Regular foam rolling can increase range of motion and reduce muscle stiffness.
- Reduced Muscle Soreness: Self-myofascial release helps alleviate muscle soreness and promotes faster recovery.
- Enhanced Performance: By improving muscle function and reducing tension, participants can experience better performance in their workouts and daily activities.
- Community Building: The class fosters a supportive environment where participants can share tips, learn from each other, and build lasting connections.

How to Participate

- Bring Your Own Foam Roller: Encourage participants to bring their own foam rollers or provide them if possible.
- Wear Comfortable Clothing: Participants should wear comfortable, stretchy clothing to allow for easy movement.
- Be Prepared to Share: Encourage participants to come prepared to

share their experiences and tips with the group.

Balance & Breakthroughs - Stability Training with Idea Sharing

The *Balance & Breakthroughs* session is a fusion of stability training and the sharing of ideas, designed to set your spirit free and ignite both your physical and mental vitality. It's a call to a new quest, a journey to reclaim your balance and unleash your inner strength, all while reveling in the joy of discovery and the thrill of transformation.

Class Structure

Warm-Up (10 minutes): Light cardio and dynamic stretching to prepare your body for the workout.

Stability Training Segments (30 minutes): Alternation between balance exercises and strength training.

Breakthrough Sessions (15 minutes): Guided discussions and reflections to share ideas and insights.

Cool Down and Final Reflection (10 minutes): Gentle stretches and a final moment of mindfulness to wrap up the class.

Key Components

Stability Training

- Physical Balance: You engage in exercises that improve your core strength, balance, and overall physical stability. This includes activities like single-leg half squats, balance boards, Bosu training, and dynamic planks.
- Mind-Body Connection: Through mindfulness and breathing techniques, you'll learn to connect your physical movements with mental focus, enhancing your overall balance and coordination.

Breakthrough Idea Sharing

- Inspiration Sessions: Throughout the class, there will be a pause for short, guided discussions where you can share personal breakthroughs, goals, or challenges. This is a space to inspire and be inspired by others.
- Mindful Reflection: After each physical segment, all will take a moment to reflect on how the exercises relate to overcoming obstacles in life. This helps integrate the physical and mental aspects of balance.

Benefits

- Improved Physical Stability: Enhance your core strength and balance through engaging exercises.
- Mental Clarity: Develop mindfulness and focus to tackle daily challenges.
- Community Support: Connect with like-minded individuals who share similar goals and aspirations.
- Innovation and Creativity: Stimulate your mind with new ideas and perspectives from fellow participants.

Appendix F: Sweatworking Master Class Outline #1

This Sweatworking master class is designed to take participants on a transformative journey that parallels the challenges and triumphs of the corporate world. This session tells a story of teamwork, perseverance, and personal growth, all while delivering an invigorating workout of movement.

Class Story: 'Climbing the Corporate Mountain'
The class is structured as a metaphorical climb up a challenging corporate mountain, with each phase of the workout representing different stages of a successful career journey.

Base Camp Preparation (Warm-up)

- Narrative: Just as a mountaineer prepares at base camp for a climb, participants warm up their bodies and minds.
- Instructor cues: "We're at the base of our mountain. Let's prepare our bodies and focus our minds for the climb ahead."

The Ascent Begins (Strength Circuit)

- Narrative: The strength circuit represents the initial challenges of starting a career.
- Instructor cues: "Each exercise is a step up the mountain. Push through the resistance, just as you would push through early career obstacles."

Teamwork at High Altitude (Partner Exercises)

- Narrative: This section emphasizes the importance of collaboration in overcoming workplace challenges.
- Instructor cues: "In the thin air of high-stakes projects, we rely on our teammates. Support each other as you would in a crucial business presentation."

Summit Push (Cardio Burst)

- Narrative: The high-intensity interval represents the final push to achieve major career goals.
- Instructor cues: "We're making our final push to the summit! Dig deep and give it your all, just as you would to close that big deal or finish a major project."

Mountain Top Reflection (Cool-down and Stretching)

- Narrative: The cool-down represents reaching career milestones and reflecting on the journey.
- Instructor cues: "As we cool down, imagine standing at the peak, looking out over all you've accomplished. Take deep breaths and appreciate your hard work."

Descend (What's Next)

- Narrative: Reaching the summit is only half the journey. The descent requires just as much focus, humility, and strategy. In your career, success isn't just about achieving goals, it's about sustaining them, mentoring others, and navigating the path forward with wisdom.
- Instructor Cues: "We've made it to the top. But our journey isn't over. Stay alert, stay grounded. This is where you lock in the lessons, manage your energy, and prepare for what comes next. Let's descend

with purpose and strength."

Throughout the session, the instructor should weave this narrative into their cues and motivation, drawing parallels between the physical challenges of the workout and the mental and emotional challenges of corporate life. They might use phrases like:

- "Each rep is building your resilience for tough meetings."
- "Partner up for this exercise. Strong partnerships are key to corporate success."
- "Push through this last set like you're racing to meet a critical deadline."

The story concludes with the post-class networking session, symbolizing the connections made and lessons learned during the journey up the corporate mountain. Participants are encouraged to share their 'climbing experiences' and how they can apply the teamwork and perseverance demonstrated in class to their daily work lives.

This narrative approach not only makes the workout more engaging but also reinforces key corporate values such as teamwork, resilience, goal-setting, and continuous improvement. It transforms a simple exercise class into a meaningful metaphor for professional growth and success.

Optional Workout Equipment

1. Yoga mats: Essential for floor exercises and stretching.
2. Resistance bands: Versatile for various strength training exercises.
3. Dumbbells: Hex dumbbells for weight training.
4. Foam rollers: For warm-up and cool-down sessions.
5. Body wheel: A small piece of equipment for stretching and more advanced exercises.

6. Sliders: Great for core workouts and adding challenge to bodyweight exercises.

Specialized Props

1. Workout gloves: To enhance grip and protect hands during exercises.
2. Half-round foam rollers: Versatile for stretching and improving posture during seated exercises.
3. Yoga bolster: Provides support for various positions and helps with floor sitting.
4. Pull-up assist bands: Can be used creatively for spinal mobility work.

Comfort and Hygiene Items

1. Water bottles: To keep participants hydrated.
2. Sweat-wicking towels: To help manage perspiration during intense workouts.

Networking Aids

1. Name tags: To facilitate easy introductions.
2. Whiteboards or notepads: For brainstorming sessions or sharing contact information after the session.
3. Healthy snacks and flavored water: For post-workout networking.

Additional Items

1. Full-length mirrors: To help participants check their form.
2. Chairs or benches: For seated exercises and resting spots.

3. Cushioned mats: For cool-down or relaxation exercises.

By incorporating these props and equipment, you can create a dynamic environment that supports both the physical workout and the networking aspects of your Sweatworking experience.

Appendix G: Sweatworking Master Class Outline #2

This Sweatworking master class is designed to provide a high-energy, full-body workout that promotes team building and networking in a corporate setting. The 45-minute session will incorporate elements of strength training, cardio, and flexibility work.

Instructor Profile
The class will be led by a highly experienced corporate wellness instructor.

Room Setup

Lighting:

- Begin with bright, energizing lights at 80% intensity
- Gradually dim to 60% during the main workout
- Lower to 40% during cool-down and stretching
- Use blue-tinted lights to enhance focus and energy

Sound System:

- High-quality speakers are placed strategically around the room
- Volume set at 60% during warm-up, increasing to 75% for main workout
- Playlist to include upbeat, instrumental tracks (120-140 BPM)
- Wireless microphone for instructor with clear, crisp audio

Aromatherapy:

- Diffuse a blend of peppermint and citrus essential oils
- Increase scent intensity gradually throughout the class
- Switch to lavender during cool-down for relaxation

Equipment Needed:

- Yoga mats
- Resistance bands of varying strengths
- Light dumbbells
- Foam rollers
- Towels and water stations

Class Structure

Warm-up (5-10 minutes)

- Dynamic stretching
- Light cardio to elevate heart rate

Strength Circuit (20 minutes)

- 4 stations with 45 seconds work, 15 seconds rest
- Exercises: Various Bodyweight exercises, strength focus
- Rotate through 3 times

Partner Exercises (10 minutes)

- Medicine ball passes
- Resistance band rows
- High-five planks

APPENDIX G: SWEATWORKING MASTER CLASS OUTLINE #2

Cardio Rush (5 minutes)

- High-intensity interval training
- 30 seconds on, 10 seconds rest
- Exercises: Various bodyweight exercises, cardio focus

Cool-down and Stretching (5 minutes)

- Static stretches
- Guided breathing exercises

Instructor Cues and Motivation

- Use clear, concise instructions for each exercise
- Provide modifications for different fitness levels
- Encourage partner interaction and support
- Use positive reinforcement and motivational phrases
- Maintain an energetic and enthusiastic tone throughout

Safety Considerations

- Remind participants to stay hydrated
- Demonstrate proper form for all exercises
- Encourage participants to work at their own pace
- Be prepared to offer individual assistance as needed

Post-Class Networking

- Allow 10-15 minutes after class for participants to mingle
- Provide healthy snacks and refreshments

SWEATWORKING

- Encourage participants to exchange contact information

By following this comprehensive outline, you'll deliver a high-quality Sweatworking experience that engages all senses and promotes both fitness and networking in a corporate environment. Remember to adapt the class as needed based on participant feedback and energy levels.

For more than 400 unique and exciting exercises, refer to the book, *Hyperfitness: 12 Weeks to Conquering Your Inner Everest and Getting Into the Best Shape of Your Life*.

Appendix H: Expected Sensory Experiences

The sensory experiences within a session are intense and multifaceted. Here's a breakdown of what you can expect.

Physical Sensations

Heat and Sweat: The most prominent sensation is the heat enveloping your body, causing you to break into a sweat. This sweating is not just a byproduct but a key feature of the experience, as it helps with detoxification and improves circulation.

Muscle Engagement: You'll feel your muscles working hard. The heat makes your muscles more pliable, allowing for deeper stretches and more intense engagement.

Skin Sensations: As you sweat, you may notice changes in your skin's texture and sensitivity. The moisture can actually improve tactile sense, especially on your palms, potentially enhancing your grip during exercises.

Mental Experience

Focus and Mindfulness: The challenging environment forces you to concentrate on the present moment, pushing aside external worries and stress. This can create a meditative-like state, promoting mindfulness and mental clarity.

Emotional Release: Many participants report feeling a sense of emotional catharsis during and after sessions. The intense physical experience can lead to a release of pent-up emotions and stress.

Social Aspects

Community Connection: Sweatworking sessions often foster a strong sense of community. Participants describe feeling connected, empowered, and part of a supportive environment.

Energy Exchange: The high-energy atmosphere is contagious, with participants feeding off each other's enthusiasm and determination.

Post-Session Sensations

Cooling Down: After the session, the process of cooling down provides its own unique sensory experience. The contrast between the intense heat and the gradual return to normal temperature can be invigorating.

APPENDIX H: EXPECTED SENSORY EXPERIENCES

Endorphin Rush: Many people experience a significant endorphin release, leading to feelings of euphoria and accomplishment.

Appendix I: Funding Options for Sweatworking Sessions

Several funding options are available for organizing Sweatworking sessions:

1. **Participant Fees**: Charge attendees a fee to cover the costs of the event.
2. **Corporate Sponsorships**: Partner with local businesses or fitness-related companies to sponsor the events in exchange for promotional opportunities.
3. **Membership Programs**: Implement a membership model where participants pay a recurring fee for access to regular Sweatworking sessions.
4. **Crowdfunding**: Utilize platforms like Kickstarter or GoFundMe to raise funds for launching a series of Sweatworking events.
5. **Grants**: Explore government or private foundation grants that support community health and networking initiatives. For instance, in the past, the National Foundation for Governors' Fitness Councils program has funded $100,000USD to gyms for qualifying schools.
6. **Fundraising Events**: Organize competitions or auctions where a portion of the proceeds goes towards funding future Sweatworking sessions.
7. **Sliding Scale Fees**: Implement a 'pay what you can' model to make the sessions accessible to individuals with varying income levels.
8. **Partnerships**: Collaborate with existing fitness facilities or community centers to share resources and reduce costs.

9. **Scholarships**: Create a scholarship program funded by wealthier participants or through separate fundraising efforts to support those who cannot afford full fees.
10. **Small Business Loans**: If planning to establish a dedicated Sweatworking business, consider applying for small business loans from banks or credit unions.

By combining these funding options, you can create a sustainable financial model for organizing and maintaining Sweatworking sessions that cater to diverse participants while fostering both wellness and professional networks.

Appendix J: Hiring Options

When organizing Sweatworking sessions, there are several hiring options to consider:

1. **Professional Trainers**: Hire a professional fitness instructor to lead the workout sessions, ensuring safety and effectiveness for participants of varying fitness levels.
2. **Specialized Instructors**: Depending on the chosen activity, you may need to hire specialized instructors for activities like yoga, barre, or kickboxing.
3. **Corporate Wellness Providers**: Some companies offer comprehensive Sweatworking packages, including trainers, equipment, and customized programs for businesses.
4. **Fitness Studio Partnerships**: Collaborate with local gyms or boutique fitness studios to host Sweatworking events, leveraging their facilities and instructors.
5. **Wellness Coaches**: Consider hiring wellness coaches who can combine fitness instruction with networking facilitation and team-building exercises.
6. **Event Planners**: For larger Sweatworking events, hiring an event planner with experience in fitness-related networking can help ensure smooth execution.
7. **Motivational Speakers**: Incorporate inspirational talks before your Sweatworking sessions by hiring motivational speakers who can address topics related to health, fitness, and professional growth, to motivate participants to attend sessions.

APPENDIX J: HIRING OPTIONS

When selecting hiring options, consider the fitness levels of participants, the desired networking outcomes, and the overall goals of your Sweatworking initiative to create an engaging and effective experience.

For more information: SeanBurch.com

Appendix K: Detailed Marketing of Your Sweatworking Session

To effectively market Sweatworking sessions, consider a combination of online and offline strategies that emphasize community engagement, unique experiences, and partnerships. Here are several marketing options:

Social Media Engagement

- **Live Sessions**: Host live Sweatworking sessions on platforms like Instagram or Facebook to attract attention and engage with your audience in real-time.
- **Challenges and Contests**: Create wellness challenges that encourage participants to share their experiences on social media, tagging your brand for increased visibility.
- **User-Generated Content**: Encourage attendees to post photos or videos from the sessions, showcasing their workouts and tagging your business to build community and authenticity.

Community Involvement

- **Local Event Sponsorships**: Sponsor or participate in local events such as health fairs or charity runs. Set up booths to promote your Sweatworking sessions and offer free trials or demonstrations.
- **Collaborate with Local Businesses**: Partner with health food stores or wellness centers to cross-promote services. Consider offering mutual discounts or co-hosting events that draw in both customer bases.

Promotional Offers

- **Introductory Discounts**: Offer special rates for first-time participants in Sweatworking sessions to encourage new sign-ups.
- **Referral Programs**: Implement a referral program where current participants can bring friends for free or at a discounted rate, incentivizing word-of-mouth marketing.

Email Marketing

- **Newsletters**: Send out bi-weekly newsletters featuring success stories, upcoming Sweatworking sessions, and fitness tips. This keeps your audience engaged and informed about your offerings.
- **Exclusive Offers**: Provide exclusive discounts or early access to new classes for subscribers, creating a sense of community and loyalty among your email list.

Content Marketing

- **Blog Posts and Videos**: Create content that highlights the benefits of Sweatworking, including success stories from participants. Share this content across your website and social media platforms to attract interest.
- **SEO Optimization**: Ensure your website is optimized for local searches related to fitness classes and Sweatworking. This will help potential clients find you more easily when searching online.

By integrating these strategies, you can effectively promote Sweatworking sessions, enhance community engagement, and ultimately grow your participant base.

Appendix L: Strategic Planning Sessions

Sweatworking offers a unique opportunity for strategic planning sessions. Here is a summary of some strategic planning options for Sweatworking sessions covered within this book:

Active Brainstorming

- **Walking Meetings**: Conduct strategic planning discussions while taking a brisk walk in a park or around the office building. This can stimulate creativity and encourage free-flowing ideas.
- **Fitness Class Planning**: Organize a group fitness class followed by a strategic planning session. The endorphin release from exercise can boost creativity and problem-solving abilities.

Team-Building Activities

- **Outdoor Challenge**: Plan a team-building obstacle course or scavenger hunt that incorporates strategic planning elements. Each checkpoint could represent a different aspect of the planning process.
- **Sports-Based Planning**: Engage in a team sport like volleyball or basketball, pausing between sets or quarters to discuss strategic objectives.

Wellness-Focused Sessions

- **Yoga and Strategy**: Combine a yoga session with strategic planning. Use the relaxation period at the end of the yoga practice for quiet reflection on long-term goals.
- **Meditation and Visioning**: Start with a guided meditation focused on the company's future, then transition into a strategic planning discussion.

Technology Integration

- **Wearable Tech Challenges**: Utilize fitness trackers to set group goals. Align achieving these fitness milestones with completing different phases of the strategic plan.
- **Time Management:** Keep Sweatworking strategic planning sessions to 2 hours or less to maintain focus and energy. Use shorter, more frequent sessions rather than long, exhaustive meetings. Incorporate brief, intense workout intervals between planning discussions to re-energize participants.

By integrating physical activity with strategic planning, these Sweatworking sessions promote enhanced engagement, creativity, and productivity. The informal environment and shared exercise experiences also cultivate stronger team bonds and foster open communication, crucial for effective planning.

Appendix M: Starting Your Own Sweatworking Business

For seasoned managers and entrepreneurs looking to enter the field of Sweatworking, there are several options to get started.

Corporate Wellness Programs

Develop and implement corporate wellness programs that incorporate Sweatworking activities. This can include:

- Organizing group fitness classes for employees
- Arranging team-building exercises that involve physical activity
- Creating inter-departmental fitness challenges

Specialized Sweatworking Events

Host exclusive Sweatworking events tailored for professionals:

- Multi-site meetups at various gym locations
- Bootcamp-style workouts for networking
- Yoga retreats combining mindfulness and business discussions

Online Fitness Coaching with Networking

Leverage digital platforms to offer remote fitness coaching services that also facilitate professional connections:

- Virtual group classes for professionals in similar industries
- Online challenges that encourage both fitness and networking
- Webinars combining wellness tips and business insights

Fitness Studio

Invest in your own wellness studio or a fitness franchise, and have specific alternative classes on professional networking. This could involve:

- Dedicated spaces for post-workout networking
- Specialized classes designed for business professionals
- Membership tiers that include networking events

Outdoor Adventure Networking

Organize outdoor fitness activities that promote both health and relationship-building:

- Group cycling events for professionals
- Hiking or trail running meetups
- Open-air bootcamps in scenic locations

Goal-Oriented Sweatworking

Set up programs where professionals can train together for a specific fitness goal:

- Training groups for upcoming 5K races or marathons
- Cycling clubs preparing for charity rides
- Exercise teams working towards competition goals

Wellness Consulting for Businesses

Offer consulting services to companies looking to integrate Sweatworking into their corporate culture:

- Develop customized Sweatworking strategies for different industries
- Create metrics to measure the impact of Sweatworking on employee productivity and satisfaction
- Design executive fitness programs that incorporate networking opportunities

Appendix N: Sweatworking Session Employee Sample Evaluation

Employee Name: _____ Date: _____
Session Type: _____ Duration: _____
Performance Metrics (Rate 1-5, 1 = Poor, 5 = Excellent)

Physical Engagement

- Effort Level: ____
- Participation: ____

Networking Skills

- Interaction with Colleagues: ____
- Conversation Initiation: ____

Team Building

- Collaboration: ____
- Support for Others: ____

Professional Conduct

- Appropriate Attire: ____
- Punctuality: ____

APPENDIX N: SWEATWORKING SESSION EMPLOYEE SAMPLE EVALUATION

Sweat Rate Calculation

Pre-session Weight: _____ lbs/kg
Post-session Weight: _____ lbs/kg
Fluid Consumed: _____ liters
Sweat Rate = (Weight loss + Fluid consumed) / Session duration
Calculated Sweat Rate: _____ liters/hour

Overall Performance:

Strengths:

Areas for Improvement:

Goals for Next Session:

1.
2.
3.

Evaluators Signature: _____ **Date:** _____

Employee's Signature: _____ **Date:** _____

This sample evaluation form combines traditional performance metrics with some unique aspects of Sweatworking, including a sweat rate calculation to promote health awareness during sessions. It allows for a broad assessment of an employee's engagement, networking skills, and professional conduct in this innovative team-building format.

Appendix O: Timeline for Your Sweatworking Business

Below is a sample timeline outlining the journey from conceptualizing your idea to successfully launching your own class:

Phase 1: Foundation (3 months)

1. Develop your fitness expertise through certifications and training.
2. Gain experience by participating in various group fitness classes.
3. Identify your niche and unique selling proposition.

Phase 2: Planning and Preparation (2 months)

1. Create your class concept and structure.
2. Develop a curriculum and playlist for your classes.
3. Practice teaching to friends and family for feedback.

Phase 3: Building Experience (6-8 months)

1. Shadow experienced instructors at local gyms or studios.
2. Start teaching as a substitute instructor to gain confidence.
3. Build rapport with clients and develop your teaching style.

APPENDIX O: TIMELINE FOR YOUR SWEATWORKING BUSINESS

Phase 4: Launch Preparation (2-3 months)

1. Secure a venue or partner with an existing fitness studio.
2. Create marketing materials and a social media presence.
3. Set up a scheduling system for your classes.

Phase 5: Launch and Growth (Ongoing)

1. Host your first class and gather feedback from participants.
2. Continuously refine your teaching style and class offerings.
3. Build a loyal community of participants.
4. Consider expanding to online platforms or creating challenges for engagement.

Your journey to mastery is uniquely shaped by your background and the local opportunities you seize. For example, I spent five years teaching martial arts classes for free while working toward my black belt in Shotokan karate. Those years of hands-on experience not only deepened my technical skills but also taught me how to lead and connect with others. This ultimately empowered me to design two original fitness programs and launch them with immediate confidence.

The key to long-term success lies in unwavering commitment and adaptability. By staying true to your vision and continuously responding to the needs of your participants, you'll foster lasting growth for both yourself and your community. Every step, whether volunteer work or innovation, is a building block toward expertise and meaningful impact.

Appendix P: Quick Stress-Relief Techniques

#1 Breathing Techniques

- Focus on five deep belly breaths inhaling and exhaling through your nose.
- Inhale through your nose for four counts, exhale through your mouth for five counts.

#2 Physical Techniques

- Take a quick walk around the block to clear your mind.
- Stretch at your desk, focusing on neck, shoulder, and chest movements.
- Do a hand massage to release tension.
- Rub your feet over a tennis ball for instant relaxation.

#3 Sensory Stress Relief

- Listen to music, especially classical tunes.
- Chew gum for stress reduction.
- Drip cold water on your wrists to calm your body.

- Squeeze a stress ball to release tension.

#4 Mental Relaxation Methods

- Practice a five-minute meditation.
- Use visual imagery to create a peaceful mental space.
- Count backward or follow your breath to interrupt stress cycles.
- Write down your emotions in a journal.

#5 Quick Mood Boosters

- Eat a small square of dark chocolate.
- Hug your pet.
- Get some sunlight for vital Vitamin D.
- Watch a funny video that makes you laugh.

Experiment with different techniques to find what works best for you. You'll need to practice these methods regularly for maximum effectiveness. The goal is to find stress-relief techniques that are quick, portable, and effective for high-pressure networking and personal situations.

Appendix Q: Stress-Release Techniques

#1 Nature Therapy

- **Forest Bathing (Shinrin-yoku)**: A Japanese practice that involves spending time in a forest environment by sitting or walking slowly, breathing deeply and engaging your senses with the surroundings.
- **Nature Meditations**: This involves purposefully relaxing and observing nature, often focusing on present natural features.
- **Engaging Senses in Nature**: Find a natural setting and engage all your senses by feeling textures, smelling scents, listening to sounds, and observing colors and patterns. This can be done by walking barefoot, touching plants, or simply sitting and observing.

#2 Conscious Eating

- **Practice Mindful Eating**: Engage all your senses while eating. Notice the colors, smells, textures, and flavors of your food. Eat slowly and without distractions, focusing on each bite to appreciate the experience fully.
- **Include a Mid-Meal Pause**: Take a moment halfway through your meal to assess your hunger level and how the food tastes. This pause can help you stop eating when you're comfortably full rather than overeating.
- **Create Balance and Honor Cravings**: Allow yourself to enjoy any

food you desire while also considering nutritional balance. Pairing indulgent foods with more nutritious options can enhance satisfaction and well-being.

#3 Digital Detox

- **Find Replacement Activities**: Engage in activities that replace screen time, such as reading, puzzles, or outdoor activities. This helps manage withdrawal symptoms and keeps you occupied without reaching for your phone.
- **Create a Tech-Free Space**: Designate areas in your home where screens are not allowed. This could be a cozy, quiet space or a dining table set up for board games. This physical separation helps break the habit of constantly checking devices.
- **Use Digital Tools for Support**: Utilize apps or tools that block access to distracting websites or social media. Additionally, turning your phone screen to greyscale can make it less appealing and reduce the urge to check it frequently.

#4 Gratitude List or Journal

- **Find New Things Each Day**: Challenge yourself to find something new to be grateful for each day. This could be a small pleasure, like a good cup of coffee, or a significant event, like a kind gesture from someone.
- **Start Broad and Get Specific**: Begin with general things you're grateful for, such as family, health, or home. Over time, add more specific details such as a good conversation with a family member or a beautiful sunset you enjoyed.

- **Elaborate on Why You're Grateful**: Instead of just listing items, explain why they are important to you. For example, if you're grateful for a friend, note how their support makes you feel.

Appendix R: Nutritional Tips for Sustained Energy

Nutritional strategies for sustained energy during long sessions (over an hour and a half) are crucial for optimal performance.

Carbohydrates

Focus on a mix of complex and simple carbohydrates to provide both immediate and sustained energy. Complex carbohydrates like whole grains, oats, and quinoa offer a gradual release of glucose, while simple carbs provide quick energy boosts.

Protein

Include protein in your nutrition plan to support muscle recovery and prevent lean-muscle cannibalization. A general consideration is a carbohydrate to protein ratio of 7:1. This has been effective for long-duration events in the past, though each individual will vary.

Hydration and Electrolytes

Maintain proper hydration by drinking fluids regularly and replenishing electrolytes lost through sweat. Electrolyte-rich ingredients and specialized electrolyte blends can help optimize hydration and prevent cramping.

Timing of Nutrition

- Pre-event: Consume a medium to small balanced meal with complex carbohydrates, lean protein, and healthy fats two hours before the event.
- During event: Eat small, healthy snacks to maintain steady energy levels. Incorporate energy-dense, easily digestible snacks. These can help stabilize blood sugar levels and provide sustained energy.
- Post-event: Focus on recovery nutrition with a combination of carbohydrates and protein to replenish glycogen stores and repair muscles.

By following these nutritional strategies, you can better help ensure sustained energy levels throughout long events, enhancing performance and reducing fatigue.

Appendix S: Proper Ergonomics

Proper posture and ergonomics are always important for making a positive impression, confidence, and maintaining comfort in everyday work life and during Sweatworking events.

In Sweatworking, confidence is a catalyst for connection, influence, and opportunity. Physical appearance, posture, and energy level all communicate silent cues that impact how you're perceived in professional settings. When you engage in movement, whether it's a hike, group workout, or wellness walk, it's good to learn to naturally elevate your posture and project a stronger, more positive presence. Research underscores that much of our perceived confidence stems not from what we say, but how we show up. This means your appearance, body language, and vitality matter, especially when you're networking, pitching ideas, or leading others in motion-based settings.

That's why Sweatworking is such a powerful tool. It puts you in environments where your confidence can be amplified through physical engagement. When you're exercising, you're not in a static, rehearsed state; you're dynamic, authentic, and often more self-assured. This physical shift not only improves how others view you, but also how you view yourself. You start to carry yourself with more assurance, speak with more clarity, and engage more genuinely.

Standing Posture

Stand like you mean it. Distribute your weight evenly across both feet. Keep your shoulders relaxed but back, and align your ears over your shoulders with a tall spine. Avoid locking your knees or slouching into one hip. Whether you're speaking to a group on a walking trail or mingling at a wellness event, grounded posture communicates presence, leadership, and vitality. These are all core values in Sweatworking settings.

Body Language

Your body speaks long before you do. Make eye contact when introducing or being introduced, and throughout conversations to demonstrate attentiveness and approachability. Use open gestures, such as keeping your palms facing outward and the area around your heart open, to be more receptive to interaction. Avoid crossing your arms or legs, which can signal defensiveness or discomfort. Lean in slightly when listening, nod to show engagement, and keep your stance approachable. In Sweatworking, where movement and connection are key, fluid and intentional body language enhances trust and encourages authentic exchanges.

Handshake

Even in an increasingly wellness-driven, casual culture, a handshake still sets the tone. A handshake is a physical expression of confidence and respect. Go for a firm, but not overpowering grip, make full palm contact, and shake once or twice while maintaining eye contact. In outdoor or active settings, adapt with a palm press or brief clasp when needed, but always deliver it with intention. All professional engagements should include a firm handshake, nothing else. We are not chimpanzees that fist-bump our way through salutations. Save that, if at all, for informal settings. I have not once fist-bumped someone when meeting them for the first time.

Eye Contact

Strong eye contact communicates credibility, attentiveness, and warmth. Aim to maintain eye contact 60–70% of the time in conversation, especially when you're listening. Avoid staring, but don't dart your eyes away either. In active Sweatworking environments, where distractions abound, maintaining eye contact helps anchor interactions and shows genuine interest in the person, not just the pitch.

Voice Tone

How you say it often matters more than what you say. Keep your tone steady, clear, and warm, especially in outdoor or group settings where background noise can distort your message. Avoid speaking too fast or too softly. Project confidence by modulating your voice with purposeful pauses and an engaging rhythm. A strong voice is an extension of a strong presence, especially when you're leading a team through a wellness experience.

Other Ergonomics To Consider While Sweatworking

Align Your Head and Neck for Clarity and Confidence

In a Sweatworking session, especially during walking meetings or hikes, keep your head balanced directly over your shoulders. Avoid jutting your chin forward, a common habit when engaging in deep conversation or checking devices. Instead, imagine a string gently pulling you up from the crown of your head. This not only relieves strain but helps you project a confident, composed presence during interactions.

Engage Your Core to Stay Grounded

Core engagement is key to stamina and upright posture, especially in movement-based networking. During active sessions, lightly draw your belly button toward your spine to activate the muscles that support your back. This prevents slouching while sitting or walking and helps you stay physically grounded and mentally focused. Incorporate core exercises into your wellness routine to build strength for any Sweatworking environment.

Optimize Your Mobile and Outdoor Workspaces

Sweatworking often happens on the move—at resorts, on trails, or in non-traditional workspaces. Whether you're gathering around an outdoor table or standing in a group, bring awareness to your body's positioning. Elevate devices to eye level when possible, keep your shoulders relaxed, and avoid hunching. Being ergonomically mindful in dynamic settings reinforces the idea that wellness and productivity are not mutually exclusive.

Break, Move, Reset

Even during the most energizing sessions, the body benefits from variety. If you're leading or attending a half-day Sweatworking event, incorporate intentional movement resets. Every 30 to 60 minutes, pause for a stretch, a brief walk, or a breathing exercise. These breaks aren't distractions; they're posture boosters that keep your mind sharp, body aligned, and energy high throughout your experience.

Use Visual and Physical Cues to Stay Aligned

Building better posture takes repetition and mindfulness. Use simple tools to reinforce good habits, such as a vibration cue or a physical reminder like a band or wearable. During Sweatworking, these cues can be subtle yet powerful nudges that help you embody strength, openness, and professionalism through body language alone.

By paying attention to posture and ergonomics, you're not just improving physical health, you're reinforcing the core philosophy of Sweatworking. How we move through the world shapes how we lead, connect, and succeed.

Appendix T: Clothing

The key to successful Sweatworking attire is balancing professionalism with comfort and functionality. Always consider the specific activities planned and adjust your outfit when necessary.

Gym/Conference/Office Setting

Tops:

- Fitted t-shirts or tank tops made of moisture-wicking fabric
- Compression shirts for increased blood flow and performance
- Sports bras for women, providing adequate support

Bottoms:

- Shorts (athletic or compression) for ventilation and movement
- Workout leggings or fitted pants for unrestricted movement
- Comfortable bike shorts (high-density padding) for cycling classes

Footwear:

- Supportive cross-training sneakers for varied activities
- Flat-footed sneakers for strength training
- Cycling shoes for cycle classes (if available)

General Tips:

- Dress in layers for temperature control.
- Choose comfortable, professional shoes for extended periods of standing or walking.
- Bring a light jacket or cardigan for air-conditioned rooms.
- Choose breathable fabrics to stay comfortable during activities.
- Choose wrinkle-resistant materials for a polished look throughout the day.
- Stick to a neutral color palette for versatility.

Outdoor Setting

Tops:

- Moisture-wicking, breathable shirts
- Long-sleeve options for sun protection
- Light, water-resistant jackets for unpredictable weather

Bottoms:

- Quick-drying shorts or pants
- Convertible pants for versatility

Footwear:

- Sturdy, comfortable athletic shoes with good traction
- Moisture-wicking socks to prevent blisters

Accessories:

- Hat or visor for sun protection

- Sunglasses
- Lightweight backpack for essentials

Acknowledgments

My sincere gratitude to Wellness Institute Press and their dedicated team for believing in me. Your support of this book's mission to merge wellness with purpose, connection with growth, to help people nurture their potential, recognize that success runs deeper than a financial bottom line, and embrace wellness as the foundation for a truly rich life, has been invaluable. Thank you for standing behind this vision and helping bring it to the world.

This book wouldn't exist without the steadfast love and unwavering support of my mother and my walking partner in more ways than one, Jeanne Lewis. With parents, you often take for granted that they'll show up when you need them, no questions asked. But what I've come to learn is that this kind of loyalty, this kind of grace, is not a given. It is a choice made over and over again. When I asked my mother to help edit this book, she didn't blink. She simply said yes—with quiet strength, patience, and that steady hand I've leaned on my entire life. That is her ethos. That is her moral compass. That is her profound gift to me, to my brother, to our family. Her belief in me—gentle, unshaken, and unconditional—helped shape every word in these pages. Thank you, Mom, for everything.

To my father, who planted the roots of business ethics in me long before I understood their value, long before I could name them, long before I desired them. Often in ways I resisted, yet now recognize these teachings as profoundly formative. I carry them with gratitude, always by your side.

To those out in the world who see something in me—even when I struggle to see it in myself—thank you. Your belief fuels my purpose, my work, and this small attempt to leave something good behind. A light. A footprint. A legacy.

To all the practicing Buddhists in the world, thank you. We hold close a knowing, a stillness, a compassion that is often invisible to the outside eye. But it's there. And it is powerful.

To those who wake up each day and try to be better than they were yesterday: I see you. I honor you. I know how hard that road is. And if my words can be a companion, a lift, or even just a moment of relief, I offer them to you, fully.

To everyone who ever truly cared—girlfriends, relatives, friends… thank you. When I said I loved you or appreciated you, I meant it. I showed it in the ways I knew how, even if they weren't always enough. But I didn't always understand the weight of what your love or friendship gave me. I didn't hold it as carefully as I should have. Perhaps that's the nature of love. It patiently waits until we are truly ready to embrace its full meaning.

To Richard Owen, my college roommate and beloved friend of 37 years—what a gift it was to walk alongside you in this life. You reappeared in my world at a moment when you needed support, and I was honored to offer it, never expecting that you would repay that kindness tenfold, again and again, with your loyalty, humor, and heart. From our first days as college freshmen, fraternity brothers, and roommates, we called each other family, and we meant it. Though your passing came far too soon and left a silence that echoes deeply, the love, light, and unwavering friendship you brought into my life will never fade. You remain, always, one of the brightest souls I've ever known.

And lastly, to my son, thank you. My pride in you grows with every breath, every sunrise, every moment you become more fully yourself. Children teach us what no book ever could: how to love without condition, without expectation, without end. You opened my heart in a way I didn't know was possible. Through you, I've learned that unconditional love isn't just a concept, it's a practice, a presence, a sacred truth we get to live out here on Earth.

What a gift.

What a blessing.

What a beautiful reason to be.

Thank you, my son, for showing me the deepest meaning of love.

About the Author

Sean Burch is an adventurer, leadership consultant, award-winning filmmaker, author, and wellness authority who holds eight world records across six countries and five continents, pushing the boundaries of human endurance. As the first Virginian to summit Mt. Everest and the winner of National Geographic Channel's "Ultimate Survival Alaska", Burch has proven his mettle in some of the world's most challenging environments.

With 25+ years of leadership experience, Burch has established himself as a sought-after speaker, workshop presenter, and leadership authority for Fortune 500 companies worldwide. He pioneered the USA's first functional fitness program to receive national attention, featured on the front page of USA Today, and is an accomplished author, having written the acclaimed self-leadership program "Hyperfitness®: 12 Weeks to Conquering Your Inner Everest," published in hardcover and softcover by Penguin Random House.

Burch has 140+ first ascents of previously unclimbed peaks, 121 of which he accomplished solo. His expertise extends to wellness instruction and personal & group coaching, where he has trained Olympic athletes, special operations personnel, C-suite executives, emerging leaders, and working professionals for over two decades.

Burch is as comfortable behind a camera as he is scaling a mountain peak. His award-winning documentaries and photographs have graced film screens worldwide, as well as major news organizations globally, from BBC to CNN, to national and local news media in the USA.

Burch's impact extends beyond personal achievements. Recognized for his humanitarian efforts, Burch was named Goodwill Ambassador to Nepal by the country's government and received the Brand Personality of the Year award from the Asia Pacific Foundation. Burch's philanthropic endeavors have raised over $1 million for developing countries collaborating with various non-profit organizations.

He is also an accomplished martial artist, with three decades of martial arts experience. Burch holds a black belt in American Shotokan Karate and instructor certifications in Jeet Kune Do and Filipino Martial Arts. He is an Explorer's Club member.

You can connect with me on:
- https://www.seanburch.com
- https://x.com/SeanBurch
- https://www.facebook.com/SeanBurchOfficial
- https://www.linkedin.com/in/seanburch

Also by Sean Burch

Hyperfitness: 12 Weeks to Conquering Your Inner Everest and Getting Into the Best Shape of Your Life (Penguin Random House)

WORLD-record holder and training expert Sean Burch, who has been hailed as "one of the fittest men on earth," (CNN International) is dedicated to reaching the greatest heights of fitness. Now Sean shares the secrets of his own success and shows you how to use his revolutionary training techniques to get yourself in better shape than you ever imagined possible.

What does *Hyperfitness* mean? It means setting goals and attaining them. It means discovering that you are stronger and tougher than you knew. And, it means taking your workout to a whole new level. The program focuses on three important, linked components:

- **Hyperstrength**: Innovative exercises and drills give you the strength, quickness, and endurance of a world-class athlete. With names like "aerial spins" and "ski-mogul master jumps," the exercises are fun and varied, and encompass three fitness levels.

- **Hyperfare**: Essential guidelines include meal plans and recipes to help your body get the nutrition needed to power through the challenging workouts.

- **Hypermind**: Mental-conditioning techniques, such as meditation and visualization, combine with the workouts so you can achieve all your physical and mental goals. In addition to the training program, Sean recounts the story of his incredible summit of Mount Everest. Encouraging and inspiring, Hyperfitness offers readers the motivation to conquer their own "inner Everest"-be it a marathon, triathlon, long hike, 5K run, or any other fitness goal.

www.ingramcontent.com/pod-product-compliance
Lightning Source LLC
Chambersburg PA
CBHW010946050426
42337CB00057B/4878